Systemic Risk and Reinsurance

Systemic Risk and Reinsurance

Special Issue Editor
Weidong Tian

MDPI • Basel • Beijing • Wuhan • Barcelona • Belgrade • Manchester • Tokyo • Cluj • Tianjin

Special Issue Editor
Weidong Tian
University of North Carolina at Charlotte
USA

Editorial Office
MDPI
St. Alban-Anlage 66
4052 Basel, Switzerland

This is a reprint of articles from the Special Issue published online in the open access journal *Risks* (ISSN 2227-9091) (available at: https://www.mdpi.com/journal/risks/special_issues/systemic-risk-reinsurance).

For citation purposes, cite each article independently as indicated on the article page online and as indicated below:

LastName, A.A.; LastName, B.B.; LastName, C.C. Article Title. *Journal Name* **Year**, *Article Number*, Page Range.

ISBN 978-3-03936-298-1 (Hbk)
ISBN 978-3-03936-299-8 (PDF)

© 2020 by the authors. Articles in this book are Open Access and distributed under the Creative Commons Attribution (CC BY) license, which allows users to download, copy and build upon published articles, as long as the author and publisher are properly credited, which ensures maximum dissemination and a wider impact of our publications.

The book as a whole is distributed by MDPI under the terms and conditions of the Creative Commons license CC BY-NC-ND.

Contents

About the Special Issue Editor vii

Preface to "Systemic Risk and Reinsurance" ix

Anna Denkowska and Stanisław Wanat
A Tail Dependence-Based MST and Their Topological Indicators in Modeling Systemic Risk in the European Insurance Sector
Reprinted from: *Risks* **2020**, *8*, 39, doi:10.3390/risks8020039 1

Irena Vodenska, Alexander P. Becker, Di Zhou, Dror Y. Kenett, H. Eugene Stanley and Shlomo Havlin
Community Analysis of Global Financial Markets
Reprinted from: *Risks* **2016**, *4*, 13, doi:10.3390/risks4020013 23

Gaël Hauton and Jean-Cyprien Héam
Interconnectedness of Financial Conglomerates
Reprinted from: *Risks* **2015**, *3*, 139–163, doi:10.3390/risks3020139 39

Gian Paolo Clemente, Nino Savelli and Diego Zappa
The Impact of Reinsurance Strategies on Capital Requirements for Premium Risk in Insurance
Reprinted from: *Risks* **2015**, *3*, 164–182, doi:10.3390/risks3020164 61

Jing Li and Mingxin Xu
Optimal Dynamic Portfolio with Mean-CVaR Criterion
Reprinted from: *Risks* **2013**, *1*, 119–147, doi:10.3390/risks1030119 79

Ekaterina Panttser and Weidong Tian
A Welfare Analysis of Capital Insurance
Reprinted from: *Risks* **2013**, *1*, 57–80, doi:10.3390/risks1020057 103

Alejandro Balbas, Beatriz Balbas and Raquel Balbas
Optimal Reinsurance: A Risk Sharing Approach
Reprinted from: *Risks* **2013**, *1*, 45–56, doi:10.3390/risks1020045 125

About the Special Issue Editor

Weidong Tian is currently a Professor of Finance and a Distinguished Professor of Risk Management and Insurance at the University of North Carolina, Charlotte. Dr. Tian served as a faculty member at the University of Waterloo and a visiting scholar at the Sloan School of Management at MIT. He also held various positions in financial institutions before joining UNC Charlotte. As a well-recognized expert in asset pricing models and risk management, his primary research interests are asset pricing, asset allocation, derivatives, and risk management. Dr. Tian has published over 30 articles in top and highly ranked academic journals in finance, mathematical finance, and risk management. The book he edited *Commercial Banking Risk Management: Regulation in the Wake of the Financial Crisis*, Palgrave Macmillan, is viewed as the most comprehensive in this area, and its Chinese translation was published in 2019.

Preface to "Systemic Risk and Reinsurance"

Since the 2008–2009 financial crisis, it is widely recognized that there exist essential flaws in the supervisory system and that further regulatory measures must be established in the financial sector. Many proposals under consideration or already embraced by regulatory authorities focus on the "systemically important financial institutions" or banks "too big/connected to fail". However, insurers and banks played markedly different roles in the financial crisis. Therefore, it is essential to study the systemic risk for the insurer and the nature of systemic risk from the reinsurance perspective. It is also important to examine how insurance business models, such as capital insurance, provide an alternative approach to systemic risk.

This present volume provides some novel approaches to systemic risk. It commences with three articles on the dynamic of indirect connections between the insurance and banking sector, and other market indices from a scientific and network perspective. Denkowska and Wanat (2020) suggest a hybrid approach to the analysis of interlinkage dynamics based on combining the copula-DCC-GARCH model and minimum spanning trees (MST). Vodenska, Becker, Zhou, Jenett, Stanley, and Havlin (2016) construct a unique network of market indices and currencies in 56 countries, and study the community formations within the network before and after the crisis period. Hauton and Heam (2015) particularly address the insurance sector and the banking sector together, and their unique roles in a financial conglomerate.

Two articles on new capital requirements follow. From a reinsurance perspective, Panttser and Tian (2013) provide a comprehensive welfare analysis of capital insurance on financial institutions and insurance companies, which can be viewed as capital too-large-to-fail. On the other hand, Clemente, Savelli, and Zappa (2015) study the impact of reinsurance strategies on new capital requirements for premium risk in insurance companies.

Two articles focus on risk measures and optimality afterward. Li and Xu (2013) solve an optimal portfolio choice problem under a widely used CVaR constraint, and this CVaR regulatory constraint is implemented by both the banking sector and the insurance sector. Finally, Balbas et al. (2013) provides a general mathematical method to deal with the coherent risk and deviation measure in one integrated framework.

Weidong Tian
Special Issue Editor

Article

A Tail Dependence-Based MST and Their Topological Indicators in Modeling Systemic Risk in the European Insurance Sector

Anna Denkowska * and Stanisław Wanat

Department of Mathematics, Cracow University of Economics, Rakowicka 27, 31-510 Cracow, Poland; wanats@uek.krakow.pl
* Correspondence: anna.denkowska@uek.krakow.pl

Received: 20 March 2020; Accepted: 17 April 2020; Published: 22 April 2020

Abstract: In the present work, we analyze the dynamics of indirect connections between insurance companies that result from market price channels. In our analysis, we assume that the stock quotations of insurance companies reflect market sentiments, which constitute a very important systemic risk factor. Interlinkages between insurers and their dynamics have a direct impact on systemic risk contagion in the insurance sector. Herein, we propose a new hybrid approach to the analysis of interlinkages dynamics based on combining the copula-DCC-GARCH model and minimum spanning trees (MST). Using the copula-DCC-GARCH model, we determine the tail dependence coefficients. Then, for each analyzed period we construct MST based on these coefficients. The dynamics are analyzed by means of the time series of selected topological indicators of the MSTs in the years 2005–2019. The contribution to systemic risk of each institution is determined by analyzing the deltaCoVaR time series using the copula-DCC-GARCH model. Our empirical results show the usefulness of the proposed approach to the analysis of systemic risk (SR) in the insurance sector. The times series obtained from the proposed hybrid approach reflect the phenomena occurring in the market. We check whether the analyzed MST topological indicators can be considered as systemic risk predictors.

Keywords: insurance sector; systemic risk; deltaCoVaR; minimum spanning trees—topological indicators; tail dependence

JEL Classification: G22; C10

---

1. Introduction

Currently, despite many studies that use different methodological and empirical approaches to identify and analyze systemic risk (SR) in the insurance sector, there is still no consistent theory to monitor it effectively. Ideal methods that could be used for this purpose should support or be associated with the essential elements of macroprudential policy and surveillance (MPS) by providing information on the build-up of system-wide vulnerabilities in time and cross-section, with an acceptable level of accuracy for both the forecast of the occurrence of a systemic event and its financial effects. The subject of this article fits into the current of research focusing on the search for such a method. We focus on the structure of interlinkages between insurance companies, which plays a key role in the spread of systemic risk in this sector.

The article is a response to the clue and task left in the work of Alves et al. (2015), which appeared in the European System Risk Board. This work contains an analysis of the network of 29 largest European insurance groups and their financial contractors. The authors note that insurance companies have direct exposures to other insurers, banks, and other financial institutions through debt, equity, and other financial instruments. These exposures can cause direct infection and thus spread of systemic risk (SR). The work cited above focuses on direct connections between EU insurers and banks. At the same time, the authors emphasize that their research does not include an analysis of linkages between insurers under reinsurance contracts, indirect connections via market price channels and information channels, nor an analysis of banks' exposure to insurers.

In the present article, we focus on the problem of indirect links between insurance companies that result from market price channels. More specifically, we examine the dynamics of these relationships. In our analysis, we assume that stock market quotations of insurance companies reflect market sentiment, which is a very important systemic risk factor. It is well known that risk infection is always accompanied by a negative market sentiment leading to customer panic in the financial industry. The results will create a vicious circle of risk and emotion. Thus, market sentiment is commonly used to forecast changes in the financial market and can be used as a systemic risk barometer (Kou et al. 2019).

Relationships between insurers and their dynamics have a direct impact on the propagation of systemic risk in the insurance sector. In our work, we propose a new hybrid approach to analyzing the dynamics of interconnections, based on combining the copula-DCC-GARCH and minimum spanning trees (MST). Using the copula-DCC-GARCH model, we determine tail dependence coefficients. Then, based on these coefficients for each analyzed period, we determine the "distance" matrix between insurance companies using the Mantegna metric (Mantegna and Stanley 1999) and construct minimum spanning trees. We analyze the dynamics using selected topological indicators for the MST obtained.

The main purpose of the work and contribution to the literature is:

(1) To check whether the time series of topological indicators of the network of connections between insurance companies obtained using the proposed hybrid approach reflect the situation on the financial market and whether they can be used as predictors of systemic risk in the insurance sector.
(2) An empirical analysis of 38 European insurance institutions selected from the top 50 insurance companies in Europe. We indicate which of the largest companies not on the G-SIIs list are of great importance in the context of SR.
(3) An analysis of the situation in the insurance sector in the context of SR, taking into account the latest political and economic situation in Europe, distinguishing four market states: The normal state, the state related to the subprime mortgage crisis, the state related to the immigration crisis in Europe, and the state related to the crises in France and Italy.
(4) An analysis of the contribution to the SR of the insurance sector.

The rest of the article is organized as follows. Section 2 reviews the subject literature devoted to systemic risk in the insurance sector. Section 3 presents the methodology and the empirical strategy used in the paper, Section 4 contains the data and a discussion of the results obtained, while Section 5 presents the conclusions.

2. Systemic Risk in the Insurance Sector

For over a decade, scientists have been trying to effectively define, study, and measure the phenomenon of systemic risk, which in the era of globalization of economics is one of the most important concepts in the prediction of economic phenomena. Most scholars base their definition of uncertainty and risk on Knight (1921, p. 233), Tversky and Kahneman (1992), Camerer and Weber (1992), and Zweifel and Eisen (2012, p. 1). In the work of Eling and Pankoke (2016) 43 definitions are given, which indicate a three-stage course of the phenomenon: Causes, events, and effects for the real economy. One of the latest approaches is the concept of systemic risk proposed by De Bandt and Hartmann (2000), in which a distinction is made between the risk of shocks based on their second-round effects (it focuses not on the institutions affected by the shock, but on the consequences on linked institution). In addition, Harrington (2009) distinguishes between systemic risk and the risk of typical shocks. According to him, only the risk of an event associated with "cross-contagious infection" (p. 802) should be considered systemic. Many researchers analyze the problem of SR in the context of the failure of a significant part of the financial sector and reduction of credit availability, e.g., Acharya et al. (2011). Adrian and Brunnermeier (2011) investigate the negative impact on credit supply; Bach and Nguyen (2012), Rodríguez-Moreno and Peña (2013) financial system failure; Baur et al. (2003), Chen et al. (2013c), Cummins and Weiss (2011, 2013), Weiß and Mühlnickel (2014) the negative impact on the real economy; Baluch et al. (2011) the chain reaction of financial difficulties; Chen et al. (2013b), Huang et al. (2009) many simultaneously defaulted pledges by large financial institutions; IAIS (2009), Jobst (2014), Radice (2010) the disruption of the flow of financial services, the negative impact on the real economy, and impairment of all or part of the financial system; Klein (2011) studies the market in the context of financial system instability, idiosyncratic events, and infection; Kress (2011) studies infection; Rodríguez-Moreno and Peña (2013) malfunctioning in the financial system and the negative impact on the real economy. In recent years, quantitative analysis of systemic risk using the described approaches has been carried out by, among others, Hautsch et al. (2015), Giglio et al. (2016), Benoit et al. (2017), Jajuga et al. (2017), Bégin et al. (2017), Jurkowska (2018).

The various concepts of systemic risk analysis presented above have inspired the creation of a number of different methods for measuring it. In the literature of the subject, several dozen measures can be indicated, which can be determined using mathematical, statistical, econometric, network modeling, and predictive analysis tools (in particular, multidimensional statistical analysis, including methods of learning with and without supervision). A review of systemic risk measures in use can be found, e.g., in the following articles: Bisias et al. (2012), Giglio et al. (2016), Di Cesare and Picco (2018).

It is worth noting that while there is quite extensive literature on the subject of systemic risk analysis in the banking sector, the insurance sector has been analyzed to a distinctly smaller extent. The reason for this was the belief that the group taking over, dispersing, and redistributing the financial effects of risk does not generate a systemic threat.

However, after the financial crisis in 2007–2009 and the European public debt crisis in 2010–2012, a significant increase in the interest in systemic risk in the insurance sector can be seen. Before the crisis, there was a clear belief among researchers that this sector is systemically insignificant. However, in the literature that emerged as a result of the crisis, although previous conviction was maintained in many studies, there appeared articles indicating the possibility of the insurance sector creating systemic risk. Examples include works in which the authors believe that insurance companies have become an unavoidable source of systemic risk (e.g., Billio et al. 2012; Weiß and Mühlnickel 2014) and in which they claim insurance companies to be systematically significant, but only due to their nontraditional (banking) activities (e.g., Baluch et al. 2011; Bednarczyk 2013; Cummins and Weiss 2014; Czerwińska 2014) and the overall systemic importance of the insurance sector as a whole is still subdued to the banking sector (e.g., Chen et al. 2013a). In turn, Bierth et al. (2015) after examining a very large sample of insurers in the long term, believe that the contribution of the insurance sector to systemic risk is relatively small, however, they claim that it peaked during the financial crisis in the period from 2007 to 2008. They also indicate that significant factors affecting the insurer's exposure to systemic risk are strong linkages between large insurance companies, leverage, losses, and liquidity (the four L's: Linkages, leverage, losses, liquidity). On the other hand, there are also studies (Harrington 2009) and (Bell and Keller 2009) claiming a complete lack of evidence for the systemic importance of the insurance industry.

After the aforementioned crises, supervisory authorities also began to pay more attention to the problem of systemic risk in the insurance industry. The Financial Stability Board (FSB), in consultation with the International Association of Insurance Supervisors (IAIS), identified nine global systemically important insurers (G-SIIs) based on the assessment methodology developed by IAIS, which includes the following five elements: Noninsurance activity of the insurer (45%), assessment of the degree of direct and indirect links of institutions within the financial system (40%), range of global activity (5%), the size of the insurance institution (5%), and product substitutability (5%).

Since the publication of this methodology and the G-SII list, questions have been raised about the appropriateness and effectiveness of the proposed framework by both the insurance sector and academia. The ongoing discussion in the literature to date tends to show that some indicators in the IAIS assessment methodology may not be able to explain the insurer's contribution to systemic risk (Weiß and Mühlnickel 2014; Bierth et al. 2015). Looking at the solutions adopted from the insurance industry, one can point to the example of MetLife, which was constantly struggling to remove the label of a "systemically important institution" and obtained a favorable ruling in the US District Court in March 2016 (Tracy and Holm 2016). Following the success of MetLife, the AIG SIFI label was withdrawn by FSOC in September 2017, and Prudential Financial dumped its brand SIFI in October 2018.

To sum up, current literature and real events show that systemic risk in the insurance sector is still a challenge waiting for precise methodological solutions. After 2014, we observe an increased involvement of scientists in the qualitative and quantitative analysis of this issue. Our paper is one of the few quantitative studies on systemic risk in the European and global insurance sector. Although SR in the financial sector is analyzed by: Bierth et al. (2015), Mühlnickel and Weiß (2015), Kanno (2016), Giglio et al. (2016), Adrian and Brunnermeier (2016), Koijen and Yogo (2016), Brownlees and Engle (2017), Kaserer and Klein (2018) and risk infection is studied by Hautsch et al. (2015), Härdle et al. (2016), Fan et al. (2018), nevertheless, none of these approaches is a hybrid approach in which the possibility of combining different measures would be analyzed on such a scale as proposed in our project.

3. Methodology

We carry out the analysis of the dynamics of interconnections between insurance companies using a new hybrid approach based on the combination of the copula-DCC-GARCH model and minimum spanning trees (MST). The construction of minimum spanning trees based on the dependencies in the tails plays a key role in it. To this end, using two-dimensional copula-DCC-GARCH models for each studied period t, $(t = 1, \ldots, T)$ and each pair of log-returns $r_{i,t}$, $r_{j,t}$, $(i, j = 1, \ldots, k, j > i)$ we estimate the bivariate joint distributions:

$$F_t(r_{i,t}, r_{j,t}) = C_{ij,t}(F_{i,t}(r_{j,t}), F_{j,t}(r_{i,t})) \qquad (1)$$

where $C_{ij,t}$ denotes the copula, while F_t and $F_{i,t}$, $F_{j,t}$, respectively, are the joint cumulative distribution function and the cumulative distribution functions (*cdf*) of the marginal distributions at time t. In turn, making use of the copulas $C_{ij,t}$ we estimate the pairwise lower tail dependence of the log-returns $r_{i,t}$, $r_{j,t}$:

$$\lambda_t^L(i,j) = \lim_{q \to 0^+} \frac{C_{ij,t}(q,q)}{q} \qquad (2)$$

Then, for each period t, we determine the "distance" matrix between insurance companies using the metric (Mantegna and Stanley 1999):

$$d_t(i,j) = \sqrt{2\left(1 - \lambda_t^L(i,j)\right)} \qquad (3)$$

and using the Kruskal algorithm (Mantegna and Stanley 1999), we construct minimum spanning trees MST_t with k vertices and $k-1$ edges.

Based on the trees thus obtained MST_t $(t = 1 \ldots T)$ we determine the time series of the following topological network indicators:

- Average path length—APL,
- Maximum degree—Max.Deg,
- The parameters α of the vertex degree distribution required to follow a power law,
- Network diameter—D,
- Rich club effect—RCE,

- Assortativity,
- Betweenness centrality—BC,
- Vertex strength (centrality),
- Vertex degree,
- Closeness centrality.

It should be mentioned that in the literature the minimum spanning trees that evolve in time are also monitored by many other topological network indicators such as the Eigenvector centrality (Tang et al. 2018), MOL (mean occupation layer) (Onnela et al. 2002, 2003), normalized tree length (Onnela et al. 2003), tree half-life (Onnela et al. 2003); survival ratio of the edges (Onnela et al. 2002; Sensoy and Tabak 2014); and agglomerative coefficient (Matesanz and Ortega 2015).

In the next stage of research, we determine a time series for the deltaCoVaR measure for each insurer. It brings along an information about the insurer's contribution to the systemic risk in the insurance sector. For this purpose, we also use two-dimensional copula-DCC-GARCH models and the empirical strategy presented in the articles: Denkowska and Wanat (2019), Wanat and Denkowska (2018, 2019). We assume that the European insurance sector is represented by the STOXX 600 Europe Insurance index. We compare the time series of deltaCoVaR measures obtained in this way with the time series of topological indicators of the MST_t from the point of view of the possibility of using the latter as systemic risk predictors in the insurance sector.

The tail dependence coefficients ($\lambda_t^L(i,j)$) and the deltaCoVaR measure, which are key to the empirical strategy presented above, are determined using two-dimensional copula-DCC-GARCH models. In the two-dimensional case in the DCC-GARCH model, the log-returns vector distribution $r_t = (r_{1,t}, r_{2,t})$, which is conditional with respect to the set Ω_{t-1} of information available up to the moment $t-1$ is modeled using the conditional copulas proposed by Patton (2006). It takes the following form:

$$r_{1,t}|\Omega_{t-1} \sim F_{1,t}(\cdot|\Omega_{t-1}),\ r_{2,t}|\Omega_{t-1} \sim F_{2,t}(\cdot|\Omega_{t-1}) \quad (4)$$

$$r_t|\Omega_{t-1} \sim F_t(\cdot|\Omega_{t-1}) \quad (5)$$

$$F_t(r_t|\Omega_{t-1}) = C_t\big(F_{1,t}(r_{1,t}|\Omega_{t-1}), F_{2,t}(r_{2,t}|\Omega_{t-1})\big), \quad (6)$$

where C_t denotes the copula, while F_t and $F_{i,t}$ ($i = 1, 2$), respectively, the two-dimensional distribution and the marginal distributions at the moment t. In general, one-dimensional log-returns can be modeled using different specifications of the average model and different specifications of the variance model (e.g., sGARCH, fGARCH, eGARCH, gjrGARCH, apARCH, iGARCH, csGARCH). In our study, the following ARMA process was used for all the series of log-returns:

$$r_{i,t} = \mu_{i,t} + y_{i,t},\ (i = 1, 2) \quad (7)$$

$$\mu_{i,t} = E(r_{i,t}|\Omega_{t-1}), \quad (8)$$

$$\mu_{i,t} = \mu_{i,0} + \sum_{j=1}^{p_i} \varphi_{ij} r_{i,t-j} + \sum_{j=1}^{q_i} \theta_{ij} y_{i,t-j}, \quad (9)$$

$$y_{i,t} = \sqrt{h_{i,t}}\, \varepsilon_{i,t}, \quad (10)$$

and the standard GARCH (sGARCH) model for the variance:

$$h_{i,t} = Var(r_{i,t}|\Omega_{t-1}),\ h_{i,t} = \omega_i + \sum_{j=1}^{p_i} \alpha_{ij} y_{i,t-j}^2 + \sum_{j=1}^{q_i} \beta_{ij} h_{i,t-j} \quad (11)$$

where $\varepsilon_{i,t} = \frac{y_{i,t}}{\sqrt{h_{i,t}}}$ are identically distributed independent random variables (in the empirical analysis we considered the following distributions: Normal, skew normal, t-Student, skew t-Student, and GED).

To describe the dependences between the log-returns $r_{1,t}$ and $r_{2,t}$ we used Student t-copulas, whose parameters were the conditional correlations R_t obtained from the DCC(m, n) model:

$$H_t = D_t R_t D_t, \tag{12}$$

$$D_t = diag\left(\sqrt{h_{1,t}}, \sqrt{h_{2,t}}\right), \tag{13}$$

$$R_t = (diag(Q_t))^{-\frac{1}{2}} Q_t (diag(Q_t))^{-\frac{1}{2}} \tag{14}$$

$$Q_t = \left(1 - \sum_{j=1}^{m} c_j - \sum_{j=1}^{n} d_j\right)\overline{Q} + \sum_{j=1}^{m} c_j\left(\varepsilon_{t-j}\varepsilon'_{t-j}\right) + \sum_{j=1}^{n} d_j Q_{t-j}. \tag{15}$$

In this model, $\overline{Q}$ is the unconditional covariance matrix of the standardized rests ε_t, while c_j $(j=1,\ldots,m)$ and d_j $(j=1,\ldots,n)$ are scalar values, where c_j describes the impact on current correlations of precedent shocks, and d_j represents the influence on current correlations of the previous conditional correlations.

We estimate the parameters of the above copula-DCC-GARCH model using the inference function for the margins (IFM) method. This method is presented in detail, among others in Joe (1997). We perform the calculations in the R environment, using the "rmgarch" package.

4. Data and Results of Empirical Analysis

The basis of the study are the stock quotes of 38 European insurance institutions. Most of them are on the list of the top 50 insurance companies in Europe based on total assets. AXA, a France-based company, is the largest insurance company in Europe and globally. It is also one of the world's largest asset managers with total assets under management of over 1.4 trillion euro. Allianz, headquartered in Munich, Germany, is the second largest European insurer in terms of assets. We include insurers analyzed in the work Alves et al. (2015) and nine additional ones[1]. We estimate the deltaCoVaR measure assuming that the European insurance sector is represented by the STOXX 600 Europe Insurance index. We analyze weekly logarithmic returns for the period from 7 January 2005 to 20 December 2019.

In order to estimate $\lambda_t^L(i,j)$, we consider various specifications for two-dimensional copula-DCC-GARCH models. Finally, following the information criteria and model adequacy tests, we adopt for all the instruments the ARMA (1,1)—sGARCH (1,1) model with the skew Student distribution. When analyzing the dynamics of the dependences between log-returns, we consider Student copulas and various DCC model specifications. As before, based on information criteria, we select the Student copula with conditional correlations obtained from the DCC (1,1) model and a constant shape parameter. We choose the same specifications for two-dimensional copula-DCC-GARCH models, which we use to estimate the deltaCoVaR measures.

In what follows, we present the results of the analysis of ten topological indicators of the MSTs, divided into two groups according to their specificity. One group consists of those that are a measure of each MST vertex: Node degree, betweenness centrality, vertex strength, and closeness centrality. The other one is formed by those that are a measure of the properties of the entire MST, such as average path length, maximum degree, parameters α of the power distribution of vertex degrees, diameter, rich club effect, and assortativity.

---

[1] These are: Achmea (Eureko Group), Aegon Group/Unirobe Meeùs Group, AGEAS, Allianz, Aviva, AXA, BNP Paribas, Grupo Catalana Occidente, CNP Assurances, Royal Bank of Scotland Group, Generali, Groupe Crédit Agricole Assurances, HDI/Talanx, If P&C Insurance, ING Group, KBC, Legal & General Group plc, Mapfre, Munich Re, Old Mutual plc, Prudential, RSA Insurance Group, SCOR, Lloyds Banking Group, Unipol, UNIQA Insurance Group, Vienna Insurance Group, Zurich Insurance, Swiss Life, Chubb Ltd, Hannover Re, Storebrand, XL Group, Helvetia Holding, Mediolanum, Sampo Oyj, Societa Cattolica di Assicurazione, Topdanmark A/S.

4.1. Degree Distribution

For an undirected network, the degree k_i of node i is defined as the total number of links incident to it, see e.g., Sensoy and Tabak (2014). The degree increases as a node becomes more connected and more central to the network. The degree distribution P(k) measures the frequency of nodes with different degrees in the network.

As depicted in Figure 1, the sample degree distribution of the minimum spanning tree is positively skewed, signaling heterogeneity in the system. Only a small portion of nodes in the network are highly interconnected (core companies), while the majority of other nodes have a relative low number of linkages (periphery companies). Such a configuration suggests the presence of several large star-like structures in the minimum spanning tree. The figure highlights examples of distributions, assigned to relevant dates, which we associated during the study as outstanding. 7 January 2005 is the period preceding the subprime crisis, 3 October 2008 is the crisis, 15 January 2010 is the date of the normal state preceding the crisis of excessive public debt in the euro area, in 3 September 2010 it is a much slender distribution graph of the vertex distribution that shows the distribution during the crisis. 18 September 2015 marks the beginning of the migrant crisis in Europe. 18 August 2017 is the beginning of the crisis related to the protests in France and the "Yellow vests' movement". Therefore, periods in which we observe a high maximum value for 1 (see Figure 1) and at the same time low values for the remaining numbers are periods during which there are many companies with only single connections and several others having a large number of links, which is a feature favoring SR. The chart reflects the market situation.

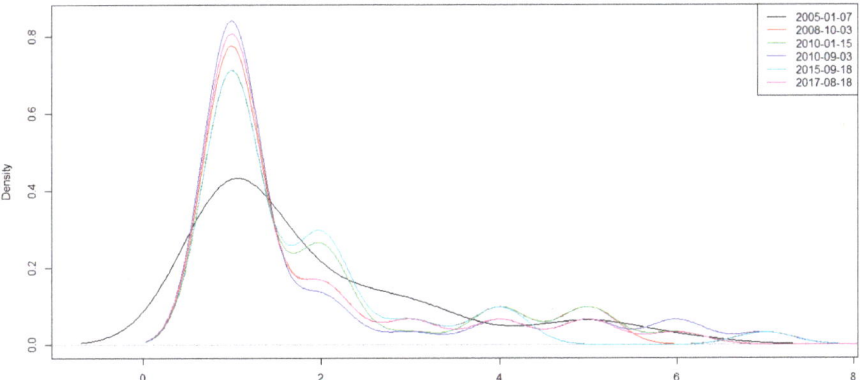

Figure 1. Degree distribution of selected minimum spanning trees. Source: Own study.

4.2. Betweenness Centrality—BC

This indicator is a measure of "being between" defined as the quotient of the number of shortest paths between vertices that pass through a given vertex and the number of all the shortest paths between vertices, see e.g., Sensoy and Tabak (2014). It determines the "most important" vertices of a given graph on a chart based on the shortest paths (e.g., the most influential insurer). For each pair of vertices in a connected graph, there is at least one path between them, so that either the number of edges that you have to pass (for unweighted graphs) or the sum of the weights of the vertices that you go through (for weighted graphs) is minimized. The BC measure of a given vertex is the number of those shortest paths that pass through it. This measure defines to what extent a given node (vertex) serves as an intermediary for other network nodes. A node with a higher BC has more control over the network because more information flows through it. Figure 2 shows the mean BC for the period under consideration and each of the insurance companies studied.

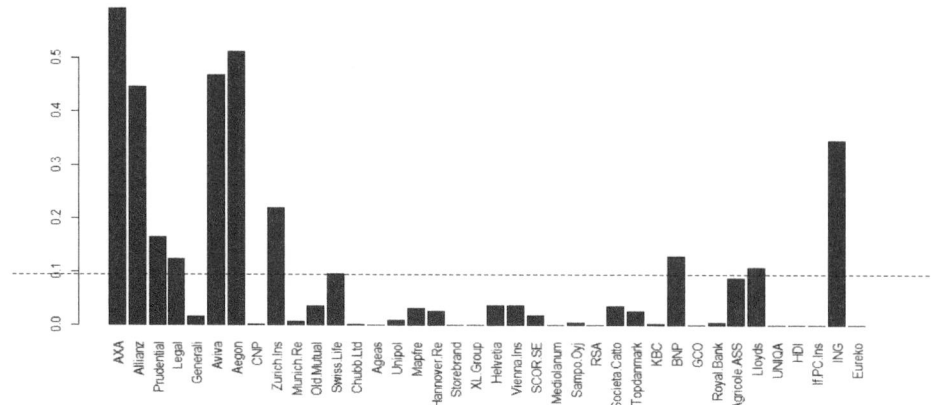

Figure 2. Average value of betweenness centrality (BC) in the period under consideration for individual insurance institutions. Source: Own study.

The analysis shows that the highest BC is held by AXA, Aegon, Allianz, Aviva, Prudential, which are companies appearing on the Financial Stability Board (FSB) 2016 list of systemically important insurers (G-SIIs), ING, and Zurich Insurance.

4.3. Vertex Strength (Centrality)

To identify the most central nodes in the system, we calculate the so-called vertex strength, which represents a weighted measure of centrality: $s_i = \sum_{j \in \psi(i)} \frac{1}{d_{ij}}$, where $\psi(i)$ is the set of all neighbors of the node i and d_{ij} is the length of the edge between two nodes, see e.g., Lautier and Raynaud (2013). It indicates how far one node is from all others in the entire network. The obtained average vertex strength of the selected insurers is presented in Figure 3.

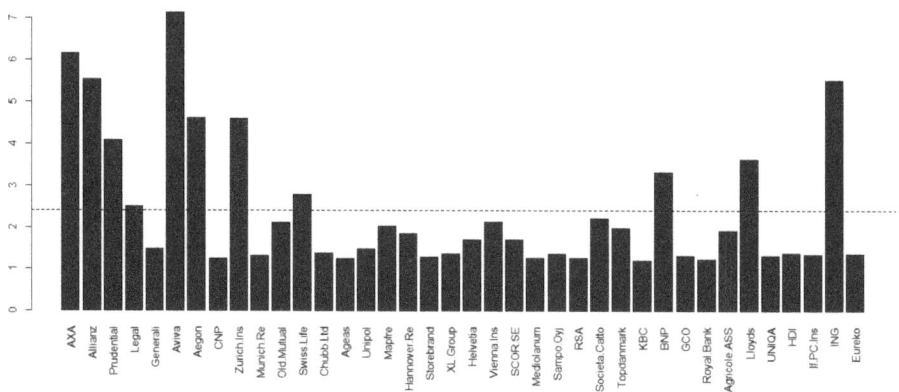

Figure 3. Average insurers strength in the period under consideration. Source: Own study.

The higher the vertex strength, the more systemically important a node is. From the diagram above we can infer that the most important are Aviva, AXA, Allianz, and ING.

4.4. Closeness Centrality

This node proximity measure is a measure calculated as the inverse of the sum of the shortest path lengths between the given node and all nodes in the network, see e.g., Bavelas (1950);

Sensoy and Tabak (2014) For MST, it is the inverse of the sum of the lengths of all edges. The more central the node is, the closer it is to all other nodes, it is thus a measure of the proximity of an insurer to the rest of the network. The average closeness centrality in the period studied and for each insurer considered is given in Figure 4.

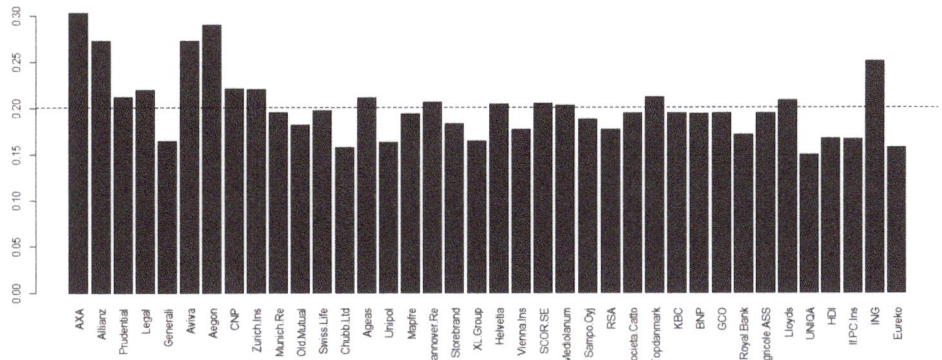

Figure 4. Average closeness centrality in the period under consideration. Source: Own study.

The diagram analysis shows that the vertices are relatively close together. This may foster contagion.

The diagram below (Figure 5) is a summary of the four-dimensional analysis of MST indicators. We present it with the intention to draw the reader's attention to the fact that there are institutions whose bars are in each case considered among the highest ones, which proves the importance of their corresponding vertex in the MST.

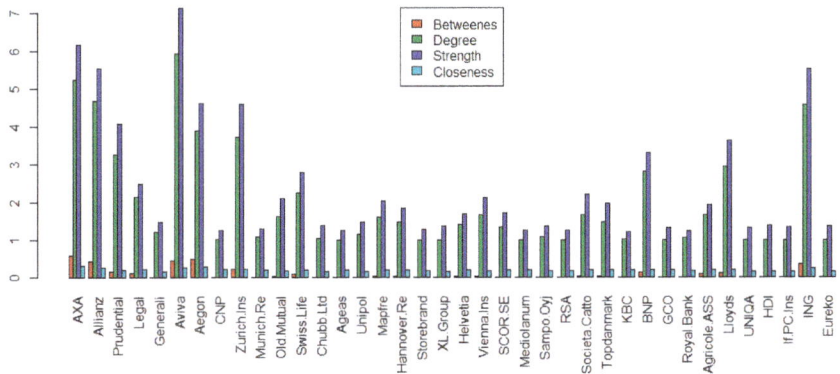

Figure 5. Average betweenness centrality, vertex degree, vertex strength, and closeness centrality. Source: Own study.

4.5. Average Path Lentgth (APL)

This indicator is defined as the average number of steps along the shortest paths for all possible pairs of network nodes. It measures the effectiveness of information flow or mass transport in a given network, see e.g., Wang et al. (2014) APL is one of the strongest measures of network topology, along with its clustering factor and degree distribution. It distinguishes an easy-to-access network from a more complex and inefficient one. The smaller the average path length, the easier the flow of information. Of course, we are talking about an average so the network itself can have several very distant nodes and many adjacent nodes. The times series obtained for the APL is presented in Figure 6.

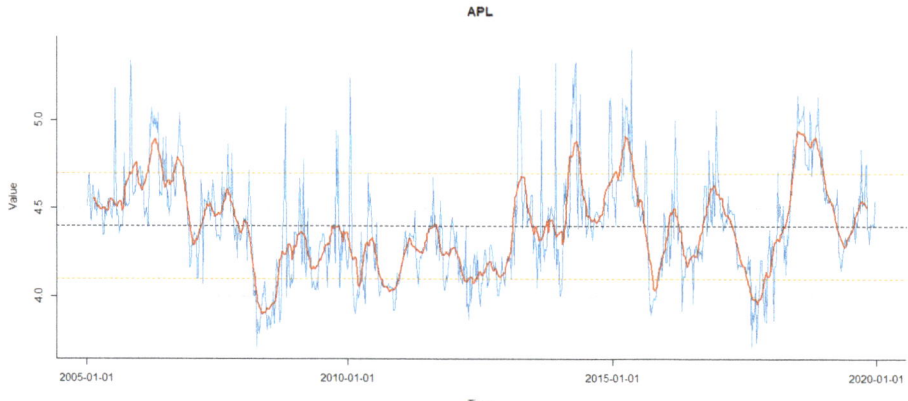

Figure 6. Average path length in the period from 7 January 2005 to 20 December 2019. Red lines depict the 13 periods of the moving average smoothed series. Source: Own study.

Note that during the crisis, the APL indicator decreases in comparison to the normal state, which means that the average path length between any pair of companies decreases.

4.6. Maximum Degree—Max.Deg

This indicator in graph theory is the maximum degree (i.e., the number of edges coming out of it, where loops count double) of a vertex of the graph; thus, it is the number of connections of a central vertex, see e.g., Wang et al. (2014).The times series obtained for the maximum degree is shown in Figure 7. This indicator in graph theory is the maximal number of connections a vertex of the graph has. By connections we mean, of course, the number of edges coming out of a vertex, with loops counting double.

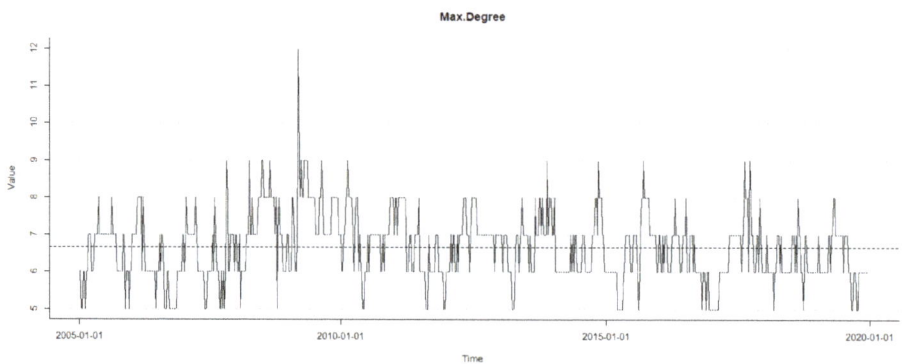

Figure 7. Maximum degree in the period from 7 January 2005 to 20 December 2019. Source: Own study.

Maximum degree grows during periods of crisis, which means that in a group of insurers during a crisis some insurer has many more connections with others than is usual in the normal state.

4.7. Parameter α of the Vertex Degree Distribution Required to Follow a Power Law

This indicator measures the scale-free behavior of a network, see e.g., Wang et al. (2014). The network is scale-free if the distribution, $P(s)$, the number of connections between the vertices, follows a power law, i.e., it has (asymptotically) the form $P(s) = C \cdot s^{-\alpha}$, $\alpha > 0$, where α is a parameter specific to the given network. The power law followed by the degree distribution gives the network a kind of fractal self-similarity property, which accounts for the name. A scale-free network is characterized by a small number of vertices having a large number of connections (such nodes are called hubs) and many vertices that have only one connection. From the point of view of our analysis, this type of network can be considered as "favorable" to the propagation of information (in our case: Of systemic risk), and the companies/hubs that it has are systemically relevant. The time series obtained for the alpha parameters is shown in Figure 8.

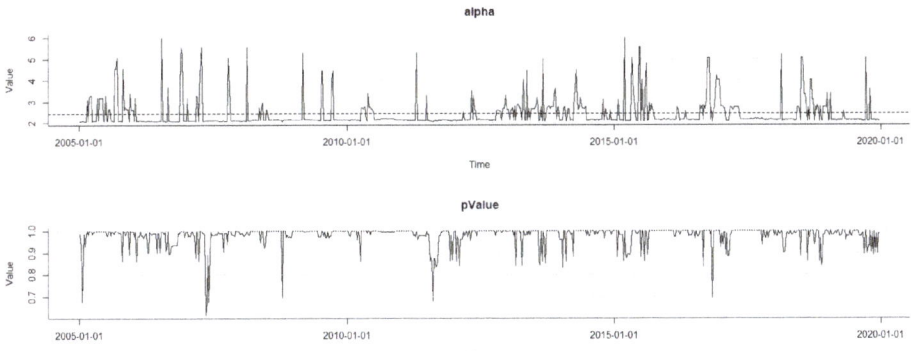

Figure 8. Estimated parameters alpha of power distribution for the minimum spanning trees (MST) from 7 January 2005 to 20 December 2019. Source: Own study.

MSTs are scale-free, but during crises the alpha value is closer to 2, which means that the structure of MST is star-shaped with outstanding hubs having a high degree, i.e., multiple edges that connect the company/hub to several companies with only one edge.

4.8. Diameter of the Network (Diameter)

It is determined by choosing from among all the shortest paths connecting any pair vertices to the longest one. For MST, this is simply the longest path in the MST. The time series obtained for the diameter is shown in Figure 9.

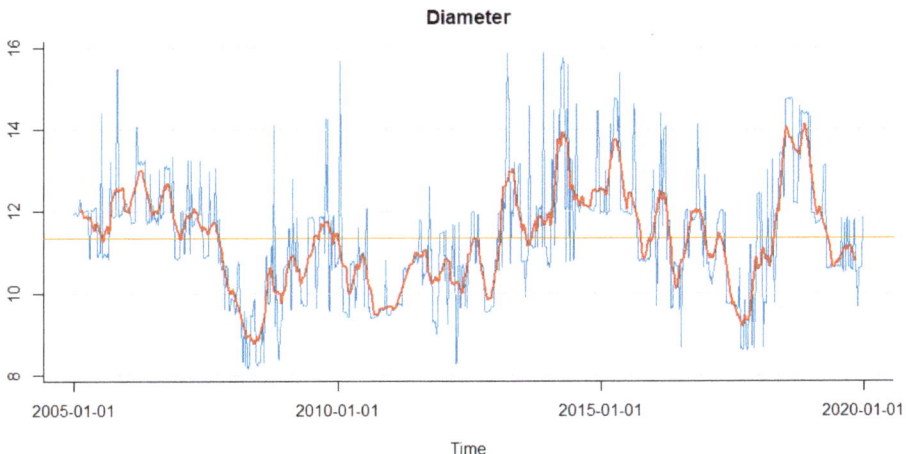

Figure 9. Diameter in the period from 7 January 2005 to 20 December 2019. Red lines depict the 13 periods of the moving average smoothed series. Source: Own study.

The diameter decreases during crises, which means that during these periods the path between the further apart lying MST vertices is shortened.

4.9. Rich Club Effect–RCE

The idea is that well-connected vertices connect also one with one another, see e.g., Colizza et al. (2006) The RCE is defined to be $\phi(k) = \frac{2E_{>k}}{N_{>k}(N_{>k}-1)}$, where $\frac{N_{>k}(N_{>k}-1)}{2}$ is the number of all the possible paths between $N_{>k}$ vertices, $E_{>k}$ is the number of vertices of $N_{>k}$ nodes having degree >k. The effect of a rich club reduces system stability, which means that if RCE increases, then a perturbation can be more easily transmitted through the network.

The times series RCE for k = 4 obtained in the study is shown in Figure 10, while its distribution in the market states determined is presented in later figure. They show the results for the dynamic MST with φ (4).

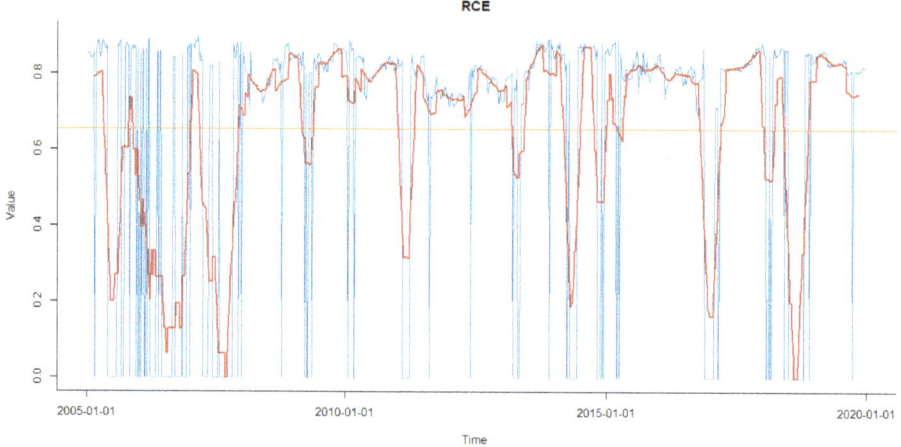

Figure 10. Rich club effect (RCE) during the period from 7 January 2005 to 20 December 2019. Red lines depict the 13 periods of the moving average smoothed series. Source: Own study.

4.10. Assortativity

The concept of assortativity was introduced by Newman (2002) and has been intensively studied since then. Assortativity is a graphic measure. It shows to what extent nodes in the network associate to one another by similarity or opposition (positive or negative mating). Basically, the network's assortatavity is determined for the degree (number of direct neighbors) of nodes in the network. Assortativity is expressed as a scalar $-1 \leq \rho \leq 1$. The network is said to be assortative when high-degree nodes are mostly connected to other high-degree nodes while low-degree nodes are mostly connected to other low-degree nodes. The network is said to be non-assortatative when high-degree nodes are connected mostly to low-degree nodes and low-degree nodes are mostly connected to high-degree nodes. Assortativity provides information on the structure of the network, but also on its dynamic behavior and robustness.

The assortativity time series is shown in Figure 11.

Assortativity is negative, which means that in each state the tree is rather non-assortatative, i.e., the vertices tend to connect rather as negative mating, which also confirms the previously described property of the network to be scale-free.

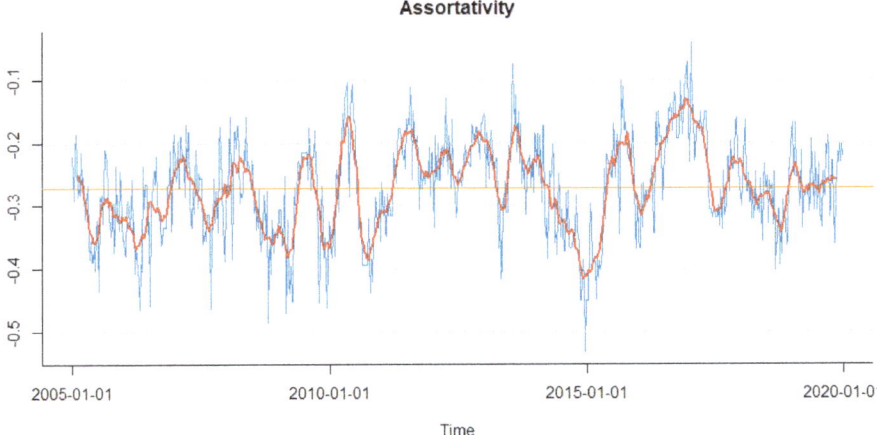

Figure 11. Assortativity during the period from 7 January 2005 to 20 December 2019. Red lines depict the 13 periods of the moving average smoothed series. Source: Own study.

Based on the time series of MST topological indicators, we determined a time partition into four periods:

- The period which we call normal state—normal (N).
- A period of two subprime crises and excessive public debt, which began in 2008 and lasted until around 2013. This period in our time series falls exactly between 8 February 2008 and 1 March 2013—subprime mortgage crisis (SMC).
- The period of crisis associated with the beginning of the migration crisis in Europe, falling on 2015/2016. This period on our time series falls exactly between 7 August 2015 and on 23 September 2016—immigrant (I).
- The period of the beginning of the crisis in the countries of the European Union related to the crisis in France associated with strikes, and in Italy due to the ever-growing public debt (which is now seven times higher than the debt in Greece), falling at the turn of 2017 and 2018. In our case it is exactly the period from 21 April 2017 until 11 May 2018—France and Italy crisis (FIC).

The charts below (Figure 12) present the expected values of the relevant MST topological indicators in the different market states. The results confirm the above description of indicators during crises and in a normal state. Putting together the indicators allows us to compare their behavior in four different states. Clearly, the indicators behave differently during crises. It is clearly apparent from the Kruskal–Wallis rank sum test results (Table 1) and the post-hoc analysis performed using the Conover–Inman test (Table 2)[2]. In the state N, APL and diameter is higher, while maximum degree is lower than in the crisis states. This means MST is stretching. The insurer with the largest number of connections has actually fewer connections than during the crises. RCE varies, but the average—marked with a red dot—is smaller, i.e., the stability of the network is higher. The network assortativity in each state is at a similar, negative level, i.e., the network does not vary, remaining constantly similar. Connections are established by negative mating. High degree companies are linked to low degree ones. Since alpha is close to 2, MSTs are scale-free, but the average alpha increases during the period N.

---

[2] We used nonparametric tests since none of the indicators satisfied the normal distribution requirement.

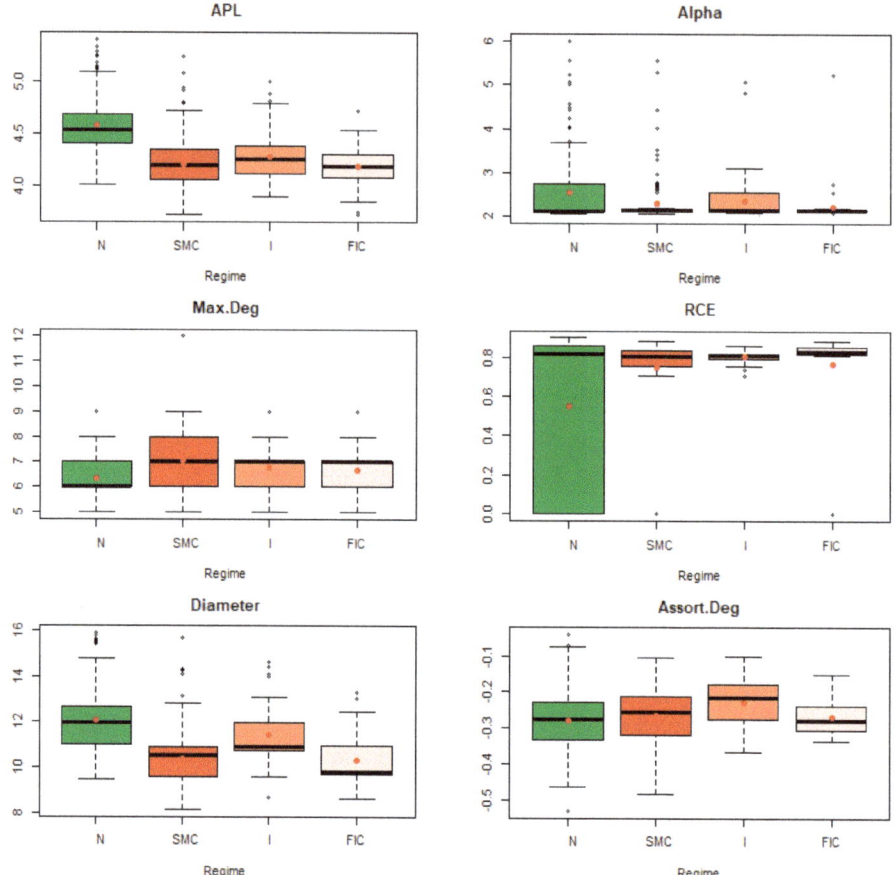

Figure 12. Distribution of MST topological indicators in different market states. Source: Own study.

Table 1. Kruskal–Wallis rank sum test results.

Indicator	Kruskal–Wallis chi-Squared	p-Value
APL	347.78	$<2.2 \times 10^{-16}$
Alpha	9.35	0.02499
Max. Deg	99.63	$<2.2 \times 10^{-16}$
RCE	15.34	0.00155
Diameter	269.03	$<2.2 \times 10^{-16}$
Assort. Deg	25.60	1.155×10^{-5}

Source: Own study.

Special attention is drawn to the RCE indicator (Figure 12), whose average value in the state N is very different from the average in the remaining distinguished states. By analyzing in more detail (Figure 13), we note that in the states presented RCE is high, which means that the way the vertices are connected to one another is such that the highest degree vertices are linked together. Potentially, this creates the possibility of transferring turbulences. In the normal states, the series shows an important variability and the average RCE is high. In the state N, the mean is lower. RCE takes the value zero many times. This means that there are no vertices with four or more edges. MST appears in the form of a stretched chain. It is then more stable than during the SMC, I, or FIC periods.

Table 2. Post-hoc analysis results (Conover–Inman test).

Compared Market States	Difference	p-Value	Signif[2].	LCL	UCL
APL					
N-SMC	307.27	0.0000	***	281.11	333.43
N-I	247.72	0.0000	***	202.00	293.45
N-FIC	318.21	0.0000	***	271.08	365.33
SMC-I	−59.55	0.0135	*	−106.77	−12.33
SMC-FIC	10.93	0.6587		−37.64	59.51
I-FIC	70.48	0.0244	*	9.11	131.85
Alpha					
N-SMC	3.36	0.9135		−57.23	63.94
N-I	−112.92	0.0366	*	−218.81	−7.03
N-FIC	−124.66	0.0252	*	−233.79	−15.53
SMC-I	−116.28	0.0372	*	−225.63	−6.92
SMC-FIC	−128.02	0.0257	*	−240.51	−15.52
I-FIC	−11.74	0.8714		−153.86	130.38
Max.Deg					
N-SMC	−166.35	0.0000	***	−197.31	−135.38
N-I	−108.68	0.0001	***	−162.81	−54.56
N-FIC	−77.98	0.0062	**	−133.76	−22.20
SMC-I	57.66	0.0432	*	1.77	113.56
SMC-FIC	88.36	0.0026	**	30.86	145.86
I-FIC	30.70	0.4070		−41.94	103.34
RCE					
N-SMC	27.31	0.1223		−7.34	61.96
N-I	25.66	0.4058		−34.90	86.23
N-FIC	−99.12	0.0019	**	−161.54	−36.70
SMC-I	−1.64	0.9589		−64.19	60.90
SMC-FIC	−126.43	0.0001	***	−190.77	−62.09
I-FIC	−124.78	0.0027	**	−206.07	−43.50
Diameter					
N-SMC	280.91	0.0000	***	252.47	309.36
N-I	107.97	0.0000	***	58.25	157.69
N-FIC	257.93	0.0000	***	206.69	309.17
SMC-I	−172.94	0.0000	***	−224.29	−121.60
SMC-FIC	−22.99	0.3932		−75.80	29.83
I-FIC	149.95	0.0000	***	83.23	216.68
Assort.Deg					
N-SMC	−46.91	0.0079	**	−81.47	−12.35
N-I	−150.22	0.0000	***	−210.63	−89.81
N-FIC	−27.48	0.3865		−89.74	34.78
SMC-I	−103.31	0.0012	**	−165.70	−40.92
SMC-FIC	19.43	0.5525		−44.75	83.61
I-FIC	122.74	0.0031	**	41.66	203.82

Source: Own study.

---

[2] We used nonparametric tests since none of the indicators satisfied the normal distribution requirement.

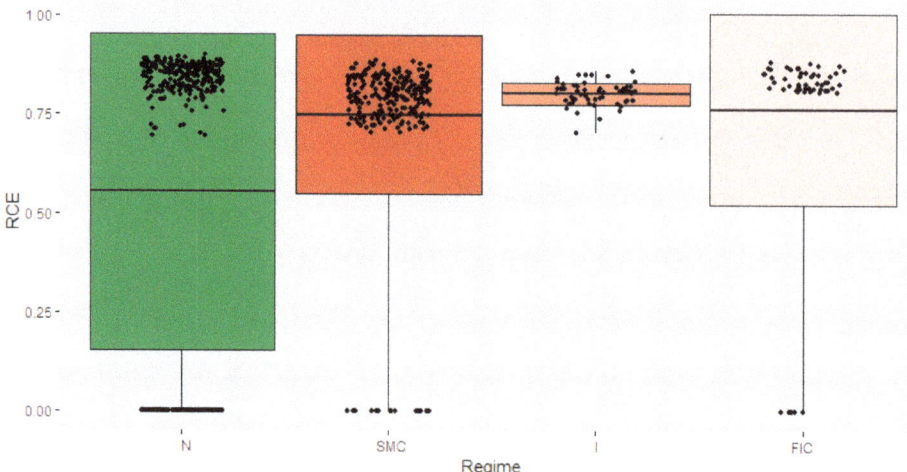

Figure 13. RCE distribution in determined market states based on the mean and the standard deviation for k = 4. Source: Own study.

Below (Figure 14) are sample MSTs at selected times: A tree that has a chain-like structure will slow down risk propagation, and one that has a star-shaped structure will foster it.

On Figures 15–17, we present the results obtained for deltaCoVaR. These are, respectively, the average deltaCoVaR value in the period studied, the distribution of this average in the different market states, and the average deltaCoVaR value for each insurer in the period under consideration. They corroborate the fact that insurance companies contribute to systemic risk. This contribution depends on the market state.

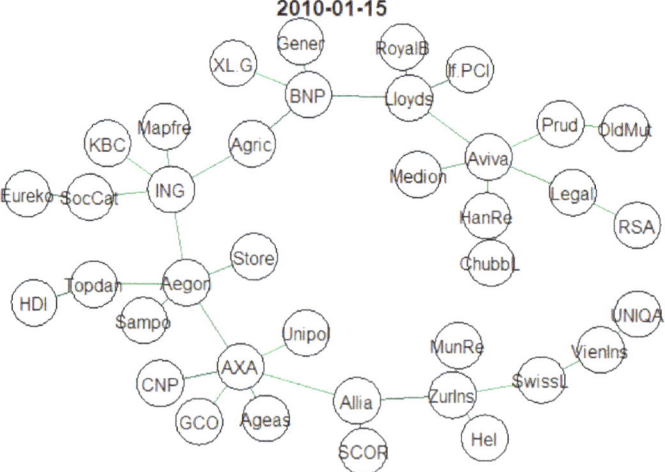

Figure 14. *Cont.*

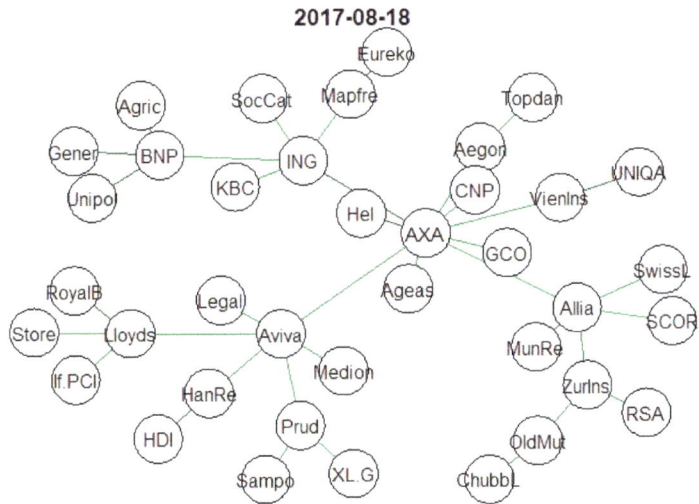

Figure 14. Sample MSTs in two chosen times. Source: Own study.

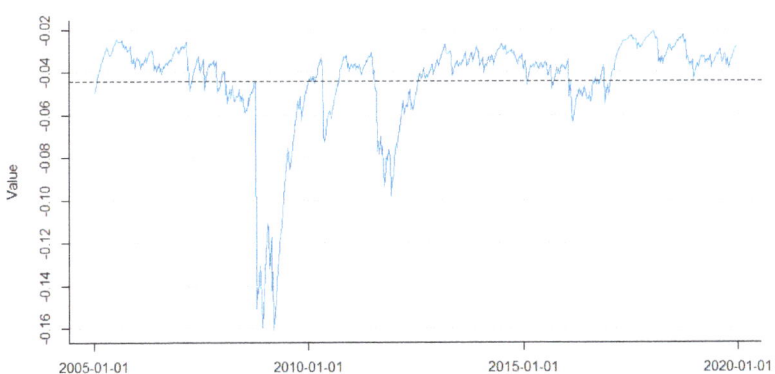

Figure 15. Mean deltaCoVaR. Source: Own study.

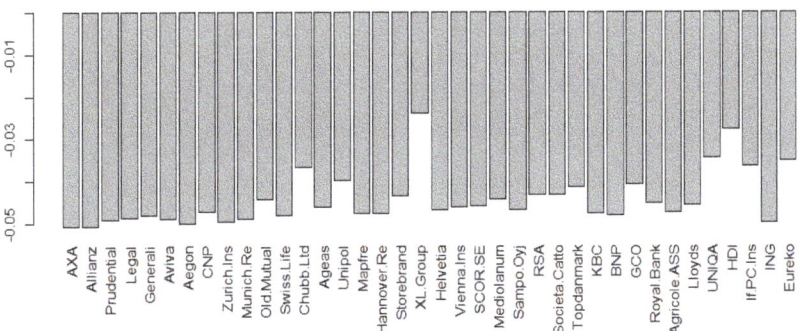

Figure 16. Mean deltaCoVaR for each insurer. Source: Own study.

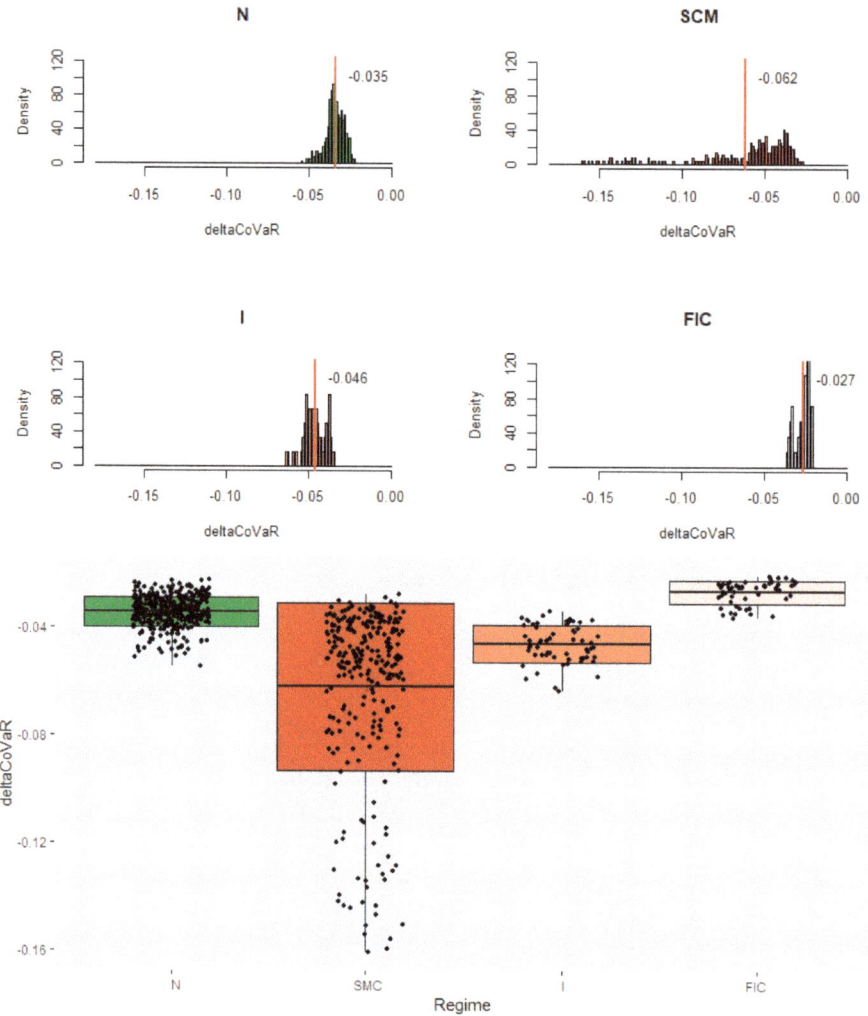

Figure 17. Mean deltaCoVaR distribution in different market states. Source: Own study.

The mean deltaCoVaR chart confirms the fact that insurance companies contribute to systemic risk. deltaCoVaR decreases in highlighted periods of crises.

On average, each company contributes to systemic risk.

The smallest contribution to SR is observed in the FIC and N periods. The largest contribution is in the SMC period. The beginning of immigration was also a period in which we notice an increased contribution to the SR.

5. Conclusions

Empirical results show the usefulness of network topology indicators for detecting and analyzing systemic risk in the insurance sector. In the proposed hybrid model, the analysis of times series, taking into account also the most recent data from the end of 2019, confirms the phenomena occurring on the market. The behavior of the time series reflects each atypical economic or political situation that influenced the insurance market. Periods corresponding to the subprime and excessive public debt crises stand out, as well as the periods of the beginning of the European immigration crisis, the UE crisis generated by the French strikes' crisis, and the growing sovereign debt crisis in Italy. In the distinguished states, the structure of MST changes along with the market situation. MSTs—their topological indicators are a tool that also allows clustering in the insurance sector and helps determine those companies that are relevant in the entire group. AXA, Allianz, Aegon, Aviva, and non-G-SIIs, ING, and Zurich Insurance play a significant role. These are institutions through which risk may be transferred. They stand out when assessing BC, strength, closeness centrality, and degree. In assessing the indicators for the entire network, we note that in the three periods of crises we have identified, APL and diameter decrease, maximum degree increases, RCE is high, and the assortment is negative. All this means that in the SMC, I, FIC states, MST becomes star-like and compact, which is accompanied by a decrease in system stability, which means that turbulence can be more easily transmitted over the network. Such a network configuration is less resistant to shocks and more susceptible to contagion and transferring the effects of collapses on the financial market. All institutions contribute to SR, and again the largest contribution is due to the previously mentioned companies. When analyzing deltaCoVaR averages, the crisis period again stands out. In the so-called period N, the contribution to SR is the smallest.

Author Contributions: Both authors (A.D., S.W.) contributed to all the sections. All authors have read and agreed to the published version of the manuscript.

Funding: The authors acknowledge support from a subsidy granted to Cracow University of Economics.

Acknowledgments: The authors would like to thank the two anonymous referees for their invaluable comments.

Conflicts of Interest: The authors declare no conflict of interest.

References

Acharya, Viral V., John Biggs, Hanh T. Le, M. Richardson, and S. Ryan. 2011. Systemic risk and the regulation of insurance companies. In *Regulating Wall Street—The Dodd-Frank Act and the New Architecture of Global Finance*. Edited by V. V. Acharya, T. F. Cooley, M. Richardson and I. Walter. Hoboken: John Wiley & Sons, pp. 241–301.

Adrian, Tobias, and Markus K. Brunnermeier. 2011. *CoVaR, Working Paper*. New York: Federal Reserve Bank of New York.

Adrian, Tobias, and Markus K. Brunnermeier. 2016. CoVar. *American Economic Review* 106: 1705–41. [CrossRef]

Alves, Ivan, Jeroen Brinkhoff, Stanislav Georgiev, Jean-Cyprien Héam, Iulia Moldovan, and Marco Scotto di Carlo. 2015. *Network Analysis of the EU Insurance Sector*. ESRB Occasional Paper Series 07. Frankfurt: European Systemic Risk Board.

Bach, Wolfgang, and Tristan Nguyen. 2012. On the systemic relevance of the insurance industry: Is a macroprudential insurance regulation necessary? *Journal of Applied Finance & Banking* 2: 127–49.

Baluch, Faisal, Stanley Mutenga, and Chris Parsons. 2011. Insurance, systemic risk and the financial crisis. *Geneva Papers on Risk and Insurance—Issues and Practice* 36: 126–63. [CrossRef]

Baur, Patrizia, Rudolf Enz, and Aurelia Zanetti. 2003. *Reinsurance—A Systemic Risk?* Zürich: Swiss Reinsurance Company.

Bavelas, Alex. 1950. Communication patterns in task-oriented groups. *The Journal of the Acoustical Society of America* 22: 725–30. [CrossRef]

Bednarczyk, Teresa. 2013. Czy sektor ubezpieczeniowy kreuje ryzyko systemowe? *Studia Oeconomica Posnaniensia* 11: 7–17.

Bégin, Jean-François, Mathieu Boudreault, Delia A. Doljanu, and Geneviève Gauthier. 2017. Credit and SystemicRisks in the Financial Services Sector: Evidence from the 2008 Global Crisis. *Journal of Risk and Insurance* 86: 263–96. [CrossRef]

Bell, Marian, and Benno Keller. 2009. *Insurance and Stability: The Reform of Insurance Regulation*. Zürich: Zurich Financial Services Group.

Benoit, Sylvain, Jean-Edouard Colliard, Christophe Hurlin, and Christophe Pérignon. 2017. Where the Risks Lie: A Survey on Systemic Risk. *Review of Finance, European Finance Association* 21: 109–52. [CrossRef]

Bierth, Christopher, Felix Irresberger, and Gregor N. F. Weiß. 2015. Systemic risk of insurers around the globe. *Journal of Banking & Finance* 55: 232–45. [CrossRef]

Billio, Monica, Mila Getmansky, Andrew W. Lo, and Loriana Pelizzon. 2012. Econometric measures of connectedness and systemic risk in the finance and insurance sectors. *Journal of Financial Economics* 104: 535–59. [CrossRef]

Bisias, Dimitrios, Mark Flood, Andrew W. Lo, and Stavros Valavanis. 2012. A Survey of Systemic Risk Analytics. *Annual Review of Financial Economics* 4: 255–96. [CrossRef]

Brownlees, Christian, and Robert F. Engle. 2017. SRISK: A Conditional Capital Shortfall Measure of Systemic Risk. *The Review of Financial Studies* 30: 48–79. [CrossRef]

Camerer, Colin, and Martin Weber. 1992. Recent developments in modelling preferences: Uncertainty and ambiguity. *Journal of Risk and Uncertainty* 5: 325–70. [CrossRef]

Chen, Fang, Xuanjuan Chen, Zhenzhen Sun, Tong Yu, and Ming Zhong. 2013a. Systemic risk, financial crisis, and credit risk insurance. *Financial Review* 48: 417–42. [CrossRef]

Chen, Hua, J. David Cummins, Krupa S. Viswanathan, and Mary A. Weiss. 2013b. Systemic Risk and the Interconnectedness between Banks and Insurers: An Econometric Analysis. *Journal of Risk and Insurance* 81: 623–52. [CrossRef]

Chen, Hua, J. David Cummins, Krupa S. Viswanathan, and Mary A. Weiss. 2013c. *Systemic Risk Measures in the Insurance Industry: A Copula Approach*. Working Paper. Philadelphia, PA, USA: Temple University.

Colizza, Vittoria, Alessandro Flammini, M. Angeles Serrano, and Alessandro Vespignani. 2006. Detecting rich-club ordering in complex networks. *Nature Physics* 2: 110–15. [CrossRef]

Cummins, J. David, and Mary A. Weiss. 2011. *Systemic Risk and the U.S. Insurance Sector*. Working Paper. Philadelphia, PA, USA: Temple University.

Cummins, J. David, and Mary A. Weiss. 2013. *Systemic Risk and Regulation of the U.S. Insurance Industry*. Working Paper. Philadelphia, PA, USA: Temple University.

Cummins, J. David, and Mary A. Weiss. 2014. Systemic Risk and the U.S. Insurance Sector. *Journal of Risk and Insurance* 81: 489–528. [CrossRef]

Czerwińska, Teresa. 2014. Systemic risk in the insurance sector. *Problemy Zarzadzania* 12: 41–63. [CrossRef]

De Bandt, Olivier, and Philipp Hartmann. 2000. *Systemic Risk: A Survey*. Working Paper. Frankfurt, Germany: European Central Bank.

Denkowska, Anna, and Stanisław Wanat. 2019. A Dynamic MST-deltaCovar Model of Systemic Risk in the European Insurance Sector. *arXiv*, arXiv:2951270.

Di Cesare, Antonio, and Anna Rogantini Picco. 2018. A Survey of Systemic Risk Indicators. In *Questioni di Economia e Finanza (Occasional Papers)*. Roma: Bank of Italy, p. 458.

Eling, Martin, and David Antonius Pankoke. 2016. Systemic Risk in the Insurance Sector: A Review and Directions for Future Research. *Risk Management and Insurance Review* 19: 249–84. [CrossRef]

Fan, Yan, Wolfgang Karl Härdle, Weining Wang, and Lixing Zhu. 2018. Single-Index-Based CoVaR with Very High-Dimensional Covariates. *Journal of Business & Economic Statistics* 36: 212–26.

Giglio, Stefano, Bryan Kelly, and Seth Pruitt. 2016. Systemic risk and the macroeconomy: An empirical evaluation. *Journal of Financial Economics* 119: 457–71. [CrossRef]

Härdle, Wolfgang Karl, Weining Wang, and Lining Yu. 2016. TENET: Tail-Event Driven NETwork Risk. *Journal of Econometrics* 192: 499–513. [CrossRef]

Harrington, Scott E. 2009. The financial crisis, systemic risk, and the future of insurance regulation. *Journal of Risk and Insurance* 76: 785–819. [CrossRef]

Hautsch, Nikolaus, Julia Schaumburg, and Melanie Schienle. 2015. Financial Network Systemic Risk Contributions. *Review of Finance* 19: 685–738. [CrossRef]

Huang, Xin, Hao Zhou, and Haibin Zhu. 2009. A framework for assessing the systemic risk of major financial institutions. *Journal of Banking & Finance* 33: 2036–49.

IAIS. 2009. *Systemic Risk and the Insurance Sector*. Basel: Bank for International Settlements, International Association of Insurance Supervisors (IAIS), October 25.

Jajuga, Krzysztof, Marta Karaś, Katarzyna Kuziak, and Witold Szczepaniak. 2017. Ryzyko systemu finansowego. Metody oceny i ich weryfikacja w wybranych krajach. In *Materiały i Studia*. Warszawa: Narodowy Bank Polski, p. 329.

Jobst, Andreas A. 2014. Systemic risk in the insurance sector: A review of current assessment approaches. *Geneva Papers on Risk and Insurance* 39: 440–70. [CrossRef]

Joe, Harry. 1997. *Multivariate Models and Dependence Concepts*. London: Chapman-Hall.

Jurkowska, Aleksandra. 2018. *Polski Sektor Bankowy Wobec Ryzyka Systemowego: Analiza Banków Giełdowych*. Kraków: Wydawnictwo Uniwersytetu Ekonomicznego w Krakowie.

Kanno, Masayasu. 2016. The network structure and systemic risk in the global non-life insurance market. *Insurance: Mathematics and Economics* 67: 38–53. [CrossRef]

Kaserer, Christoph, and Christian Klein. 2018. Supplementary Material to 'Systemic Risk in Financial Markets: How Systemically Important Are Insurers? *Journal of Risk and Insurance* 86: 729–59. [CrossRef]

Klein, Robert W. 2011. Insurance Market Regulation: Catastrophe Risk, Competition and Systemic Risk. In *Handbook of Insurance*, 2nd ed. Working Paper. Edited by G. Dionne. New York: Springer.

Knight, Frank H. 1921. *Risk, Uncertainty and Profit*. Chicago: Chicago University Press.

Koijen, Ralph S. J., and Motohiro Yogo. 2016. Shadow Insurance. *Econometrica* 84: 1265–87. [CrossRef]

Kou, Gang, Xiangrui Chao, Yi Peng, Fawaz E. Alsaadi, and Enrique Herrera-Viedma. 2019. Machine learning methods for systemic risk analysis in financial sectors. *Technological and Economic Development of Economy* 25: 716–42. [CrossRef]

Kress, Jeremy C. 2011. Credit default swaps, clearinghouses, and systemic risk: Why centralized counterparties must have access to central bank liquidity. *Harvard Journal of Legislation* 48: 49–93.

Lautier, Delphine, and Franck Raynaud. 2013. Systemic risk and complex systems: A graph-theory analysis. In *Econophysics of Systemic Risk and Network Dynamics*. Milano: Springer, pp. 19–37.

Mantegna, Rosario N., and H. Eugene Stanley. 1999. *Introduction to Econophysics: Correlations and Complexity in Finance*. Cambridge: Cambridge University Press.

Matesanz, David, and Guillermo J. Ortega. 2015. Sovereign public debt crisis in europe. a network analysis. *Physica A: Statistical Mechanics and Its Applications* 436: 756–66. [CrossRef]

Mühlnickel, Janina, and Gregor N. F. Weiß. 2015. Consolidation and Systemic Risk in the International Insurance Industry. *Journal of Financial Stability* 18: 187–202. [CrossRef]

Newman, M. 2002. Assortative mixing in networks. *Physical Review Letters* 89: 11. [CrossRef]

Onnela, Jukka Pekka, Anirban Chakraborti, Kimmo Kaski, and Janos Kertesz. 2002. Dynamic asset trees and portfolio analysis. *The European Physical Journal B-Condensed Matter and Complex Systems* 30: 285–88. [CrossRef]

Onnela, Jukka Pekka, Anirban Chakraborti, Kimmo Kaski, Janos Kertesz, and Antti Kanto. 2003. Asset trees and asset graphs in financial markets. *Physica Scripta* 2003: 48. [CrossRef]

Patton, Andrew J. 2006. Modelling asymmetric exchange rate. *International Economic Review* 47: 527–56. [CrossRef]

Radice, Marc Philippe. 2010. *Systemische Risiken im Versicherungssektor?* Working Paper. Bern, Switzerland: FINMA.

Rodríguez-Moreno, Maria, and Juan Ignacio Peña. 2013. Systemic Risk Measures: The Simpler theBetter? *Journal of Banking & Finance* 37: 1817–31.

Sensoy, Ahmet, and Benjamin M. Tabak. 2014. Dynamic spanning trees in stock market networks: The case of Asia-Pacific. *Physica A: Statistical Mechanics and Its Applications* 414: 387–402. [CrossRef]

Tang, Yong, Janson Jie Xiong, Zi-Yang Jia, and Yi-Cheng Zhang. 2018. Complexities in financial network topological dynamics: Modeling of emerging and developed stock markets. *Complexity* 2018: 4680140. [CrossRef]

Tracy, Ryan, and Erik Holm. 2016. Metlife Wins Bid to Shed 'Systemically Important' Label. *Wall Street Journal*, March 30.

Tversky, Amos, and Daniel Kahneman. 1992. Advances in prospect theory: Cumulative representation of uncertainty. *Journal of Risk and Uncertainty* 5: 297–323. [CrossRef]

Wanat, Stanisław, and Anna Denkowska. 2018. Dependencies and Systemic risk in the European Insurance Sector: Some New Evidence Based on Copula-DCC-GARCH Model and Selected Clustering Methods. *arXiv*, arXiv:1905.03273.

Wanat, Stanisław, and Anna Denkowska. 2019. Linkages and Systemic Risk in the European Insurance Sector: Some New Evidence Based on Dynamic Spanning Trees. *arXiv*, arXiv:1908.01142.

Wang, Gang-Jin, Chi Xie, Peng Zhang, Feng Han, and Shon Chen. 2014. Dynamics of Foreign Exchange Networks: A Time-Varying Copula Approach. In *Hindawi Publishing Corporation Discrete Dynamics in Nature and Society*. London: Hindawi, 11p.

Weiß, Gregor, and Janina Mühlnickel. 2014. Why do some insurers become systemically relevant? *Journal of Financial Stability* 13: 95–117. [CrossRef]

Zweifel, Peter, and Roland Eisen. 2012. *Insurance Economics*. Heidelberg: Springer.

© 2020 by the authors. Licensee MDPI, Basel, Switzerland. This article is an open access article distributed under the terms and conditions of the Creative Commons Attribution (CC BY) license (http://creativecommons.org/licenses/by/4.0/).

Article
Community Analysis of Global Financial Markets

Irena Vodenska [1,2,*], Alexander P. Becker [1], Di Zhou [1], Dror Y. Kenett [1], H. Eugene Stanley [1] and Shlomo Havlin [3]

1. Center for Polymer Studies and Department of Physics, Boston University, 590 Commonwealth Avenue, Boston, MA 02215, USA; apbecker@bu.edu (A.P.B.); zhou@buphy.bu.edu (D.Z.); drorkenett@gmail.com (D.Y.K.); hes@bu.edu (H.E.S.)
2. Administrative Sciences Department, Metropolitan College, Boston University, 808 Commonwealth Avenue, Boston, MA 02215, USA
3. Department of Physics, Bar-Ilan University, Ramat-Gan 52900, Israel; havlin@ophir.ph.biu.ac.il
* Correspondence: vodenska@bu.edu; Tel.: +1-617-358-0005

Academic Editor: Weidong Tian
Received: 9 February 2016; Accepted: 6 May 2016; Published: 13 May 2016

Abstract: We analyze the daily returns of stock market indices and currencies of 56 countries over the period of 2002–2012. We build a network model consisting of two layers, one being the stock market indices and the other the foreign exchange markets. Synchronous and lagged correlations are used as measures of connectivity and causality among different parts of the global economic system for two different time intervals: non-crisis (2002–2006) and crisis (2007–2012) periods. We study community formations within the network to understand the influences and vulnerabilities of specific countries or groups of countries. We observe different behavior of the cross correlations and communities for crisis *vs.* non-crisis periods. For example, the overall correlation of stock markets increases during crisis while the overall correlation in the foreign exchange market and the correlation between stock and foreign exchange markets decrease, which leads to different community structures. We observe that the euro, while being central during the relatively calm period, loses its dominant role during crisis. Furthermore we discover that the troubled Eurozone countries, Portugal, Italy, Greece and Spain, form their own cluster during the crisis period.

Keywords: community structure; complex networks; financial markets

1. Introduction

Financial crisis can cause substantial damages and economic losses not only locally, but also in other countries through trade relations, currency policies, financial contracts, and cross-country investments. Some examples of such crises are the 1997 Asian financial crisis, 1998 Russian bond crisis, 2001 dot-com bubble, 2007–2008 global financial crisis, and 2010 EU sovereign debt crisis, all spilling over to various parts of the world. Similar to the transmission of a disease, small financial shocks initially affecting only a particular sector of the economy or geographic region can spread to other economic sectors and other countries with quite healthy economic outlook Lin *et al.* (1994).

Many research studies have examined the connections among countries by exploring correlations of various financial time series data Smith (2009); Forbes and Rigobon (2002); Flavin *et al.* (2002); Solnik *et al.* (1996); Ramchand and Susmel (1998); Boyer *et al.* (2006); Bonanno *et al.* (2000 2003 2004); Sheedy (1998); Meese (1990); Longin and Solnik (1995); Arshanapalli and Doukas (1993); Kenett *et al.* (2010 2011 2012); Onnela *et al.* (2003); Sandoval and Franca (2012); Sandoval (2014); Curme *et al.* (2014); Aste *et al.* (2010); Tumminello *et al.* (2007). Moreover, many studies have analyzed relationships between stock and foreign exchange markets, given the significant increase in global capital flows in the last two decades Dornbusch and Fischer (1980); Dooley and Isard (1982); Morley (2002); Nieh and Lee (2002);

Bae et al. (2003); Gagnon and Karolyi (2006); Cappiello and De Santis (2005); Granger et al. (2000); Pan et al. (2007); Ning (2010); Zhao (2010); Katechos (2011); Lin (2012). Other studies have focused on global stock market return predictability offering diverse findings across different regions and time periods Cohen and Frazzini (2008); Cochrane (2008); Fama and French (1988 1989); Welch and Goyal (2008); Ferson and Harvey (1993); Dahlquist and Hasseltoft (2013); Breen et al. (1989); Harvey (1991); Bekaert et al. (2009); Rapach et al. (2013).

There have been dramatic advances in the field of complex networks in many research fields. The world-wide-web, the Internet, highway systems, and electric power grids are all examples of networks that can be modeled using coupled systems Barabási and Albert (1999); Buldyrev et al. (2010); Mantegna (1999); Watts and Strogatz (1998); Albert and Barabási (2002); Amaral et al. (2000); Li et al. (2015); Kenett et al. (2012), where the connectivity between network components is essential. Similarly, the economic system is composed of many agents, interacting at different levels. The agents in the system could be individual traders, firms, banks, financial markets, or countries, hence the global financial system can be well represented by using a complex network model. Recently, researchers have used network theory to study economic systems as well as systemic risk propagation through the financial network Billio et al. (2012); Gai et al. (2011); Anand et al. (2012); Haldane and May (2011); Battiston et al. (2012); Huang et al. (2013); Schweitzer et al. (2009); Glasserman and Young (2015); Acemoglu et al. (2013 2012); Dehmamy et al. (2014); Ellis et al. (2014). We develop and analyze a two-layer interdependent network, where each layer represents a different financial market and interactions exist not only within the same market, but also between the two layers. Because of these interdependences, failure in a certain network node can trigger global systemic risk and crisis propagation to other nodes in the network. In this study, we select major global stock market indices and their corresponding currencies as the two layers in our coupled network model.

Stock markets are a common trade place for company shares thus reflecting companies' performances and investors' perceptions of company values. Moreover, stock markets are considered leading economic indicators and therefore useful as predictors of the economy. The foreign exchange market is the largest financial market in the world, with market participants actively involved in currency trading 24 h a day except weekends, with daily turnover of over 5 trillion US dollars, according to the Bank for International Settlement for International Settlements (2013). These two financial markets capture important aspects of a country's economic status, and therefore, we use them as a centerpiece of our research. We use a complex network approach to model the interaction between stock and foreign exchange markets to capture the topology as well as the dynamics in this coupled financial system. We study 56 stock market indices and 45 distinct currencies since 12 of the countries in our dataset use the euro as their official currency. Our analysis reveals novel insights and interesting features of the interactions among global stock and currency markets. We divide the entire period of 2002 to 2012 into two time intervals, non-crisis (2002–2006) and crisis (2007–2012) periods. We find that correlations exhibit different behavior during the crisis period such as higher stock market correlations and lower foreign exchange correlations when compared to the non-crisis period.

The objective of this article is to study community formations in global financial markets and to investigate the systemic importance of countries and their influence on other countries or regions. The rest of the paper is organized as follows: In Section 2, we present our correlation-based community analysis results for two different sub-periods, non-crisis period (2002–2006) and crisis period (2007–2012); in Section 3, we offer a discussion of our findings. The data set and the methods we use are described in Section 4.

2. Results

2.1. Pearson Correlation Analysis

In order to see how the cross-correlation trends change with time, we divide the data into 11 annual periods. Figure 1a shows a heat map of the yearly stock market correlations. The x-axis represents the years, and the y-axis shows the 1540 unique pairwise correlations, excluding the diagonal of the correlation matrix. We use the color bar to show the magnitude of the correlations, where red means $C = 1$ and the two series are perfectly positively correlated, while blue means $C = -1$ and the two series are perfectly negatively correlated. Green means $C = 0$, or the two series are not correlated.

From Figure 1a, we can see that the overall correlation of the global stock markets trends upward starting in 2006, reaches its peak in 2008, and stays at a high level thereafter. These increasing correlation trends match the global financial crisis of 2007–2008 and could possibly be regarded as indicators of increased co-movements heading towards financial crisis.

In Figure 1b, the heat map for foreign exchange markets is plotted. It is generated in the same way as the heat map for the stock markets; however, the number of entries is lower due to the lower number (45) of distinct currencies among the 56 countries. Hence, we have 990 distinct correlations for the currency correlation matrix, excluding the diagonal. Generally, foreign exchange markets shows stronger correlation compared to stock markets. It seems that the overall foreign exchange correlation falls during the financial crisis period, contrary to the stock market correlation trend.

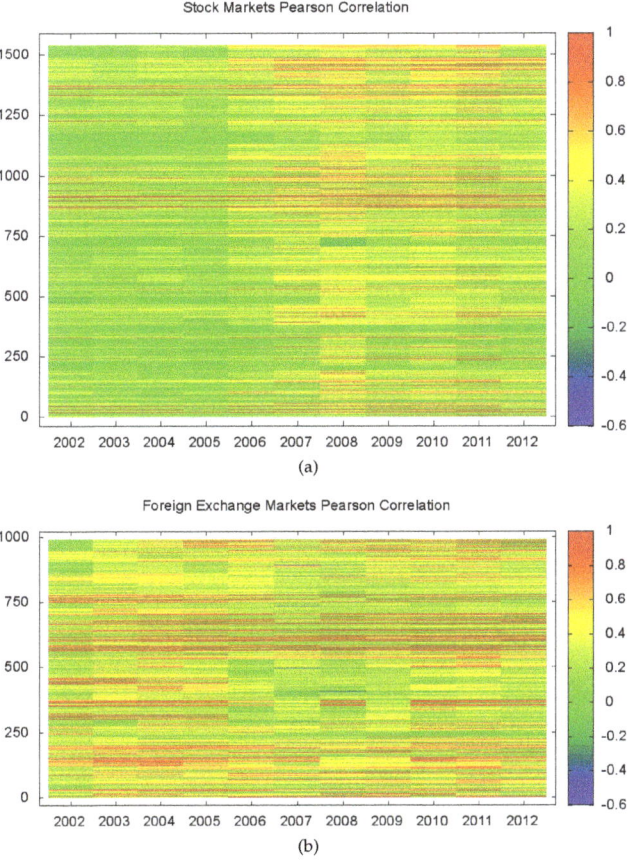

Figure 1. Heat maps of the annual Pearson correlations for (**a**) stock markets and (**b**) foreign exchange markets logarithmic returns. For the stock markets, we consider all 56 countries; for the foreign exchange markets, we consider the 45 distinct currencies. The color shows the value of the correlations for different years, where red indicates strong positive correlation, blue indicates strong negative correlation, while green means that the correlation is weak.

2.2. Summary Statistics

To study the statistical characteristics of the correlations, we calculate the first moment (mean) and the second moment (standard deviation) of any of the correlation distributions for the 11 years for all three cases, including Pearson correlations for stock market layer, currency layer, as well as inter-layer correlations.

In Figure 2, we show that the mean value of stock market correlations exhibits a peak during the crisis period (2007–2012). This finding suggests (similar to Figure 1a) that during crisis, the overall correlation increases, and the stock markets tend to move together. This could be due to portfolio re-balancing, reducing equity market exposures and increasing allocations in the bond market. The re-balancing in global portfolios occurs across different countries and thus produces declining stock market trends internationally.

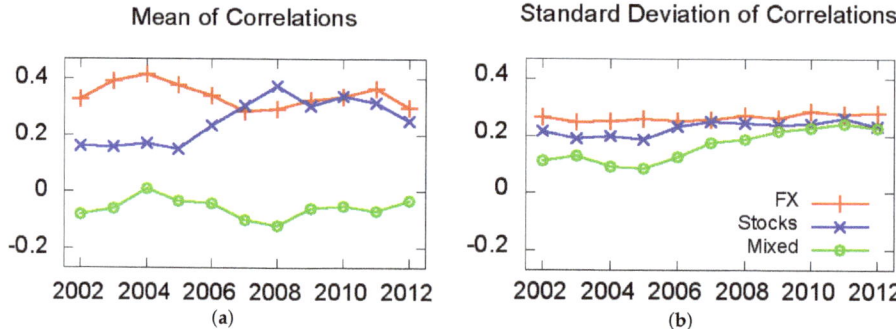

Figure 2. (a) Annual mean correlation and (b) annual standard deviation for stock markets (x), foreign exchange markets (+), and between stock and foreign exchange markets (o). We observe that the stock markets are more correlated during the crisis period, whereas the foreign exchange market correlation are higher in the non-crisis period. The correlation between stock and foreign exchange markets is lowest during the crisis. The standard deviation for both, stock and foreign exchange markets remains fairly constant, while we observe an increase in the standard deviation for the interlayer correlations.

The means of the foreign exchange market Pearson correlations are low during the crisis period, while, in contrast, we observe a peak during the non-crisis period. This finding suggests that, in general, the correlations among currencies are low during crises and high during non-crisis periods, contrary to the stock market behavior. For both, however, the standard deviation of the correlations remains fairly constant, which suggests uniform increase (decrease) of the correlations in the stock markets (foreign exchange markets) throughout the entire time period.

In order to confirm this qualitative description that the means of the correlation are in fact different for the years in the calm period and for the years in the crisis period, we perform Student's t-test. The null hypothesis is that the annual mean correlations are the same for both periods and that any differences come from the standard deviation. We apply the two-sample Student's t-test. It rejects the null hypothesis that the two means are equal, p-value is 0.0002; thus, the alternative hypothesis that the means are not equal is accepted.

The mean value of Pearson correlations between stock and foreign exchange markets exhibits a local minimum during the crisis period, which could be interpreted as positive stock market returns corresponding to currency appreciations. Overall the interlayer correlation does not change much throughout the entire period. The increase in standard deviation, however, indicates a larger spread in correlation values between the two layers during the crisis (Table 1).

Table 1. Statistics for the pre-crisis and the crisis periods.

	Stocks		Currency	
	2002–2006	2007–2012	2002–2006	2007–2012
Mean	0.175	0.315	0.370	0.318
Standard Deviation	0.208	0.249	0.260	0.279
Minimum	−0.320	−0.340	−0.155	−0.575
Maximum	0.965	0.966	1.000	1.000

We distinguish between two different markets in our analysis, the network of stock market indices and the network of foreign exchange markets. Besides their obvious differences, the two markets also exhibit different correlation distributions, as visual inspection of Figure 1a,b hints. The two-sample Kolmogorov-Smirnov test (K-S test) allows us to statistically confirms this, with the null hypothesis being that the two sample data are from the same continuous distribution. The K-S test rejects this null hypothesis at a significance level $\alpha = 0.001$. Therefore, we can conclude that the correlation distributions of stock markets and of foreign exchange markets are different.

2.3. Community Formation and Cluster Analysis

In our analysis we focus on two periods: a period of relative economic calmness (2002–2006) and a period of economic crisis (2007–2012). Using the correlation information, we depict the network structure of the stock markets and of the foreign exchange markets for each of these time periods. Since countries have different peak trading times due to their respective geographical locations and different time zones, lagged correlations allow us to infer information about regional influences. We separate the 56 countries and 45 currencies into three groups according to their geographical location. When we consider synchronous correlations, we use the returns at time t for every country. In that case, the Asian markets are the first to trade, then the European markets, and finally the American markets. A shock originating in the US, for example, would then not show its immediate effect on the other markets because the stock markets in other parts of the world are closed for most or all of the trading hours of the NYSE. When we consider lagged correlations, we use the returns at time t for the American countries and at time $t + 1$ for the other countries of the world. In that case, it is as if the American markets were first to trade, followed by the Asian and then the European markets. A shock from the US would then be very visible. For both, the stock and the foreign exchange markets, we first consider the synchronous correlations and then compare the results to those of the lagged correlations.

We use Planar Maximally Filtered Graphs (PMFG) Tumminello et al. (2005); Di Matteo et al. (2010) to study the properties of stock and foreign exchange market correlations. PMFG is useful for filtering meaningful correlations from the bulk of the 1540 correlation pairs, as it suppresses small correlations while maintaining the overall network structure. In order to build the graph, we order the correlations $C_{i,j}$ from largest to smallest. First, the pair with the largest correlation is connected. In subsequent steps we connect the countries i, j under the condition that a link between them maintains the planar structure of the graph; if it does not, the pair is skipped. This procedure results in an adjacency matrix with unweighted links from which the graph is plotted. We use *Wolfram Mathematica* to investigate the communities in the network, which are detected with respect to their modularity.

2.3.1. Stock Markets

Synchronous Correlations

Figure 3a shows the PMFG for the period from 2002 to 2006, where we identify five clusters which seem to be organized by geographical locations. The cluster on the top left is led by Singapore, a financial hub, and Saudi Arabia, which connects to many other OPEC countries in the cluster. The second Asian cluster is centered around Hong Kong and Japan. The third cluster contains smaller

European countries, organized around the Scandinavian countries. The fourth cluster contains the major European economies, except for Italy and Germany which are closely connected to the American countries in the fifth cluster, particularly through ties to the US and Canada. These four countries exhibit particularly strong connections within and, in case of Germany and Italy, to countries outside the cluster. The communities change significantly during the crisis period, where Singapore and Hong Kong lead a large Asian cluster, as illustrated in Figure 3b. The American cluster formed during the non-crisis period becomes more mixed during the crisis period, as Norway, Iceland and Russia become part of this cluster. The change in the community comprised of mostly American countries suggest that Italy and Germany influence the performance of the American markets in the non-crisis period, while during the crisis period, Norway and Russia seem to increase their influence. The majority of the European countries, connected through France, form another cluster, strongly linked to the countries in the American cluster. These observations are in line with the coordinated responses to the crisis from the US, large European economies, and the ECB; at the same time the Asian countries do not become more closely connected to them NYT (2008). Most notably, however, two new clusters appear: one with the troubled Eurozone countries Portugal, Italy, Greece and Spain, and another consisting of rather less connected countries like Slovakia, Mauritius and Tunisia.

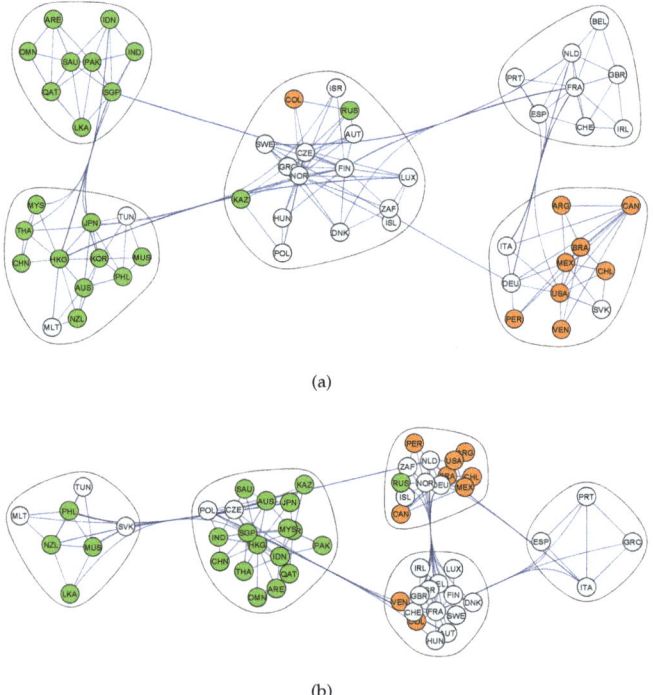

Figure 3. Planar maximally filtered graph (PMFG) for the stock markets obtained using synchronous correlations during (**a**) the economically calm period and (**b**) crisis period. The countries are denoted by their three-letter symbols and are color-coded according to their geographical locations: green for Asia, light blue for Europe and orange for the Americas. During the calm period, we detect five large clusters which are mostly geographically divided. The clusters significantly change during the crisis period. Most notably the troubled Eurozone countries, Italy, Spain, Greece and Portugal, form their own cluster. The Asian countries form one larger cluster centered around Hong Kong and Singapore. We also observe a smaller cluster containing a diverse group of less connected countries.

Lagged Correlations

As pointed out before, lagged correlations are an important measure to study the influences of financial markets. They allow us to consider effects originating in one region and spreading to another. In the following, we consider the correlation calculated for the returns for the Americas at time t, and for Asia and Europe at time $t + 1$. In other words, we focus on how the index movements in the Americas will affect the index movements in the rest of the world. Please note that this does not change the correlations within one geographical region, nor will the correlations between Asian and European countries change. However, due to the PMFG algorithm, larger correlations that appear for countries in the Americas with countries in the rest of the world can change the structure of the network.

The European clusters remain mostly unchanged in the calm period, except that Germany and Italy no longer form a community with American countries, when considering lagged correlations compared to synchronous correlations. Since here we consider the Americas at time t and Europe and Asia at time $t + 1$, it seems that the American countries, including the US, do not affect Italy and Germany significantly. The Netherlands, Italy, France, and the Scandinavian countries still manifest themselves as the most connected European countries. We do, however, observe large changes in the American cluster on the very right in Figure 4a; Australia and New Zealand, economically close to the US, have moved from the Asian community to connect more tightly to the American countries. Different responses by central banks, leading to higher interest rates particularly in Australia, can be considered a reason for this DailyFX (2012). They are joined by smaller countries, such as Sri Lanka and the Philippines, that we have previously identified as countries with weak links to other Asian countries. The Asian cluster is led by Singapore, Hong Kong and Japan, which display the most significant correlations to countries outside of their community. The community structure changes significantly when we consider the years of economic turmoil in Figure 4b. Most obviously, the number of communities reduces to three because the two European clusters from the non-crisis period mostly merge. Netherlands, United Kingdom and France are at the center of the European community in the crisis period. Portugal, Italy, Greece and Spain are found at the periphery of this cluster. Using synchronous correlations, Germany and Netherlands were tightly connected to the American cluster during the crisis period, while when considering lagged correlations, they belong to the large European cluster. We observe that Japan, Australia and New Zealand, among others, form a community with the American countries during the crisis, which suggests that the major financial markets in the Pacific follow the trends of the American stock markets. The importance of the US stock market is emphasized by the largest number of connections in this cluster. Australia is the second most connected country in this community.

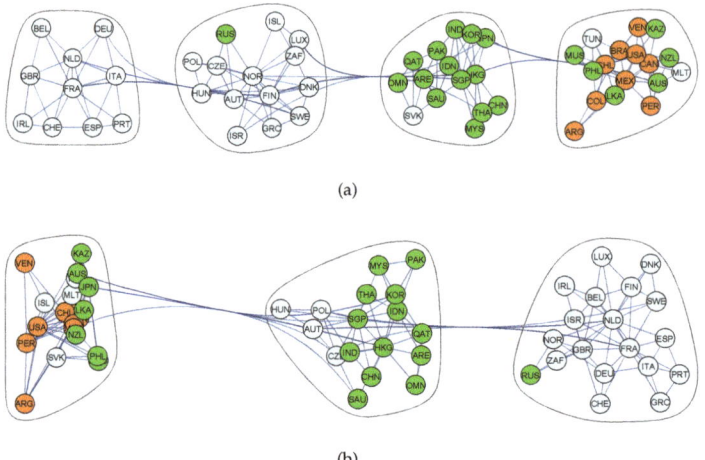

(a)

(b)

Figure 4. Planar maximally filtered graph (PMFG) for the stock markets obtained using lagged correlations during (**a**) the economically calm period and (**b**) crisis period. The countries are denoted by their three-letter symbols and are color-coded according to their geographical locations: green for Asia, light blue for Europe and orange for the Americas. During the calm period, we observe four large clusters, while in the crisis period the number of communities changes to three, as the two European clusters merge.

2.3.2. Foreign Exchange Markets

While we analyze a total of 56 global stock market indices, we only investigate 45 currencies because 12 countries use the euro.

Synchronous Correlations

Figure 5a shows the dominant role that the euro has played in Europe prior to the crisis. Together with the Danish krone, pegged to the euro via the European Exchange Rate Mechanism, the euro is connected with all European currencies, and it exhibits close ties to the Canadian dollar, the Australian dollar, and the New Zealand dollar. With 19 links each, the node for the euro and the node for the US dollar show the highest interconnectedness among all currencies in the calm period. The US dollar is at the center of the cluster comprised of the majority of the American currencies and the oil-exporting countries. In Figure 5b we observe that the clear structure and hierarchy of the European community during the calm period falls apart during crisis. In addition, a fourth cluster appears, comprised of European and South and Central American currencies, like the Brazilian real, the Mexican peso and the Chilean peso, which were closely connected to the US dollar in the non-crisis period. As the financial crises unfolded, the Fed and its European counterparts employed "quantitative easing" as monetary policy, which in turn has been eliciting strong criticism in the BRIC countries, as QE corresponds to currency devaluation Telegraph (2012). The US dollar maintains its strong ties with the currencies of oil-exporting countries. Its cluster is joined by the Japanese yen and the Chinese yuan. China moved to a managed floating regime during the crisis period Reuters (2012), whereas the Japanese government tried to stimulate its economy with policies similar to QE, known as "Abenomics" BBC (2011).

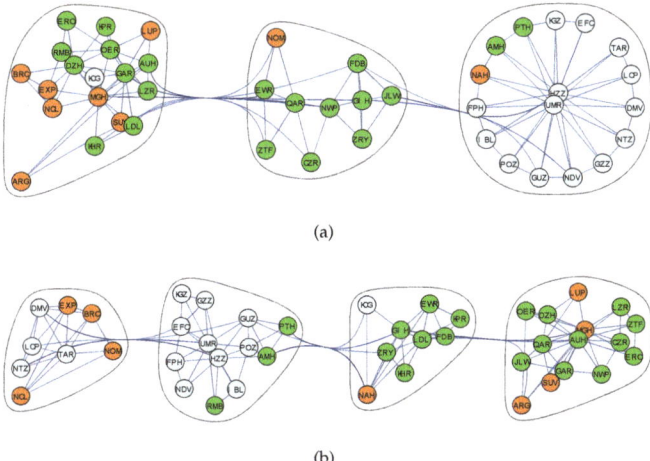

(a)

(b)

Figure 5. Planar maximally filtered graph (PFMG) for the foreign exchange markets obtained using synchronous correlations during (**a**) the economically calm period and (**b**) crisis period. The currencies are denoted by their three-letter symbols and color-coded according to their geographical locations: green for Asia, light blue for Europe, orange for the Americas. During the calm period, we detect three large clusters. Most distinctive is the European cluster on the right, with the euro and the Danish krone, which is pegged to the euro, at the center. The Asian countries split in two different clusters, with major oil-exporting countries being closely associated with the US dollar which is at the center of its community. The remaining Asian countries form the third cluster. During the crisis, the hierarchy of the euro cluster collapses. The community around the US dollar still contains the oil-exporting countries. It is joined by the Chinese yuan and the Japanese yen. The Brazilian real, Mexican peso and Chilean peso, however, are no longer part of the US dollar-centered community during the crisis period.

Lagged Correlations

In Figure 6a, using lagged correlations during the non-crisis period, we observe that the Euro is at the center of the cluster of European currencies. The Japanese yen joins this cluster. The US dollar and the currencies of the Asian (Middle Eastern) oil-exporting countries no longer share close ties. We notice in Figure 6b, during the crisis period, that there is a mixed cluster comprised of all the American currencies and a group of Asian currencies, including India, Singapore and Korea, while the South East Asian currencies form their own community using synchronous correlations, as observed in Figure 5b. The number of connections of the nodes comparing the two different periods remains stable; the majority of the currencies do not gain or lose more than two connections. Instead we find that different connections develop within the clusters. For example, Hong Kong loses the link with countries like India and Russia during the crisis, but becomes more closely connected to Singapore, the Philippines and Thailand.

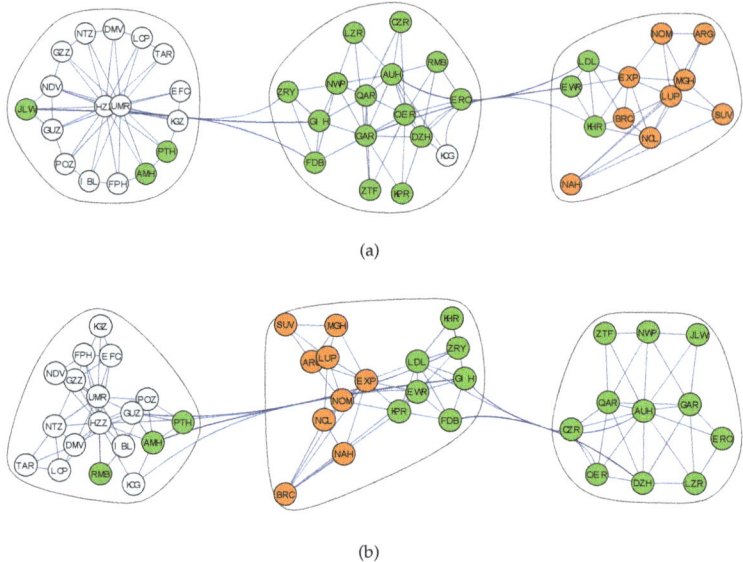

(a)

(b)

Figure 6. Planar maximally filtered graph (PMFG) for the foreign exchange markets obtained using lagged correlations during (**a**) the economically calm period and (**b**) crisis period. The currencies are denoted by their three-letter symbols and color-coded according to their geographical locations: green for Asia, light blue for Europe, orange for the Americas. For lagged correlations we use time t for the Americas and time $t+1$ for Europe and Asia. During both periods, we detect three large clusters. In the non-crisis period we observe that the clusters are determined by the geographical currency location, except for the Japanese yen, New Zealand dollar and Australian dollar. Iceland appears in the predominantly Asian cluster, while Malaysia, the Philippines and Indonesia are part of the American community. During the crisis period the interconnectedness between American and South East Asian currencies increases as they belong to the same community. The purely Asian cluster comprises the Japanese Yen along with the currencies of the oil-exporting countries. The Russian ruble joins the European cluster.

Any currency is traded during every hour of the day, therefore any sudden changes should be reflected in all the currencies on a time scale shorter than one full day. In fact, one would expect the strong correlations to correspond to shorter time scales. Hence the community structure of the currencies is depicted by synchronous correlations, while when using lagged correlations, the true structure of the network disappears.

3. Discussion

In this study, we investigate the daily logarithmic returns in the stock and foreign exchange markets of 56 countries and 45 currencies. We use network theory and community analysis to understand the structure of the coupled financial network formed by global stock market indices and currencies. We define weighted links within a network layer and between the two layers (stock markets on one hand and currencies on the other) using Pearson correlation. The overall correlations within stock markets increase during the crisis period, and the overall correlations within foreign exchange markets, as well as the correlations between stock and foreign exchange markets decrease during this period. We investigate statistical properties of our results by presenting correlation summary statistics and performing the K-S test to closely study the characteristics of the correlation distributions. We apply the PFMG method to discover distinct community formations and categorize the countries into clusters. We identify the importance of the countries according to their relative positions in the communities and the strength of their links with other member of the community as well as the strength of their external links with countries that do not belong to their cluster. In our analysis, we distinguish between synchronous and lagged correlations. We divide the countries in three geographical regions, Asia, Europe and Americas. To study lagged correlations, we consider the returns at time t in the Americas, and the returns at time $t + 1$ in Asia and Europe. The comparison of the network and community structures allows us to infer influences from one region to another, in both, crisis and non-crisis periods. Using synchronous correlations we identify five clusters in the stock market during the non-crisis period. These clusters change their structure during the crisis period, where, for example, four of the five troubled Eurozone countries, Portugal, Italy, Spain and Greece, form their own community. In the case of lagged correlations, we observe four clusters in the stock market layer during the non-period period and only three communities during the crisis period. We observe that the American countries are most closely connected to Asian countries. The introduction of a time lag and the onset of the crisis cause the European countries to become more tightly connected. Unlike stock markets, which are bound to different time zones, currencies trade around the clock. Any influences among currencies are immediately reflected in their returns, hence synchronous correlation define the true network structure of the foreign exchange markets. We observe that the Euro plays a central role among the European currencies during the non-crisis period, while it loses its central position during the crisis-period. The US dollar is closely linked to the currencies of the major oil-exporting countries, both, during non-crisis and crisis periods.

These findings could have policy implications and could be helpful for central bankers, policy makers and regulators, offering a tool for identifying tightly related communities of countries by stock market performance and by currency dynamics. If, for instance, a financial crisis originates in a specific country, the most vulnerable countries, where the crisis might spread first, are the countries with stronger links with the originating country, most likely belonging to the same community. If policy makers have knowledge of these communities, they might be able to focus needed bailout funds or implement temporary preventative measures in the most vulnerable countries, thus reducing the impact of inherent global financial crisis to the rest of the world and preventing the propagation of the crisis before severe damages cripple the entire economic system.

4. Materials and Methods

4.1. Data

We acquired the data from the Boston University Bloomberg terminal provided by Bloomberg L.P. for academic research. In our analyss, we use a time range of 11 years from January 1, 2002 to December 31, 2012, with daily frequency. We use the daily closing price. We exclude the weekends, and for holidays we repeat the closing price of the previous day. We select 56 representative countries, which include developed as well as emerging countries.

When a country has more than one well-known major stock market index, we use the following criteria to select the most representative index: first we select the stock market indices that are widely used in the financial industry, and from that subset, we select the index that includes most of the companies listed on the respective exchange, covering mostly large capitalization stocks but in some instances including some mid or small capitalization stocks as well. Using this criteria, we have selected one single index for each country, such as the S&P 500 for the US, Nikkei 225 for Japan, STI for Singapore, *etc.*

For the foreign exchange rates, we use the closing mid price, which is the average of the closing bid and ask prices. The foreign exchange market convention is for the majority of the currencies to be expressed in terms of USD, except for the British pound, Australian dollar, New Zealand dollar, and the euro that are expressed as USD per currency. In our analysis, for consistency, we have converted these four currencies to be expressed in terms of USD. For any country in the eurozone that has adopted the euro at a later date than January 1, 2002, we keep the separate currencies up to the date before the actual euro adoption, and replace them with euro after the adoption day. This is becuase before the adoption of the euro, these currencies moved independently from the euro to some extent NBS (2005); 200 (2004). Examples like these include the Maltese lira and Slovak koruna, which were replaced by the euro on January 1, 2008 and January 1, 2009 respectively.

In order to also include the US dollar as part of our analysis, we have expressed all currencies as currency over SDR. The SDR is an international reserve asset, created by the International Monetary Fund (IMF) in 1969 to supplement its member countries' official reserves. Its value is based on a basket of four key international currencies, and SDRs can be exchanged for freely usable currencies. Though it is not a currency, *per se* the SDR can be used as a currency unit in our study Frankel *et al.* (1993 1995). The IMF fixes the value of one SDR in terms of US dollars daily.

4.2. Pearson Correlation Analysis

For all analyzed time-series, we first obtain the logarithmic returns as follows. $P(t)$ is the value of the time series at time t, where $t = 1, 2, \ldots, N$, and $N = 2866$ days is the size of the time series. The logarithmic return of time series i is

$$R_i(t) = \ln \frac{P_i(t+1)}{P_i(t)} \qquad (1)$$

We then normalize $R_i(t)$ to have zero mean and unit standard deviation,

$$r_i(t) = \frac{R_i(t) - \overline{R_i}}{\sigma_{R_i}} \qquad (2)$$

where $\overline{R_i}$ and σ_{R_i} are the mean value and standard deviation of time series i.

For stock market indices, the dimension of the logarithmic return time series matrices is 56×2865. For foreign exchange markets, it is 45×2865 since we group all Eurozone countries together. We calculate the cross-correlation matrix C, and the value of each cell $C_{i,j}$ as follows,

$$C_{i,j} = \langle r_i r_j \rangle \qquad (3)$$

where $C_{i,j}$ represents the Pearson correlation between logarithmic return time series for a pair of countries i and j.

4.3. Analyzed Countries

Country	Currency	Index Label	Currency Label	Country	Currency	Index Label	Currency Label
Argentina	Argentine peso	ARG	ARS	Malta	Maltese lira	MLT	MTL/EUR
Australia	Australian dollar	AUS	AUD	Mauritius	Mauritian rupee	MUS	MRO
Austria	euro	AUT	EUR	Mexico	Mexican peso	MEX	MXN
Belgium	euro	BEL	EUR	Netherlands	euro	NLD	EUR
Brazil	Brazilian real	BRA	BRL	New Zealand	New Zealand dollar	NZL	NZD
Canada	Canadian dollar	CAN	CAD	Norway	Norwegian krone	NOR	NOK
Chile	Chilean peso	CHL	CLP	Oman	Omani rial	OMN	OMR
China	Chinese yuan	CHN	CNY	Pakistan	Pakistani rupee	PAK	PKR
Colombia	Colombian peso	COL	COU	Peru	Peruvian nuevo sol	PER	PEN
Czech Republic	Czech koruna	CZE	CZK	Philippines	Philippine peso	PHL	PHP
Denmark	Danish krone	DNK	DKK	Poland	Polish zloty	POL	PLN
Finland	euro	FIN	EUR	Portugal	euro	PRT	EUR
France	euro	FRA	EUR	Qatar	Qatari riyal	QAT	QAR
Germany	euro	DEU	EUR	Russia	Russian ruble	RUS	RUB
Greece	euro	GRC	EUR	Saudi Arabia	Saudi riyal	SAU	SAR
Hong Kong	Hong Kong dollar	HKG	HKD	Singapore	Singapore doller	SGP	SGD
Hungary	Hungarian forint	HUN	HUF	Slovakia	Slovak koruna	SVK	SKK/EUR
Iceland	Icelandic krona	ISL	ISK	South Africa	South African rand	ZAF	ZAR
India	Indian rupee	IND	INR	Spain	euro	ESP	EUR
Indonesia	Indonesian rupiah	IDN	IDR	Sri Lanka	Sri Lankan rupee	LKA	LKR
Ireland	euro	IRL	EUR	Sweden	Swedish krona	SWE	SEK
Israel	Israel new shekel	ISR	ILS	Switzerland	Swiss franc	CHE	CHF
Italy	euro	ITA	EUR	Thailand	Thai baht	THA	THB
Japan	Japanese yen	JPN	JPY	Tunisia	Tunisian dinar	TUN	TND
Kazakhstan	Kazakhstani tenge	KAZ	KZT	Utd. Arab Emirates	UAE dirham	ARE	AED
Korea	South Korean won	KOR	KRW	United Kingdom	British pound	GBR	GBP
Luxembourg	euro	LUX	EUR	United States	US dollar	USA	USD
Malaysia	Malaysian ringgit	MYS	MYR	Venezuela	Venezuelan bolivar	VEN	VEF

Acknowledgments: We thank the DTRA, NSF (grants CMMI 1125290, CHE-1213217 and SES 1452061), Keck Foundation, European Commission FET Open Project (FOC 255987, FOC-INCO 297149) and Office of Naval Research for financial support. S.H. acknowledges the European LINC and MULTIPLEX (EU-FET project 317532) projects, the Deutsche Forschungsgemeinschaft (DFG), the Israel Science Foundation, ONR and DTRA for financial support.

Author Contributions: Authors contributed equally to the writing of the paper.

Conflicts of Interest: The authors declare no conflict of interest.

References

Lin, W.L.; Engle, R.F.; Ito, T. Do Bulls and Bears Move Across Borders? International Transmission of Stock Returns and Volatility as the World Turns. *Rev. Financ. Stud.* **1994**, *7*, 507–538.

Smith, R.D. The spread of the credit crisis: View from a stock correlation network. *J. Korean Phys. Soc.* **2009**, *54*, 2460–2463.

Forbes, K.J.; Rigobon, R. No contagion, only interdependence: Measuring stock market comovements. *J. Financ.* **2002**, *57*, 2223–2261.

Flavin, T.J.; Hurley, M.J.; Rousseau, F. Explaining stock market correlation: A gravity model approach. *Manch. Sch.* **2002**, *70*, 87–106.

Solnik, B.; Boucrelle, C.; Le Fur, Y. International market correlation and volatility. *Financ. Anal. J.* **1996**, *52*, 17–34.

Ramchand, L.; Susmel, R. Volatility and cross correlation across major stock markets. *J. Empir. Financ.* **1998**, *5*, 397–416.

Boyer, B.H.; Kumagai, T.; Yuan, K. How do crises spread? Evidence from accessible and inaccessible stock indices. *J. Financ.* **2006**, *61*, 957–1003.

Bonanno, G.; Vandewalle, N.; Mantegna, R.N. Taxonomy of stock market indices. *Phys. Rev. E* **2000**, *62*, R7615–R7618.

Bonanno, G.; Caldarelli, G.; Lillo, F.; Mantegna, R.N. Topology of correlation-based minimal spanning trees in real and model markets. *Phys. Rev. E* **2003**, *68*, 046130.

Bonanno, G.; Caldarelli, G.; Lillo, F.; Miccichè, F.; Vandewalle, N.; Mantegna, R.N. Networks of equities in financial markets. *Eur. Phys. J. B* **2004**, *38*, 363–371.

Sheedy, E. Correlation in currency markets a risk-adjusted perspective. *J. Int. Financ. Mark. Inst. Money* **1998**, *8*, 59–82.

Meese, R. Currency fluctuations in the post-Bretton Woods era. *J. Econ. Perspect.* **1990**, *4*, 117–134.

Longin, F.; Solnik, B. Is the correlation in international equity returns constant: 1960–1990. *J. Int. Money Financ.* **1995**, *14*, 3–26.

Arshanapalli, B.; Doukas, J. International stock market linkages: Evidence from the pre-and post-October 1987 period. *J. Bank. Financ.* **1993**, *17*, 193–208.

Kenett, D.Y.; Shapira, Y.; Madi, A.; Bransburg-Zabary, S.; Gur-Gershgoren, G.; Ben-Jacob, E. Dynamics of stock market correlations. *AUCO Czech Econ. Rev.* **2010**, *4*, 330–341.

Kenett, D.Y.; Shapira, Y.; Madi, A.; Bransburg-Zabary, S.; Gur-Gershgoren, G.; Ben-Jacob, E. Index cohesive force analysis reveals that the US market became prone to systemic collapses since 2002. *PLoS ONE* **2011**, *6*, e19378.

Kenett, D.Y.; Raddant, M.; Lux, T.; Ben-Jacob, E. Evolvement of uniformity and volatility in the stressed global financial village. *PLoS ONE* **2012**, *7*, e31144.

Onnela, J.P.; Chakraborti, A.; Kaski, K.; Kertesz, J.; Kanto, A. Dynamics of market correlations: Taxonomy and portfolio analysis. *Rev. Mod. Phys.* **2003**, *68*, 056110.

Sandoval, L.; Franca, I.D.P. Correlation of financial markets in times of crisis. *Phys. A Stat. Mech. Appl.* **2012**, *391*, 187–208.

Sandoval, L. To lag or not to lag? How to compare indices of stock markets that operate on different times. *Phys. A Stat. Mech. Appl.* **2014**, *403*, 227–243.

Curme, C.; Tumminello, M.; Mantegna, R.N.; Stanley, H.E.; Kenett, D.Y. Emergence of statistically validated financial intraday lead-lag relationships. *SSRN Electron. J.* **2015**, *15*, 1375–1386.

Aste, T.; Shaw, W.; Di Matteo, T. Correlation structure and dynamics in volatile markets. *New J. Phys.* **2010**, *12*, 085009.

Tumminello, M.; Di Matteo, T.; Aste, T.; Mantegna, R.N. Correlation based networks of equity returns sampled at different time horizons. *Eur. Phys. J. B* **2007**, *55*, 209–217.

Dornbusch, R.; Fischer, S. Exchange rates and the current account. *Am. Econ. Rev.* **1980**, *70*, 960–971.

Dooley, M.; Isard, P. A portfolio-balance rational-expectations model of the dollar-mark exchange rate. *J. Int. Econ.* **1982**, *12*, 257–276.

Morley, B. Exchange rates and stock prices: Implications for European convergence. *J. Policy Model.* **2002**, *24*, 523–526.

Nieh, C.C.; Lee, C.F. Dynamic relationship between stock prices and exchange rates for G-7 countries. *Q. Rev. Econ. Financ.* **2002**, *41*, 477–490.

Bae, K.H.; Karolyi, G.A.; Stulz, R.M. A new approach to measuring financial contagion. *Rev. Financ. Stud.* **2003**, *16*, 717–763.

Gagnon, L.; Karolyi, G.A. Price and volatility transmission across borders. *Financ. Mark. Inst. Instrum.* **2006**, *15*, 107–158.

Cappiello, L.; De Santis, R.A. *Explaining Exchange Rate Dynamics: The Uncovered Equity Return Parity Condition*; ECB Working Paper, 2005. Available online: http://ssrn.com/abstract=804924 (accessed on 19 October 2005).

Granger, C.W.; Huangb, B.N.; Yang, C.W. A bivariate causality between stock prices and exchange rates: Evidence from recent Asianflu*. *Q. Rev. Econ. Financ.* **2000**, *40*, 337–354.

Pan, M.S.; Fok, R.C.W.; Liu, Y.A. Dynamic linkages between exchange rates and stock prices: Evidence from East Asian markets. *Int. Rev. Econ. Financ.* **2007**, *16*, 503–520.

Ning, C. Dependence structure between the equity market and the foreign exchange market—A copula approach. *J. Int. Money Financ.* **2010**, *29*, 743–759.

Zhao, H. Dynamic relationship between exchange rate and stock price: Evidence from China. *Res. Int. Bus. Financ.* **2010**, *24*, 103–112.

Katechos, G. On the relationship between exchange rates and equity returns: A new approach. *J. Int. Financ. Mark. Inst. Money* **2011**, *21*, 550–559.

Lin, C.H. The comovement between exchange rates and stock prices in the Asian emerging markets. *Int. Rev. Econ. Financ.* **2012**, *22*, 161–172.

Cohen, L.; Frazzini, A. Economic links and predictable returns. *J. Financ.* **2008**, *63*, 1977–2011.

Cochrane, J.H. The dog that did not bark: A defense of return predictability. *Rev. Financ. Stud.* **2008**, *21*, 1533–1575.

Fama, E.F.; French, K.R. Dividend yields and expected stock returns. *J. Financ. Econ.* **1988**, *22*, 3–25.

Fama, E.F.; French, K.R. Business conditions and expected returns on stocks and bonds. *J. Financ. Econ.* **1989**, *25*, 23–49.

Welch, I.; Goyal, A. A comprehensive look at the empirical performance of equity premium prediction. *Rev. Financ. Stud.* **2008**, *21*, 1455–1508.

Ferson, W.E.; Harvey, C.R. The risk and predictability of international equity returns. *Rev. Financ. Stud.* **1993**, *6*, 527–566.

Dahlquist, M.; Hasseltoft, H. International bond risk premia. *J. Int. Econ.* **2013**, *90*, 17–32.

Breen, W.; Glosten, L.R.; Jagannathan, R. Economic significance of predictable variations in stock index returns. *J. Financ.* **1989**, *44*, 1177–1189.

Harvey, C.R. The world price of covariance risk. *J. Financ.* **1991**, *46*, 111–157.

Bekaert, G.; Hodrick, R.J.; Zhang, X. International stock return comovements. *J. Financ.* **2009**, *64*, 2591–2626.

Rapach, D.E.; Strauss, J.K.; Zhou, G. International stock return predictability: What is the role of the United States? *J. Financ.* **2013**, *68*, 1633–1662.

Barabási, A.L.; Albert, R. Emergence of scaling in random networks. *Science* **1999**, *286*, 509–512.

Buldyrev, S.V.; Parshani, R.; Paul, G.; Stanley, H.E.; Havlin, S. Catastrophic cascade of failures in interdependent networks. *Nature* **2010**, *464*, 1025–1028.

Mantegna, R.N. Hierarchical structure in financial markets. *Eur. Phys. J. B* **1999**, *11*, 193–197.

Watts, D.J.; Strogatz, S.H. Collective dynamics of 'small-world' networks. *Nature* **1998**, *393*, 440–442.

Albert, R.; Barabási, A.L. Statistical mechanics of complex networks. *Rev. Mod. Phys.* **2002**, *74*, 47.

Amaral, L.A.N.; Scala, A.; Barthélémy, M.; Stanley, H.E. Classes of small-world networks. *Proc. Natl. Acad. Sci. USA* **2000**, *97*, 11149–11152.

Li, D.; Fu, B.; Wang, Y.; Lu, G.; Berezin, Y.; Stanley, H.E.; Havlin, S. Percolation transition in dynamical traffic network with evolving critical bottlenecks. *Proc. Natl. Acad. Sci. USA* **2015**, *112*, 669–672.

Kenett, D.Y.; Preis, T.; Gur-Gershgoren, G.; Ben-Jacob, E. Dependency network and node influence: Application to the study of financial markets. *Int. J. Bifurc. Chaos* **2012**, *22*.

Billio, M.; Getmansky, M.; Lo, A.W.; Pelizzon, L. Econometric measures of connectedness and systemic risk in the finance and insurance sectors. *J. Financ. Econ.* **2012**, *104*, 535–559.

Gai, P.; Haldane, A.; Kapadia, S. Complexity, concentration and contagion. *J. Monet. Econ.* **2011**, *58*, 453–470.

Anand, K.; Gai, P.; Kapadia, S.; Brennan, S.; Willison, M. *A Network Model of Financial System Resilience*; Technical Report; Bank of England: London, UK, 2012.

Haldane, A.G.; May, R.M. Systemic risk in banking ecosystems. *Nature* **2011**, *469*, 351–355.

Battiston, S.; Delli Gatti, D.; Gallegati, M.; Greenwald, B.; Stiglitz, J.E. Liaisons dangereuses: Increasing connectivity, risk sharing, and systemic risk. *J. Econ. Dyn. Control* **2012**, *36*, 1121–1141.

Huang, X.; Vodenska, I.; Havlin, S.; Stanley, H.E. Cascading Failures in Bi-partite Graphs: Model for Systemic Risk Propagation. *Sci. Rep.* **2013**, *3*, 1219.

Schweitzer, F.; Fagiolo, G.; Sornette, D.; Vega-Redondo, F.; White, D.R. Economic Networks: What do we know and what do we need to know? *Adv. Complex Syst.* **2009**, *12*, 407–422.

Glasserman, P.; Young, H.P. How likely is contagion in financial networks? *J. Bank. Financ.* **2015**, *50*, 383–399.

Acemoglu, D.; Ozdaglar, A.; Tahbaz-Salehi, A. *Systemic Risk and Stability in Financial Networks*; Technical Report; National Bureau of Economic Research: Cambridge, MA, USA, 2013.

Acemoglu, D.; Carvalho, V.M.; Ozdaglar, A.; Tahbaz-Salehi, A. The network origins of aggregate fluctuations. *Econometrica* **2012**, *80*, 1977–2016.

Dehmamy, N.; Buldyrev, S.V.; Havlin, S.; Stanley, H.E.; Vodenska, I. A Systemic Stress Test Model in Bank-Asset Networks. *arXiv Preprint* **2014**, arXiv:1410.0104.

Ellis, L.; Haldane, A.; Moshirian, F. Systemic risk, governance and global financial stability. *J. Bank. Financ.* **2014**, *45*, 175–181.

Bank for International Settlements. Triennial Central Bank Survey of foreign exchange turnover in April 2013—Preliminary results released by the BIS. 2013. Available online: http://www.bis.org/press/p130905.htm (accessed on 10 April 2016).

Tumminello, M.; Aste, T.; Di Matteo, T.; Mantegna, R.N. A tool for filtering information in complex systems. *Proc. Natl. Acad. Sci. USA* **2005**, *102*, 10421–10426.

Di Matteo, T.; Pozzi, F.; Aste, T. The use of dynamical networks to detect the hierarchical organization of financial market sectors. *Eur. Phys. J. B* **2010**, *73*, 3–11.

NYT. The U.S. Financial Crisis Is Spreading to Europe. Available online: http://www.nytimes.com/2008/10/01/business/worldbusiness/01global.html (accessed on 10 April 2016).

DailyFX. Why is the Australian Dollar Correlated to the US S&P 500? Available online: https://www.dailyfx.com/forex/technical/article/forex_correlations/2012/03/27/forex_correlations_australian_dollar_us_dollar.html (accessed on 10 April 2016).

Telegraph. BRICs attack QE and urge Western leaders to be 'responsible'. Available online: http://www.telegraph.co.uk/finance/economics/9174292/BRICs-attack-QE-and-urge-Western-leaders-to-be-responsible.html (accessed on 10 April 2016).

Reuters. Timeline: China's reforms of yuan exchange rate. Available online: http://www.reuters.com/article/2012/04/14/us-china-yuan-timeline-idUSBRE83D03820120414 (accessed on 17 April 2015).

BBC. Japan government and central bank intervene to cut yen. Available online: http://www.bbc.co.uk/news/business-14398392 (accessed on 10 April 2016).

NBS. Slovak Koruna Included in the ERM II. Available online: http://www.nbs.sk/PRESS/PR051128.HTM (accessed on 17 April 2015).

OECD. *OECD Economic Surveys: Euro Area 2004*; OECD Publishing: Paria, France, 2004.

Frankel, J.A.; Wei, S.J. *Is There a Currency Bloc in the Pacific?*; Department of Economics, University of California: Berkeley, CA, USA, 1993.

Frankel, J.A.; Wei, S.J.; Canzoneri, M.; Goldstein, M. *Emerging Currency Blocks*; Springer: Berlin/Heidelberg, Germany, 1995.

© 2016 by the authors. Licensee MDPI, Basel, Switzerland. This article is an open access article distributed under the terms and conditions of the Creative Commons Attribution (CC BY) license (http://creativecommons.org/licenses/by/4.0/).

Article
Interconnectedness of Financial Conglomerates

Gaël Hauton [1] and Jean-Cyprien Héam [1,2,*]

[1] Autorité de Contrôle Prudentiel et de Résolution (ACPR), 61 rue Taitbout, Paris 75009, France; gael.hauton@acpr.banque-france.fr

[2] Centre de Recherche en Économie et Statistique (CREST), 15 Boulevard Gabriel Péri, Malakoff 92240, France

* Author to whom correspondence should be addressed; jean-cyprien.heam@acpr.banque-france.fr; Tel.: +33-1-49-95-46-99.

Academic Editor: Weidong Tian
Received: 26 March 2015; Accepted: 11 May 2015; Published: 21 May 2015

Abstract: Being active in both the insurance sector and the banking sector, financial conglomerates intrinsically increase the interconnections between the banking sector and the insurance sector. We address two main concerns about financial conglomerates using a unique database on bilateral exposures between 21 French financial institutions. First, we investigate to what extent to which the insurers that are part of financial conglomerates differ from pure insurers. Second, we show that in the presence of sovereign risk, the components of a financial conglomerate are better off than if they were distinct entities. Our empirical findings bring a new perspective to the previous results of the literature based on using different types of data.

Keywords: interconnectedness; financial conglomerate; contagion; systemic risk

JEL Classification: G22; G28

---

1. Introduction

In the aftermath of the financial crisis, the Financial Stability Board (FSB) pinpointed interconnectedness as a key indicator of the systemic dimension of financial institutions (see FSB [1]). Figure 1 illustrates the importance of interconnections between financial institutions. It represents the aggregate asset allocation of European insurers and banks. The exposures of insurance companies to the financial sector represent about 25% of their total investments, while the exposures of banks represent about 15% of their total credit exposures. In addition, exposures to sovereign risk appear important. Sovereign exposures of banks are as large as their exposures to financial institutions. Sovereign exposures of insurance account for more than 55% of the total investments. These key facts explain the concern for the contagion risk between the banking sector and the insurance sector.

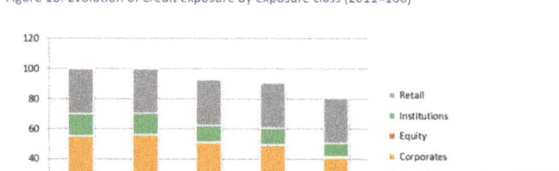

Source: Figure 25 in EIOPA [2]. Source: Figure 18 in EBA [3].

Figure 1. Aggregate breakdown of exposure allocation of the main European insurers and banks. (**a**) Investment allocation (in %) for debt and other fixed income securities for the European insurance sector; (**b**) evolution for credit exposure by exposure class (2011 = 100) for the European banking sector.

At a global level, the general guidelines proposed by the FSB to identify systemic institutions have been derived separately for banks (see BCBS [4]) and for insurance companies (see IAIS [5]), although there exist financial conglomerates.[1] In contrast, European regulation takes into account the existence of financial conglomerates (see OJEU [6]). About 70 European institutions are classified as conglomerates. On top of complying with the banking and insurance regulations, they must meet capital adequacy requirements for their whole activities. These capital adequacy requirements do not address interconnectedness, but rather risk concentration. One natural concern is therefore that financial conglomerates may be contagion pathways between the banking sector and the insurance sector. The French financial sector presents an interesting situation, since it includes several major financial conglomerates.

Our paper is an extended version of the second part of the working paper Hauton and Héam [7]. The first part of the working paper provides a comparison of several methodologies to measure the interconnectedness between financial institutions on a consolidated basis (such as the identification of core-periphery structure, for instance). The second part, which we extend here, focuses on financial conglomerates. The objective of our paper is to address two major questions: To what extent are insurers part of conglomerates different from pure insurers? To what extent are financial conglomerates modifying the vulnerability of the financial sector to contagion? Previous literature answers these questions using either market data or stand-alone accounting data. The originality of our paper is to use a new type of data: we analyze a database on the bilateral exposures of 21 French financial institutions encompassing six conglomerates, four pure banks and eleven pure insurers. The exposures of the banking and insurance components of financial conglomerates, as well as the sovereign exposures were specifically investigated for this paper.

The paper is organized as follows. Section 2 presents the literature on interconnections to highlight where our contribution lies. Section 3 presents the database. It heavily relies on Hauton and Héam [7]. Section 4 uses statistical measures of exposure closeness in order to assess to what extent the insurer parts of conglomerates are different from pure insurers. Section 5 uses contagion models to analyze the risk of contagion within the financial sector. Section 6 concludes.

---

[1] Note that we adopt the continental European point of view: a conglomerate is a group with banking and insurance activities. This wording contrasts with an Anglo-Saxon view where "conglomerate" is often synonymous with "universal bank" (a bank mixing traditional banking activity and investment activity).

2. Literature Review

Firstly, we present the main theoretical arguments explaining the emergence of financial conglomerates. These motivations are similar to the explanation of linkages between banks and insurers. Before addressing in greater detail the specific motivations, the business models of banking and insurance explain a different general profile of interconnectedness. Maturity transformation leads banks to borrow partly from other financial institutions and to invest in typically non-financial firms and households. The insurance companies are expected to be exposed to the financial sector, since they invest the proceeds of the policyholders' premium. Their liabilities are mostly composed of commitments to the policyholders; thus, the exposures of other financial institutions to insurers should be low. Being a financial conglomerate benefits from revenue enhancement and cost savings through diversification effects (see Berger and Ofek [8,9]). For instance, a bank can use its knowledge of clients, as well as its offices to sell insurance products, too. Another motive for interconnections between banks and insurers may be risk transfers, such as reinsurance or securitization (see Subramanian and Wang [10]). This motive is less relevant for conglomerates, since risks are transferred to other subsidiaries, but remain in the same group. General opinion about the interconnection between financial institutions refers to liquidity management (see Holmstrom and Tirole [11], Rochet [12], Tirole [13]). Liquidity issues are relevant for short-term relationships, such as interbank overnight loans. Their relevance for financial conglomerates is much less clear. It is hard to narrow the advantages of being a conglomerate to a simple advantage in liquidity management. However, this strand of literature provides results worth being kept in mind when analyzing conglomerates. In particular, Allen and Gale [14] show that the degree of interconnection has an ambiguous effect on financial stability. When institutions are exposed to small and diversified shocks, the optimal structure is a complete network: the interconnections are actually generating an insurance scheme. However, when institutions are exposed to large shocks, a complete network is the worst situation. In that case, interconnections are the support of contagion: the shock is propagated to all institutions, leading to a massive cascade of defaults.

Second, most papers exploiting bilateral exposure data consider only banks. In contrast, our scope includes also financial conglomerates and insurers. Moreover, most papers analyze one national banking sector.[2] In general, little evidence of solvency contagion is found. When liquidity channels are considered, contagion risk may become prominent. Liquidity channels consist of fire sales (see Cifuentes *et al.* [15] for instance) and liquidity hoarding (see Fourel *et al.* [16] for instance). These channels are relevant for banks for which core activity is maturity transformation. For insurance, liquidity concerns are less important. The unique case of international analysis is Alves *et al.* [17], where the interconnections between 53 major European banks are analyzed. Researchers use market data (stock prices) or accounting data (profits, turnover, *etc.*) to circumvent the scarcity of bilateral exposure data. Concerning contagion between insurance and banks, Schmid and Walter [18] investigate the profitability of U.S. financial firms between 1985 and 2004. One of their most relevant results for our paper is that commercial banks do not benefit from developing insurance activity. Brewer and Jackson [19] analyze the impact of three announcements in 1990 on the abnormal returns of U.S. commercial banks and U.S. life-insurers. Their empirical findings provide mixed results due to an overlapping of information effects and competitiveness effects. They show that there is less contagion risk from the insurance sector to the banking sector than from the banking sector to the insurance sector. Still on the U.S. market, Filson and Olfati [20] analyze abnormal returns following mergers of U.S. banks between 2001 and 2011. This date range includes the 1999 Gramm-Leach-Bliley Act authorizing commercial banks to perform also investment banking, securities brokerage and insurance

---

[2] See, among others: Furfine [24] for the USA, Wells [25] for the U.K., Upper and Worms [26] for Germany, Lublóy [27] for Hungary, van Lelyveld and Liedorp [28] for the Netherlands, Degryse and Nguyen [29] for Belgium, Toivanen [30] for Finland, Mistrulli [31] for Italy, Gauthier *et al.* [32] for Canada, Cont *et al.* [33] for Brazil, Fourel *et al.* [16] for France, *etc.*

activities. They show that diversification creates value, contrasting with Schmid and Walter [18]. Analyzing extreme stock return co-movements between major financial firms of the U.S., Germany and U.K. between 1990 and 2003, Minderhoud [21] shows that correlation during normal periods is significantly different from correlation during crisis periods. Interpreting extreme co-movements as contagion phenomena, he concludes that there is contagion risk from the insurance sector to the banking sector, despite the results of Brewer and Jackson [19]. His results are two-fold: there is no diversification pattern during crisis time, but a diversification advantage may exist in standard periods. Stringa and Monks [22] study six events in the U.K. financial market between 2002 and 2003 to assess the risk of contagion from the insurance sector to the banking sector. They pinpoint the heterogeneity of banks' responses to a distress. In particular, financial conglomerates are much more affected than pure banks. A key paper concerning European financial conglomerates is van Lelyveld and Knot [23]. The authors compare the market performances of major European financial conglomerates with the market performances of major EU banks and insurances between 1995 and 2005. They investigate if a conglomerate has a better performance than the sum of its banking part and of its insurance part. They find that the diversification effect is only a recent phenomenon. Moreover, there is a large heterogeneity of the diversification discount. The authors interpret their results as the outcome of a combination of diversification and opacity.

Empirical papers about financial conglomerates or, more generally, about spill over effects between the banking sector and the insurance sector present contrasting results. The results based on the stock returns of publicly-traded firms unveil market participants' assessments of financial conglomerates. To the best of our knowledge, our paper is the first paper to provide an empirical analysis based on a specific type of data: bilateral exposure data. Market or accounting data are a collection of individual data. Although very informative, the links that are put in evidence with such data are statistical links, such as correlation or Granger causality. In contrast, bilateral exposures are structural financial links. One aspect of our contribution is therefore to bring a new perspective to the questions previously analyzed in the literature.

3. Data

The perimeter includes all French banking groups and insurance groups with total assets larger than €10 bn, as of December 2011. We exclude publicly-oriented firm, such as development banks. This perimeter accounts for more than 85% of the French financial sector. Consequently, the dataset is composed of bilateral exposures of the 21 largest French banks and insurance groups: BNP, Crédit Agricole, Société Générale, BPCE, Crédit Mutuel and La Banque Postale are financial conglomerates; HSBC, Crédit Logement, CRHand Oseo are banks; AG2R-La Mondiale, Aviva, Axa, Allianz, CNP, Generali, Groupama, Covea, Maif, Macif and Scor are insurers. This low number of firms is explained by the high concentration of the French financial sector. For instance, the top five banking groups account for about 80% of the French banking sector. A secondary explanation is that institutions are considered on a consolidated basis aggregating potential hundreds of financial subsidiaries. This restriction comes from the used regulatory reports. In terms of size, conglomerates account for about half of the sample, while the remaining half is almost equally split between banks and insurers. We do not identify the financial institutions in the remainder of the paper due to confidentiality restrictions. Since our database is one snapshot of 2011, the representative character of this specific year is a natural concern. Since we do not have access to other snapshots of bilateral exposures, we cannot bring adamant comparisons. However, we situate year 2011 using ancillary data in Appendix A. Except for conglomerates, institutions are considered on a fully consolidated basis, gathering all classes and area of activity. For conglomerates, we distinguish a fully consolidated basis, where banking activity and insurance activity are merged, from a partially consolidated basis, where the banking component is separated from the insurance component. When conglomerates are considered on a partially consolidated basis, the sample size is 27. We collect balance sheet data from regulatory reports when available or from public financial statements otherwise. For banks and banking components of conglomerates, the exposures are derived from "large exposures" regulatory reports. These reports contains the list of all exposures larger than €300 mn or 10% of capital. In that report, an exposure to a counterpart is a double aggregation: it is the sum over all of the banking subsidiaries of all individual financial instruments associated with any subsidiaries of this specific counterpart. Each exposure is then broken down into broad financial instrument classes. We identify in the list of counterparts the financial institutions of our perimeter. In addition, we also keep major sovereign exposures. The exposures of insurers are based on security-by-security reports of French insurance entities. We identify the same counterparts as we do for banks. Since we can only access French insurance subsidiaries, there is downward bias. The impact of the bias varies across insurers according to their area of activity: the bias is almost null for domestic-oriented insurers and larger for globally-active insurers. The exposures are broken down between debt instruments and equity instruments. Debt instruments consist of debt securities, loans, deposits, *etc*. Equity instruments gather share securities, equity investments, *etc*. Note that the French financial conglomerates are banking dominant. The equity associated with the banking components represents about 90% of the total equity of the groups. Therefore, we expect the banking component to be similar to a banking group and are more interested in the behavior of the insurance component.

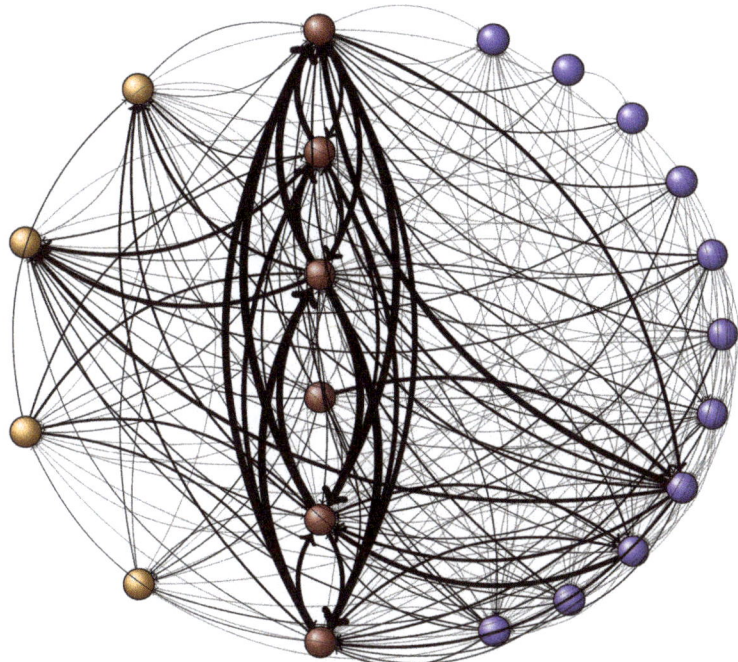

Figure 2. Network of French financial institutions for total exposures on a consolidated basis. The node color indicates the institution class (red for conglomerates, blue for pure insurers and yellow for pure banks); the edge width is proportional to exposure. The arrow starts from the owner of the exposure and ends at the counterpart with a left bent profile. Source: ACPRdata, authors' computation.

A total of €227 bn is reported. Among the 420 possible bilateral exposures, 261 are non-zero. The ratio of the two figures is called the density. With a density of 62%, the French financial network is very dense. For a comparison, the density of the banking network is about 1% in Germany (see Craig and von Peter [34]), 8% in the Netherlands (see van Lelyveld and Veld [35]), 3% in the U.K. (see Langfield *et al.* [36]) and varies between 10% and 20% in Italy (see Fricke and Lux [37]). This high density may be explained by the presence of insurers. Figure 2 represents the network of total exposures where institutions are considered on a full-consolidated basis. Institutions are represented by nodes. In the center, the six red nodes are the conglomerates. On the left part, the four blue nodes are the pure banks. On the right part, the eleven yellow nodes are the insurers. The arrows represent exposures between institutions. Identifying a clear pattern is a challenge. Conglomerates appears to have the largest exposures and to be connected to banks and insurers. However, we observe many exposures between insurers. Figure 3 represents the volume of exposure between sub-sectors. About 50% of the €227 bn are exposures between financial conglomerates. About 20% of the exposures are exposures of pure insurers to conglomerates. The exposures of conglomerates to the banks and to the insurers account for about 10% each. We consider that the banking component of one financial conglomerate is the parent company of the insurance component when we analyze the exposures between components of the same conglomerate. The exposure of the banking component to the insurance component is consequently composed of equity. Overall, the exposures from one component to another are approximately balanced. In a majority of cases, the insurance component is slightly more exposed to the banking component than the banking component to the insurance component. In any case, the main difference between intra-group exposures is the instrument: the bank component holds equity issued by the insurance component, whereas the insurance component holds debt instruments issued by the banking component.

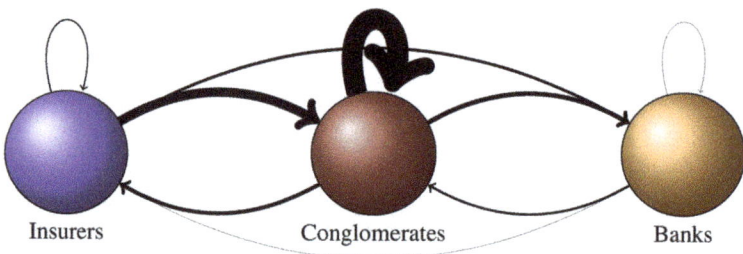

Figure 3. Volume of total exposures allocation between sectors. The node color indicates the institution class (red for conglomerates, blue for pure insurers and yellow for pure banks); the edge width is proportional to exposure. The arrow starts from the owner of the exposure and ends at the counterpart with a left bent profile. Loop arrows represent exposure within the class considered. Source: ACPR Data, authors' computation.

This basic analysis of the exposure shows first that the network is very dense. High density is a double-edged sword. On the one hand, this feature can be seen as a diversification pattern that points towards resilience. On the other hand, Allen and Gale [14] show that a dense network is prone to widespread contagion when shocks are extreme. This dichotomy between a positive effect during normal times and a negative aspect during bad times corresponds to the empirical findings in Minderhoud [21]. Second, this analysis shows that the financial conglomerates are key players in terms of the size of institutions and exposures. At first glance, contagion can hardly occur without involving at least one of them.

4. To What Extent Are Insurers within a Conglomerate Different from Pure Insurers?

In this section, we address the similarity in terms of interconnectedness between the insurer part of a conglomerate and a stand-alone insurer. To do so, we use a distance metric between each financial institutions to see if the insurer part of a conglomerate are close to the stand-alone insurer.

4.1. Methodology

We compare the interconnectedness between financial institutions using two concepts: network integration and network substitutability (see Hauton and Héam [7]). Two institutions are said to be close in terms of network integration when they have similar exposures independent of their counterparts. Two institutions are said to be close in terms of network substitutability when they have similar exposures to the same counterparts. Network substitutability is more stringent than network integration: if two institutions are close in terms of network substitutability, they are necessarily close in terms of network integration. To illustrate the differences between these two concept, we consider a fictitious example represented by the exposure matrix given in Table 1. An exposure matrix gathers the exposures between a set of financial institutions, such that coefficient (i, j) represents the exposure of institution i to institution j. Let us consider institutions A and C. Their common exposures, which are exposures to institutions B, D, E and F, are reported in Table 2. The exposure series are similar, since each amount in the exposures of institution A can be mapped to an exposure of institution C: 2.7 with 2.9, 5.0 with 5.1, 2.1 with 2.0 and 3.2 with 3.1. Let us now consider institutions A and B. Their common exposures, which are exposures to institutions C, D, E and F, are reported in Table 3. The exposures are very similar, since the amounts are roughly the same and concern the same counterpart. Institution A and institution B are considered close in terms of substitutability and in terms of integration (Table 3): they lend similar volumes to the same counterparts. By contrast, institution A and institution C are close in terms of integration, but distant in terms of substitutability (Table 2): they lend similar volume,s but not to the same counterparts.

Table 1. Fictitious example for network integration and network substitutability.

	A)	B)	C)	D)	E)	F)
A)	0	2.7	3.0	5.0	2.1	3.2
B)	2.0	0	2.9	4.9	2.2	3.3
C)	1.9	2.9	0	3.1	5.1	2.0
D)	0.5	0.1	0.6	0	2.1	0.7
E)	1.1	1.5	1.3	1.9	0	1.9
F)	2.0	4.1	4.9	3.7	2.1	0

Table 2. Fictitious example: common exposures of institutions A and C.

	A)	B)	C)	D)	E)	F)
A)	X	2.7	X	5.0	2.1	3.2
C)	X	2.9	X	3.1	5.1	2.0

Table 3. Fictitious example: common exposures of institutions A and B.

	A)	B)	C)	D)	E)	F)
A)	X	X	3.0	5.0	2.1	3.2
B)	X	X	2.9	4.9	2.2	3.3

In line with these two concepts, Hauton and Héam [7] propose two metrics to quantify each dimension. These metrics are derived from a statistical background that goes beyond the scope of this paper (see Appendix B for more details). Intuitively, the metrics are based on comparing the size of exposure with or without taking into account the counterparts. The main idea is that we can build two distance matrices describing the closeness of any pair of institutions with respect to network integration and network substitutability. An interesting feature is that this process can be carried out by considering gross exposure (exposures in €), or by scaling exposures by the owner's size (exposures in % of owner's equity), or by scaling exposures by the issuers' size (exposures in % of issuer's equity).

These three processes are not expected to provide the same results, as they are three distinct vantage points to look at exposures. Examining exposures in € is the basic analysis that provides insights into the stock of inter-financial assets. One drawback of this vantage point is the risk that we capture size effects rather than interconnection effects: it is natural that two institutions of similar total asset size have similar exposures. The second vantage point is adopting a credit risk perspective. Instead of considering the size of the exposure, we look at how much the exposure represents of the owner's equity. A €10 mn loan granted from a small institution will be different from a €10 mn loan granted by a large institution. From that perspective, if two institutions appear close, they take similar risk in investing. In that approach, we have controlled for size effects. The third and last vantage point is adopting a funding risk perspective. Exposure is expressed as the percent of the equity of the issuers. Following this line, two closed institutions have similar funding strategies. Note that the two first approaches are examining the asset side, whereas with the last approach, the focus is on the liability side. Since analyzing manually a distance matrix between 27 institutions is cumbersome, we use cluster analysis. The objective is to categorize institutions, so that institutions of the same cluster are very alike. Intuitively, clusters are built step-by-step through aggregating individuals to the closest cluster. The graphical representation of a cluster analysis is a dendrogram. The $y-$axis is the threshold distance between clusters, while individuals are represented on the $x-$axis. Figure 4 presents a toy example of clustering analysis results. There are various technical ways to process the aggregation of individuals. We present the results using the Ward criterion that minimizes the inner variance (see Ward [38]). We check that our results are robust using the other following aggregating criteria: complete (that minimizes the furthest distance), group average (that minimizes the unweighted average distance) and weighted (that minimizes a weighted average distance). See Hartigan [39] for a textbook on clustering methods.

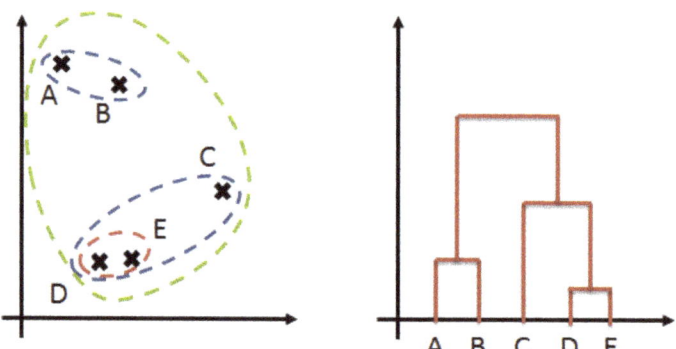

Figure 4. Cluster analysis example. The left panel represents a population of five individuals (*A* to *E*) with the successive clusters. The right panel represents the corresponding dendrogram.

4.2. Results on Network Integration

Figure 5 presents the dendrograms for network integration when exposures are considered in € (Figure 5a), normalized by the size of the owner (Figure 5b), and normalized by the size of the issuer (Figure 5c). Each label on the x-axis represents one institution. Pure banks are labeled from PB1 to PB4; pure insurers are labeled from PI1 to PI11. The banking component of financial conglomerate i is labeled BCi, while the insurance component is labeled ICi. We use an arbitrary threshold identifying at most three clusters to ease the discussion. We distinguish three clusters for gross exposures (Figure 5a). The first cluster (on the left) is composed of all pure institutions, except for two pure insurers that form a second cluster (in the middle) and except for one insurance component. The last cluster (on the right) is composed of all components of the financial conglomerates (except the insurance component, which is in the first cluster). Therefore, the components of financial conglomerates tend to be exposed to similar volumes. These volumes are different from the volumes of pure banks and pure insurers. The volume perspective is informative, but since the size of institutions is not controlled for, we may only grasp the cluster of institutions with a similar size. Let us look at Figure 5b, where exposures are scaled by the size of the owner. Two clusters are spotted. The first one (on the left) is composed of all financial components and one pure insurer. The second cluster gathers all pure institutions (except one pure insurer). The picture is therefore similar to the analysis in terms of volumes. The components of financial conglomerates are very alike, independent of their banking or insurance activities. Finally, we adopt a funding perspective in Figure 5c. Here, almost all banking components of financial conglomerates are gathered into one cluster (on the right). Insurance components are mixed with pure banks and several pure insurers (on the left). One last cluster (in the middle) regroups five pure insurers. In a funding perspective, the components of financial conglomerates have a clearer stand: insurance components are close to insurers, while banking components form a distinct homogeneous group.

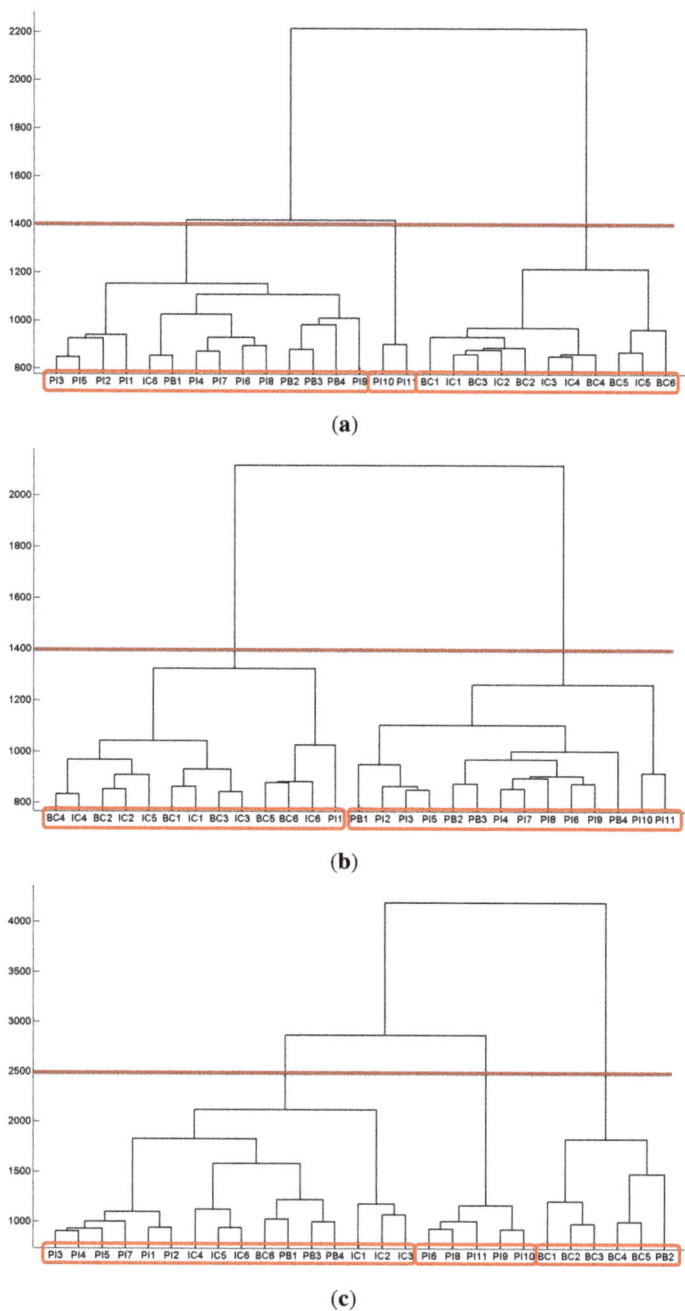

Figure 5. Dendrograms for network integration. Legend: PIx indicates the x-th pure insurer; PBy indicates the y-th pure bank; ICz the insurance component of the z-th financial conglomerate; and BCz the banking component of the z-th financial conglomerate. Source: ACPR data, authors' calculation. (**a**) Volume (exposures in €); (**b**) credit risk (exposures in % of owner's equity); (**c**) funding risk (exposures in % of issuer's equity).

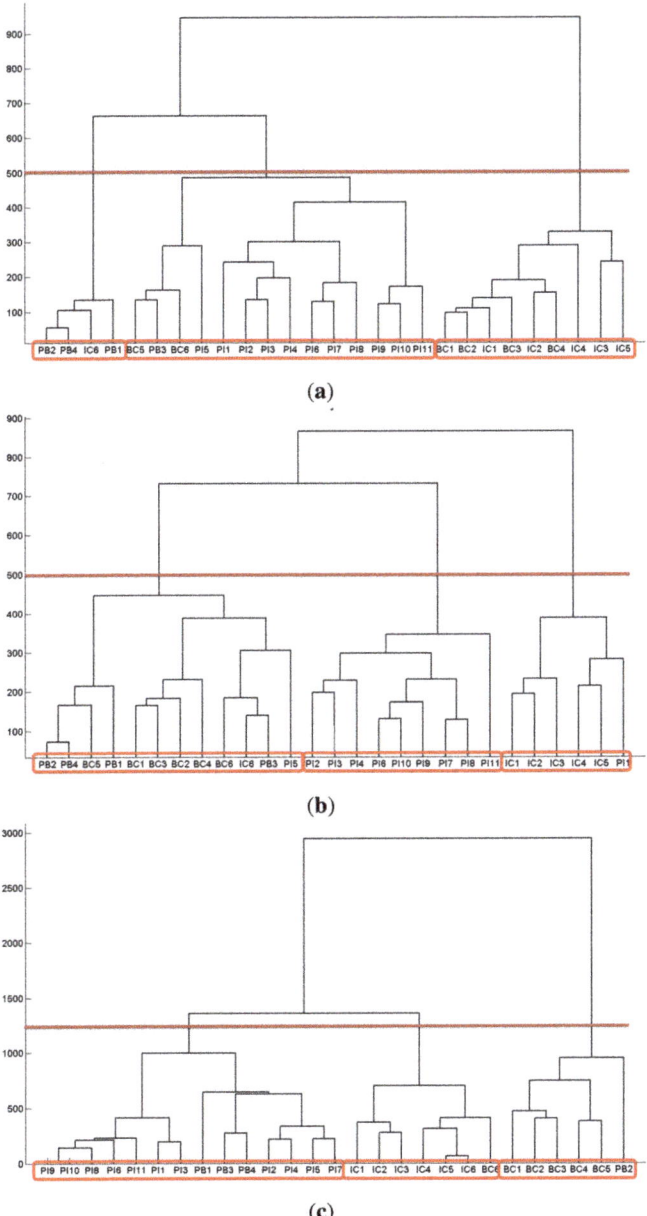

Figure 6. Dendrograms for network substitutability. Legend: PIx indicates the x-th pure insurer; PBy indicates the y-th pure bank; ICz the insurance component of the z-th financial conglomerate; and BCz the banking component of the z-th financial conglomerate. Source: ACPR data, authors' calculation. (**a**) Volume (exposures in €); (**b**) credit risk (exposures in % of owner's equity); (**c**) funding risk (exposures in % of issuer's equity).

4.3. Results on Network Substitutability

Figure 6 presents the dendrograms for network substitutability when exposures are considered in € (Figure 6a), normalized by the size of the owner (Figure 6b) and normalized by the size of the issuer (Figure 6c). Compared to network integration, the distance metric encompasses a comparison of the size of exposures associated with a similarity of counterparts. The substitutability in terms of volumes is analyzed in Figure 6a. Nine out of twelve components of conglomerates form a cluster (on the right). The two last clusters mix different institutions (on the left and in the middle). From that perspective, insurance components of conglomerates tend to lend similar amounts (in €) to the same counterparties as their banking homologous do. This proximity disappears when examining credit risk represented in Figure 6b. Except for a few cases, three groups can be identified: a group formed by a banking component and pure banks, a group of pure insurers and a group of insurance components. Insurance components are therefore different from their banking homologous in risk taking, but also different from pure insurers. With respect to funding risk in Figure 6c, the insurer components shape a cluster (in the middle) that is distinct from the cluster banking components (on the right) and the cluster of pure institutions (on the left). The reading is similar to the features identified for credit risk.

4.4. Conclusion on Likeliness of Insurers

The comparison of the results on network substitutability and the results on network integration leads us to draw a few stylized facts. On the asset side, the banking components and insurance components of financial conglomerates appear to have similar exposures. This proximity may come from an economy of scale in counterparty risk monitoring. However, their portfolio allocations differ. Insurance components have a clear profile distinct from their homologous and distinct from pure insurers. This feature may be explained by a diversification constraint at a group level. On the liability side, the nature of the activity is a clear discriminant. The insurance components' funding strategy is much more like pure insurers' strategy than that of their banking homologous. This analysis of financial assets and liabilities suggests that insurers that are part of conglomerates differ specifically and moderately from pure insurers. They tend to be more exposed than pure insurers. However, their exposures are diversified from their banking peers. On the liability side, there is a clear insurance profile where insurance components are very distinct from the banking components of conglomerates. Their funding strategy is similar to any pure insurers. Let us emphasize that the comparison is only carried out with respect to interconnectedness and brings no insight in terms of the riskiness of investments, marketing strategies, *etc.*

5. To What Extent Are Conglomerates Modifying Contagion Risk?

Since conglomerates are active in the banking sector and the insurance sector, a natural concern is the risk that they could facilitate the propagation of a crisis from one sector to another. Using market data, Stringa and Monks [22] or Brewer and Jackson [19] shed light on the perception of this specific concern by market participants. To bring evidence based on granular bilateral data, we use a network stress test approach. We consider specific shocks to briefly analyze the risk that the default of one institution may trigger a default cascade. We also apply common shocks based on sovereign exposures that affect simultaneously all institutions.

5.1. Methodology

A network stress test exercise is composed of a contagion model and the design of external shocks. We use the contagion model developed in Gouriéroux *et al.* [40]. This structural model extends the model of Eisenberg and Noe [41] by distinguishing a contagion channel based on equity instruments from a contagion channel based on debt instruments. The motivation to use the model of Gouriéroux *et al.* [40] is that alternative models consider only contagion based on debt instruments. Equity instruments are necessary for our analysis, since equity is a major instrument for the exposures between the components of a financial conglomerate. Using a network stress test has the advantage of comparison, since most academic papers using bilateral exposure data include a network stress test application. A network stress test is also in line with stress test exercises run by the industry, such as the 2014 stress test for European banks organized jointly by the European Banking Authority and the European Central Bank or the 2014 stress test for European insurers organized by the European Insurance and Occupational Pensions Authority. Moreover, we design simple scenarios that are easy to explain. The main drawback of stress test comes from the so-called "static balance sheet assumption". We apply a shock and look at its propagation through the system without considering any reactions of financial institutions. It is as if the shock were unexpected and sudden. We acknowledge that this assumption is a caveat for the result interpretation. However, modeling the reaction of financial institutions in a network perspective goes far beyond the scope of our paper. Let us present briefly the model of Gouriéroux et al. [40]. Consider n financial institutions interconnected through equity instruments and debt instruments. On the liability side, we denote Y_i the value of the equity of institution i and L_i the value of the debt of institution i. On the asset side, we denote $\pi_{i,j}$ the fraction of equity instruments issued by institution j owned by institution i, $\gamma_{i,j}$ the fraction of debt instruments issued by institution j owned by institution i and Ax_i the value of all others assets of institutions i (loans to households, sovereign exposures, etc). For instance, $\pi_{1,2} = 0.5$ means that Institution 1 owns 50% of the equity of Institution 2. The balance sheet of institution i is represented in Table 4. Denoting L_i^* the nominal debt of institution i, Merton's model written for each bank provides the following $2n$−equation system:

$$\left\{ L_i = \min\left[\sum_{j=1}^n \left(\pi_{i,j} Y_j\right) + \sum_{j=1}^n \left(\gamma_{i,j} L_j\right) + Ax_i \right] \right. \tag{1}$$

System (??) defines a liquidation equilibrium. Gouriéroux et al. [40] show that under mild assumptions, there exists one unique liquidation equilibrium (Y, L) for any choice of Ax and L^*. The parameters $\pi_{i,j}, \gamma_{i,j}$ and L^* are calibrated on the dataset, as well as the pre-shock values of external assets Ax. Specifying the shock corresponds to computing the liquidation equilibrium with a shocked value Ax. Let us emphasize that we consider only deterministic shocks: we analyze what happens in a given situation without quantifying the likelihood of this situation.

Table 4. Balance sheet of institution i in Gouriéroux et al. [40].

		Asset	Liability		
interbank cross shareholding	↔ {	$\pi_{i,1} Y_1$ ⋮ $\pi_{i,n} Y_n$	L_i	↔	debt
interbank lending	↔ {	$\gamma_{i,1} L_1$ ⋮ $\gamma_{i,n} L_n$	Y_i	↔	equity
external asset	↔		Ax_i		

5.2. Stress Test with Individual Shocks

The very first concern about contagion risk and conglomerates is the risk that the default of one component is propagated to the other component, initiating a cross-sector chain of defaults. In that perspective, we consider sequentially that the external assets of each component of the six financial conglomerates are totally wiped out by assuming $Ax_i = 0$. For four of the financial conglomerates, the default of the banking component implies the default of the insurance component. For the last two conglomerates, the default of the banking component is not sufficient to put the insurance component into default. On the contrary, the default of the insurance component never triggers the default of the banking component. This result is in line with the fact that the banking component is much more important than the insurance component for the French conglomerates. In light of this stress test exercise, the contagion risk within a financial conglomerate is therefore clear: the insurance component is exposed to the banking component, but the reverse is false.

5.3. Stress Test with Common Shocks

Considering individual shocks is informative, but they correspond to very particular situations, which may not be representative of anticipated shocks. More realistically, we consider that contagion risk is prominent when there is a common shock that weakens all institutions. The contagion is a second-round effect that pushes the impact further. We consider shocks composed of the decrease of 50% of the sovereign exposures on major countries, since first, sovereign debt is a massive investment part of banks and insurers (especially for insurers) and, second, sovereign risk is one current major concern. We sequentially shock sovereign exposures on Germany, Spain, France, the United Kingdom, Ireland, Italy, Portugal and the United States of America.[3] The figure of 50% corresponds to the 2011 agreement on the Greek sovereign debt (see Erlanger and Castle [42]). Sovereign exposures encompass all "official" counterparties: state debt, federal debt, municipalities bonds, hospital debt, *etc*. For each country, we compare the setup where financial conglomerates are split and the setup where financial conglomerate are one group. In the first setup, the two components of one conglomerate are considered as different entities, albeit exposed to one another, whereas in the second setup, they share the same fates. There is no general argument to tell which situation is the most resilient. We emphasize that the first set-up is not a perfect counter-factual representation of what may happen if conglomerates were legally split, since exposures are endogenous. If conglomerate were to be split, the exposures between the banking component and the insurer component would be somehow reallocated. This caveat should be kept in mind when interpreting the results. Although not perfect, we believe this counter-factual representation brings informative insights. Robustness checks are provided in Appendix C. Results are presented in Table 5. For Germany, Spain, the United Kingdom, Ireland, Portugal and the United States of America, the losses do not lead any institutions to default, whatever the setup. Even the U.S. and the U.K., of which sovereign debt may be used as collateral for exchange with the corresponding financial sectors, do not lead any institution to default. For Italy, one insurance component is in default (in the split setup), whereas on a fully consolidated setup, no institution is in default. Therefore, only one insurer benefits from being part of a conglomerate. The recovery rate on the debt of this insurance component is 98%. There is a clear home bias. For France, the losses generate the default of all insurances components and one banking component in the split setup. In the consolidated setup, one financial conglomerate is in default. Consequently, five (out of six) insurers somehow benefit from being part of a conglomerate. The recovery rate on defaulted institutions is 90% for insurer components, 97% for banking components and 98% for conglomerates. With respect to these scenarios, financial conglomerates strengthen the resilience of the French financial sector, since policyholders, who are debt holders, are less likely to suffer losses.

---

[3] NB: for these counterparts, we get all of the exposures of insurance subsidiaries whether they are French or not, using a specific regulatory template for a financial conglomerate.

Table 5. Sovereign exposure stress test results. Equity recovery is the average over the non-defaulted institutions of the ratio of equity after shock and equity before shock. Debt recovery is the average over the defaulted institutions of the ratio of debt value after shock and before shock. "." indicates that the value cannot be computed.

Country	DE	ES	FR	UK	FR	IE	IT	PT	US
No. of Defaults									
Insurance Component	0	0	6	0	0	0	1	0	0
Banking Component	0	0	1	0	0	0	0	0	0
Conglomerate	0	0	1	0	0	0	0	0	0
Equity Recovery (%)									
Insurance Component	93	75	.	100	94	93	61	83	99
Banking Component	91	96	71	99	99	99	86	97	86
Conglomerate	92	96	66	99	99	99	87	97	86
Debt Recovery (%)									
Insurance Component	.	.	90	.	.	.	98	.	.
Banking Component	.	.	97	.	.	.	.	.	.
Conglomerate	.	.	98	.	.	.	.	.	.

5.4. Conclusion on Contagion Risk

Using a contagion model to assess the impact of several deterministic scenarios, we find that insurance components are dependent on the banking component within the same group. Second, we find evidence towards a positive role of financial conglomerates that increases the resilience of insurers. One interpretation is that the dependence link is negative for an Armageddon scenario (such as designed for individual shock), but positive for extreme adverse shocks, such a significant sovereign crisis.

6. Conclusions

Financial conglomerates are not standard financial institutions and have been raising lively debates. We shed light on some specific aspects of these discussions. First, we compare the insurance components of financial conglomerates to pure insurers. On the liability side, we find a proximity between insurance components and pure insurers. On the asset side, insurance components appear more exposed than pure insurers, but this higher level of exposure seems offset by a diversification scheme at a group level. Second, we analyze the contagion risk. We show that for French conglomerates, which are dominated by banking activity, the insurance component is exposed to the banking component, whereas the banking component does not depend on the insurance component. However, when considering common shocks that affect both components, conglomerates appear in general more resilient than separate structures. The downside aspect of the dependence does not appear for these very adverse shocks. We exploit a unique type of database of bilateral exposures to contrast previously-established results. Moreover, most previous papers used data prior to the last financial crisis, whereas we have a snapshot of 2011. We believe it is unproductive to set the points of view against each other. Minderhoud [21] found that market participants do not value the diversification dimension of a financial conglomerate during a crisis. Our application using a stress test approach, which we believe is closer to fundamental risk, goes in the opposite direction. The explanation may lie in the argument of van Lelyveld and Knot [23], stating that the diversification bonus of financial conglomerates comes with an opacity drawback, for market participants. This opacity may appear to be more important during crisis, when market agents are said to be feverish, leading to the negative effect shown by market data. However, balance sheet data and stress test scenarios are not influenced by "animal spirits". Another partial explanation may be that previous authors analyzed the market value of equity, while we are more concerned with debt holders (or policyholders in the case of insurers). In line with this paper, further work to understand how a financial conglomerate allocates its assets between its banking and insurance components would be interesting. Our contribution is on the risk analysis of financial conglomerates and other types of concerns, such as competitiveness, pricing or cross-sale, which would be worth taking into account.

Acknowledgments: The opinions expressed in the paper are only those of the authors and do not necessarily reflect those of the Autorité de Contrôle Prudentiel et de Résolution.

We thank the anonymous referees for their insightful remarks and Ivan Alves, Olivier de Bandt, Monica Billio, Serges Darolles, Dominique Durant, Laure Frey, Henri Fraisse, Sarah Gandolphe, Christian Gouriéroux, Anne-Laure Kaminski, Claire Labonne and the participants of the Workshop on Stress Test organized by the Advisory Technical Committee of the European Systemic Risk Board (Frankfurt, Germany, 2014), the 7th Risk Forum (Paris, France, 2014), 14th Credit Risk Evaluation Designed for Institutional Targeting in finance Conference (Venise, Italy, 2014), the 3rd Research Workshop (London, UK, 2014), the 6th IMF Forum on Stress Test (London, UK, 2014) and the Université de Besançon Seminar for their helpful comments. This paper has also benefited from the excellent research assistance of Farida Azzi.

Appendix A. French Financial Situation in 2011

In this paper, we analyze one snapshot of the French financial sector, as of December 2011. We present here background figures on the size of interconnections and the size of sovereign exposures in order to situate the representativeness of our database.

A.1. Financial Exposures

First, Alves *et al.* [17] developed the empirical analysis of bilateral exposure between 53 large European banks as of December 2011. About half of the exposures (in €) between these 53 large European banks have a remaining maturity higher than one year. Second, Figure A1 reports the volume of credit exposures of the French banking sector between 2008 and 2012. There is a moderate decreasing trend of the exposures to other banks ("credit institutions" category in green). This trend is confirmed over 2012 and 2013 (see Section 3.1 in ACPR [43]).

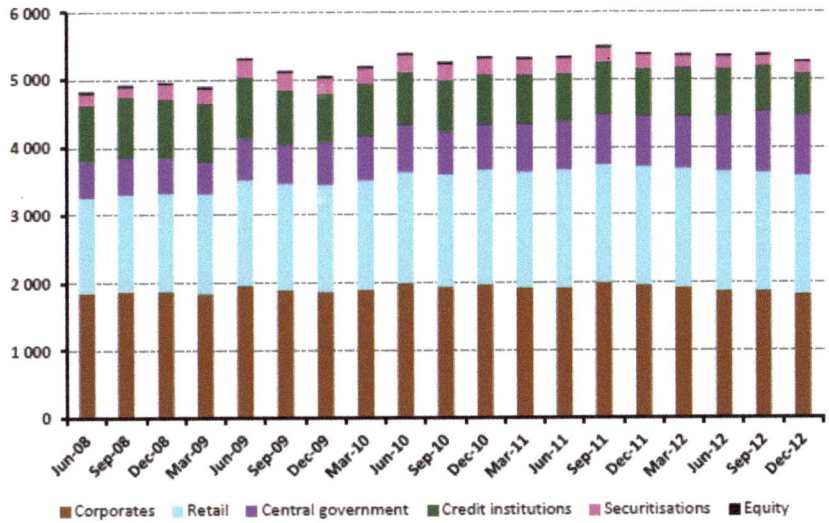

Figure A1. Credit exposures of the French banking sector (€bn) between 2008 and 2012. Source: Chart 28 in ACP [44].

Third, Figure A2 reports the volume of investment of the 12 major French insurers between 2008 and 2014. The presented breakdown does not match our scope perfectly: the category "deposits" (in mallow) is part of the exposures to banks, but the category "other debt securities" (in intermediate blue) encompasses bonds issued by banks, insurers and industrial firms. We complement this aggregate view by reporting the annual evolution of investment in debt securities issued by banks in Figure A3. Since most nodes are slightly above the 45° line, we see a moderate decreasing trend in the exposures of insurers to banks.

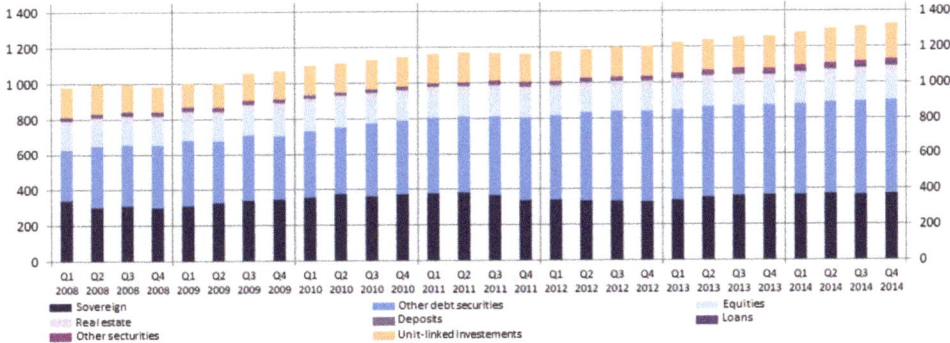

Figure A2. Credit exposures of the French banking sector (€bn) between 2008 and 2012. Source: Chart 6 in ACPR [45].

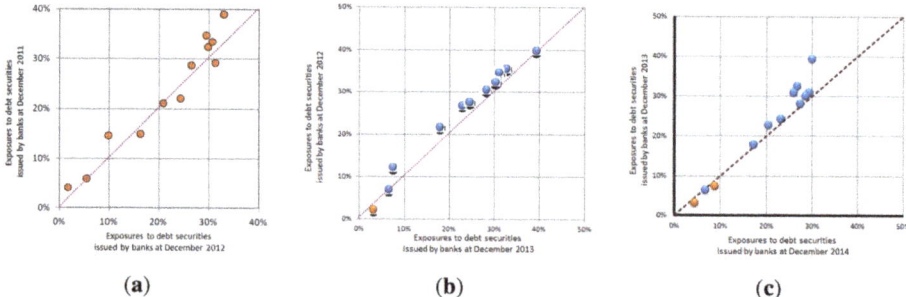

Figure A3. Annual change of investment of the major French insurers through debt securities between December 2011 and December 2014. Each dot represents one insurer. When dots are colored, a blue dot indicates a decrease, while a yellow dot indicates an increase. Sources: ACP [46] for (**a**), ACPR [47] for (**b**) and ACPR [45] for (**c**). (a) Between 2011 and 2012; (b) between 2012 and 2013; (c) between 2013 and 2014.

These three pieces of anecdotal evidence shed light on the total intra-financial assets of French banks and insurers. The year 2011 does not appear as one exceptional year, but a regular point in the evolution of the French financial sector characterized by a slightly decreasing trend of the size of exposures. This information on the volume of exposure is not informative for the allocation of these exposures, that is the evolution of the network structure. As shown by Cocco *et al.* [48], there is a certain level of persistence between the banking relationship on the inter-bank market, even if loans are typically overnight loans. Considering that the network structure is constant for long-term exposures seems an acceptable first-order approximation.

A.2. Sovereign Exposures

Figure A4 reports the evolution of exposures of European peripheral countries for major French banks and insurers, after 2011. For banks, there is a clear decrease of sovereign exposures between 2010 and 2011, followed by a stabilization period (see also Chart 31 in ACPR [43]). For insurers, there is an off-peak of exposures to Spain and Italy. Exposures to Greece, Ireland and Portugal decrease and stabilize. Moreover, exposures to sovereign debt are regularly disclosed by financial institutions. Consequently, the year 2011 is representative of current exposures to peripheral sovereign debt.

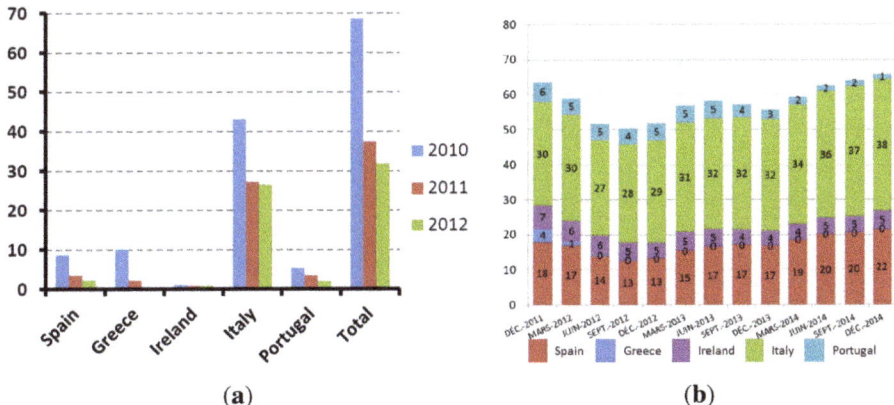

Figure A4. Exposures to European peripheral countries for major French banks and insurers (€bn). Sources: ACP [44] for (**a**) and ACPR [45] for (**b**). (**a**) Exposures of major French banks to European peripheral countries; (**b**) exposures of major French insurers to European peripheral countries.

Appendix B. Distance Metrics

B.1. Network Integration

We call $DNI(i_0, i_1)$ the distance between institution i_0 and institution i_1 with respect to network integration. Denoting $E(i, j)$ the exposure of institution i to institution j, $DNI(i_0, i_1)$ is defined as:

$$DNI(i_0, i_1) = max\left[\sum_{i \neq i_0, j \neq i_1} 1\!\!1_{E(i_0,i) - E(i_1,j) > 0}; \sum_{i \neq i_0, j \neq i_1} 1\!\!1_{E(i_1,i) - E(i_0,j) > 0}\right].$$

Intuitively, $DNI(i_0, i_1)$ is the number of exposure of one institution (either i_0 or i_1) that are larger than the exposures of the other institutions (either i_1 or i_0). If the two institutions have the same exposures, then DNI is $n(n+1)/2$, where n is the number of institutions. When one institution has all of its exposures larger than the other one, then DNI is n^2. Therefore, DNI varies between $n(n+1)/2$ and n^2.

B.2. Network Substitutability

Similarly, we call $DNS(i_0, i_1)$ the distance between institution i_0 and institution i_1 with respect to network substitutability. $DNS(i_0, i_1)$ is defined as:

$$DNS(i_0, i_1) = max\left[\sum_k k(1\!\!1_{Z_{(k)} > 0}; \sum_k k 1\!\!1_{Z_{(k)} < 0}\right],$$

where $Z_j = E(i_0, j) - I(i_1, j)$, ordered according to $|Z_{(1)}| \leq |Z_{(2)}| \leq ....$ Loosely speaking, DNS is the (weighted) sum of discrepancies of exposures of institutions i_0 and i_1 to the same counterparties.

B.3. Gross Exposures, Credit Risk Exposures and Funding Risk Exposures

Let us denote M the matrix where $M(i, j)$ is the amount (in €) of institution i on institution j, and denote K_i the equity of institution i. When we analyze gross exposures, the distance matrices DNI and DNS are computed with $E(i, j) = M(i, j)$. When we analyze credit risk exposures, the distance matrices DNI and DNS are computed with $E(i, j) = M(i, j)/E(i)$. When we analyze funding risk exposures, the distance matrices DNI and DNS are computed with $E(i, j) = M(j, i)/E(j)$.

Appendix C. Robustness Check on Stress Test Exercise

In the stress test exercise for sovereign risk, we considered a haircut of 50% in line with the outcome of the Greek sovereign debt crisis. For the robustness check, we run the same exercise varying the haircut between 10% and 100%. We observe some defaults of conglomerates or some defaults of their components only in scenarios where France or Italy are shocked. For Germany, Spain, the United Kingdom, Ireland, Portugal and the United States of America, losses never lead to default. Table A1 provides the number of defaults for different haircut levels on the Italian sovereign debt. Up to three insurance components may be in default. However, banking components and conglomerates are in no cases in default. Table A2 provides the number of defaults for different haircut levels on the French sovereign debt. The home bias is clearly present. Insurance components are more affected than banking components. For a shock up to 80%, all conglomerates are more resilient than their split-up version. For extreme shocks at haircuts of 90% and 100%, we observe two conglomerates in default, while only one banking component is in default.

Table A1. Number of defaults for a shock on Italian sovereign debt: robustness check. When the Italian sovereign debt loses 40% of its value, one insurance component is in default, zero banking components are in default and zero conglomerates are in default.

Haircut	Insurance Component	Banking Component	Conglomerate
10%	0	0	0
20%	0	0	0
30%	0	0	0
40%	1	0	0
50%	1	0	0
60%	1	0	0
70%	1	0	0
80%	1	0	0
90%	3	0	0
100%	3	0	0

Table A2. Number of defaults for a shock on French sovereign debt: robustness check. When the French sovereign debt loses 40% of its value, four insurance components are in default, one banking component is in default and one conglomerate is in default.

Haircut	Insurance Component	Banking Component	Conglomerate
10%	1	0	0
20%	2	0	0
30%	3	1	1
40%	4	1	1
50%	6	1	1
60%	6	1	1
70%	6	1	1
80%	6	1	1
90%	6	1	2
100%	6	1	2

Author Contributions: G. Hauton and J.C. Héam designed and realized the data collection ensuring that the different data bases are merged consistently. J.C. Héam designed IT tools. G. Hauton and J.C. Héam analyzed the results. J.C Héam wrote the paper.

Author Contributions: The authors declare no conflict of interest.

References

1. FSB. *Guidance to Assess the Systemic Importance of Financial Institutions, Markets and Instruments: Initial Consideration*. Basel, Switzerland: Financial Stability Board, 2009.
2. EIOPA. "Part I." *Financial stability report* 14-105 (2014): 6–43.
3. EBA. *EU-wide 2014 stress-test report*. London, UK: European Banking Authority, 2014.
4. BCBS. *Global Systemically Important Banks: Updated Assessment Methodology and the Higher Loss Absorbency Requirement*. Basel, Switzerland: Basel Committee on Banking Supervision, 2013.
5. IAIS. *Global Systemically Important Insurers: Initial Assessment Methodology*. London, UK: International Association of Insurance Supervisors, 2013.
6. OJEU. *Directive on the Supplementary Supervision of Credit Institutions, Insurance Undertakings and Investment Firms in a Financial Conglomerate*. Aberdeen, UK: Official Journal of the European Union, 2002.
7. G. Hauton, and J.C. Héam. "How to measure interconnectedness between banks, insurers and financial conglomerates?" In *Débats Économiques et Financiers*. Paris, France: Autorité de Contrôle Prudentiel et de Résolution, 2014.
8. P.G. Berger, and E. Ofek. "Diversification's effect on firm value." *Journal of financial economics* 37 (1995): 39–65. [CrossRef]
9. I. van Lelyveld, and A. Schilder. "Risk in financial conglomerates: Management and supervision." *Brookings-Wharton Pap. Finan.* 2003 (2003): 195–224. [CrossRef]
10. A. Subramanian, and J. Wang. "Catastrophe risk transfer." Check on ISSN: http://ssrn.com/abstract=2321415.
11. B.R. Holmstrom, and J. Tirole. "Private and public supply of liquidity." *J. Political Econom.* 106 (1998): 1–40. [CrossRef]
12. J.C. Rochet. "Macroeconomic shocks and banking supervision." *J. Financ. Stabil.* 1 (2004): 93–110. [CrossRef]
13. J. Tirole. *The theory of corporate finance*. Princeton, NJ, USA: Princeton University Press, 2010.
14. F. Allen, and D. Gale. "Financial contagion." *J. Political Econom.* 108 (2000): 1–33. [CrossRef]
15. R. Cifuentes, G. Ferrucci, and H.S. Shin. "Liquidity risk and contagion." *J. Euro. Econ. Assoc.* 3 (2005): 556–566. [CrossRef]
16. V. Fourel, J.C. Héam, D. Salakhova, and S. Tavolaro. *Domino Effects when Banks Hoard Liquidity: The French network*. Paris, France: Banque de France, 2013, Volume 432.
17. I. Alves, S. Ferrari, P. Franchini, J.C. Héam, P. Jurca, S. Langfield, S. Laviola, F. Liedorp, A. Sanchez, S. Tavolaro, and G. Vuillemey. *The Structure and Resilience of the European Interbank Market*. Frankfurt, Germany: European Systemic Risk Board, 2013, Volume 3.
18. M.M. Schmid, and I. Walter. "Do financial conglomerates create or destroy economic value?" *J. Financ. Intermed.* 18 (2009): 193–216. [CrossRef]
19. E. Brewer, and W.E. Jackson. *Inter-Industry Contagion and the Competitive Effects of Financial Distress Announcements: Evidence from Commercial Banks and Life Insurance Companies*. Chicago, IL, USA: Federal Reserve Board of Chicago, 2002, volume 2–3.
20. D. Filson, and S. Olfati. "The impacts of Gramm–Leach–Bliley bank diversification on value and risk." *J. Bank. Financ.* 41 (2014): 209–221. [CrossRef]
21. K. Minderhoud. *Extreme Stock Return Co-movements of Financial Institutions: Contagion or Interdependence?* Amsterdam, The Netherlands: De Nederlandsche Bank, 2003, volume 2003-16.
22. M. Stringa, and A. Monks. *Inter-industry contagion between UK life insurers and UK banks: an event study*. London, UK: Bank of England, 2007, volume 325.
23. I. van Lelyveld, and K. Knot. "Do financial conglomerates create or destroy value? Evidence for the EU." *J. Bank. Financ.* 33 (2009): 2312–2321. [CrossRef]
24. C.H. Furfine. "Interbank exposures: Quantifying the risk of contagion." *J. Money Credit Bank.* 35 (2003): 111–128. [CrossRef]
25. S. Wells. *Financial Interlinkages in the United Kingdom's Interbank Market and the Risk of Contagion*. London, UK: Bank of England, 2002.
26. C. Upper, and A. Worms. "Estimating bilateral exposures in the German interbank market: Is there a danger of contagion?" *Euro. Econ. Rev.* 48 (2004): 827–849. [CrossRef]
27. Á. Lublóy. "Domino effect in the Hungarian interbank market." *Hungarian Econ. Rev.* 52 (2005): 377–401.

28. I. van Lelyveld, and F. Liedorp. "Interbank contagion in the Dutch banking sector: A sensitivity analysis." *Int. J. Cent. Bank.* 2 (2006): 99–133. [CrossRef]
29. H. Degryse, and G. Nguyen. "Interbank exposures: An empirical examination of contagion risk in the Belgian banking system." *Int. J. Cent. Bank.* 3 (2007): 123–171.
30. M. Toivanen. *Financial Interlinkages and Risk of Contagion in the Finnish Interbank Market.* Helsinki, Finland: Bank of Finland, 2009.
31. P.E. Mistrulli. "Assessing financial contagion in the interbank market: Maximum entropy versus observed interbank lending patterns." *Journal of Banking* 35 (2011): 1114–1127. [CrossRef]
32. C. Gauthier, A. Lehar, and M. Souissi. "Macroprudential capital requirements and systemic risk." *J. Financ. Intermed.* 21 (2012): 594–618. [CrossRef]
33. R. Cont, A. Mousa, and E. Bastos e Santos. "Network structure and systemic risk in banking systems." In *Handbook of Systemic Risk.* Edited by J. Fouque and J. Langsam. Cambridge, UK: Cambridge University Press, 2013, chapter 11.
34. B. Craig, and G. von Peter. "Interbank tiering and money center banks." *J. Financ. Intermed.* 23 (2014): 322–347. [CrossRef]
35. I. van Lelyveld, and D.i. Veld. *Finding the core: Network structure in interbank markets.* Amsterdam, The Netherlands: De Nederlandse Bank, 2012, volume 348.
36. S. Langfield, Z. Liu, and T. Ota. "Mapping the UK interbank system." *J. Bank. Financ.* 45 (2014): 288–303. [CrossRef]
37. D. Fricke, and T. Lux. "Core–periphery structure in the overnight money market: Evidence from the e-mid trading platform." *Comput. Econ.* 45 (2015): 359–395. [CrossRef]
38. J.H. Ward. "Hierarchical grouping to optimize an objective function." *J. Am. Stat. Assoc.* 58 (1963): 236–244. [CrossRef]
39. J.A. Hartigan. *Clustering Algorithms.* Hoboken, NJ, USA: Wiley, 1975.
40. C. Gouriéroux, J.C. Héam, and A. Monfort. "Bilateral exposures and systemic solvency risk." *Can. J. Econ.* 45 (2012): 1273–1309. [CrossRef]
41. L. Eisenberg, and T.H. Noe. "Systemic risk in financial systems." *Management Sci.* 47 (2001): 236–249. [CrossRef]
42. S. Erlanger, and S. Castle. "Merkel called bankers' bluff, getting Europe a financial plan." *New-York Times* 10/27/2011 (2011): A1.
43. ACPR. *French banks' performance in 2013; Analyse et Synthèse.* Paris, France: Autorité de Contrôle Prudentiel et de Résolution, 2014, volume 29.
44. ACP. *French Banks' Performance in 2012,Analyse et Synthèse.* Paris, France: Autorité de Contrôle Prudentiel, 2013, volume 23.
45. ACPR. *Monitoring Inflows and Investements of 12 Major Life-Insurers as of December 2014; Analyse et Synthèse.* Paris, France: Autorité de Contrôle Prudentiel et de Résolution, 2015, volume 43.
46. ACP. *Monitoring Inflows and Investements of 12 Major Life-Insurers as of December 2012; Analyse et Synthèse.* Paris, France: Autorité de Contrôle Prudentiel, 2013, volume 12.
47. ACPR. *Monitoring Inflows and Investements of 12 Major Life-Insurers as of December 2013, Analyse et Synthèse.* Paris, France: Autorité de Contrôle Prudentiel et de Résolution, 2014, volume 25.
48. J.F. Cocco, F.J. Gomes, and N.C. Martins. "Lending relationships in the interbank market." *J. Financ. Intermed.* 18 (2009): 24–48. [CrossRef]

 © 2015 by the authors. Licensee MDPI, Basel, Switzerland. This article is an open access article distributed under the terms and conditions of the Creative Commons Attribution (CC BY) license (http://creativecommons.org/licenses/by/4.0/).

Article

The Impact of Reinsurance Strategies on Capital Requirements for Premium Risk in Insurance

Gian Paolo Clemente [1,†,*], Nino Savelli [1,†] and Diego Zappa [2,†]

1 Department of Mathematics, Finance and Econometrics, Università Cattolica del Sacro Cuore, 20123 Milano, Italy; nino.savelli@unicatt.it
2 Department of Statistical Sciences, Università Cattolica del Sacro Cuore, 20123 Milano, Italy; diego.zappa@unicatt.it
* Author to whom correspondence should be addressed; gianpaolo.clemente@unicatt.it; Tel.: +39-027-2343-726.
† These authors contributed equally to this work.

Academic Editor: Weidong Tian
Received: 31 March 2015; Accepted: 26 May 2015; Published: 3 June 2015

Abstract: New risk-based solvency requirements for insurance companies across European markets have been introduced by Solvency II and will come in force from 1 January 2016. These requirements, derived by a Standard Formula or an Internal Model, will be by far more risk-sensitive than the required solvency margin provided by the current legislation. In this regard, a Partial Internal Model for Premium Risk is developed here for a multi-line Non-Life insurer. We follow a classical approach based on a Collective Risk Model properly extended in order to consider not only the volatility of aggregate claim amounts but also expense volatility. To measure the effect of risk mitigation, suitable reinsurance strategies are pursued. We analyze how naïve coverage as conventional Quota Share and Excess of Loss reinsurance may modify the exact moments of the distribution of technical results. Furthermore, we investigate how alternative choices of commission rates in proportional treaties may affect the variability of distribution. Numerical results are also figured out in the last part of the paper with evidence of different effects for small and large companies. The main reasons for these differences are pointed out.

Keywords: capital requirement for premium risk; collective risk model; reinsurance strategies; Solvency II

1. Introduction

On 10 October 2014, the European Commission adopted a Delegated Act (see [1]) regarding implementing rules for Solvency II. This document was published in the Official Journal of European Union on 17 January 2015, as Commission Delegated Regulation n. 2015/35, after approval of the European Parliament and Council. The new system will lay down new quantitative requirements and a proper methodology to evaluate them. These new criteria will come in force from next 1 January 2016.

Usually for a Non-Life insurer, the Underwriting Risk module (and, in particular, Premium and Reserve sub-module) has the greatest impact on Solvency II Capital Requirement (SCR—Solvency Capital Requirement). In the valuation of these requirements, the risk mitigation effect of proportional and non-proportional reinsurance will be recognized. In this framework, the aim of this paper is to describe the risk profile of a general multi-line insurer in order to show the effect of reinsurance, one of the most crucial aspects of risk management strategies.

In order to describe the risk profile of a general multi-line insurer, we start by adopting the structure of a classical risk theoretical model where, by known relations in actuarial literature[1], only premium risk is dealt with. We extend the relation to consider also the volatility of expenses to evaluate the impact on both exact moments of technical results and capital requirements.

Furthermore, to analyze the effect on both profit and losses and capital requirement of alternative reinsurance strategies[2], two classical proportional and non-proportional treaties have been introduced by extending classical relations. We derive moments of combined ratios by considering both the cases of Quota-Share (QS) and Excess of Loss (XL) treaties (see [2–4]). According to Quota-Share, we analytically describe how alternative methodologies[3] to identify ceding commissions have an effect on the moments of the probability distribution of combined ratios and on the capital requirements for Premium Risk.

Indeed, in the management practice, the insurer must usually choose among different efficient reinsurance strategies, taking into account either profitability sacrifice or capital saving.

A case study based on two different multi-line Non-Life insurers allows the comparison of the effect of wide strategies on both profitability and allocated capital. Parameters of the model have been calibrated in order to assure a realistic and consistent comparison between insurers and alternative reinsurance strategies.

In particular, Section 2 briefly describes the structure of the Standard Formula defined by Delegated Acts [1] focusing only on a sub-module of Premium and Reserve risk. In Section 3, we provide the general framework needed to develop the internal model. Section 4 analytically shows the effect of two alternative reinsurance strategies as Quota-Share and Excess of Loss. Finally, in Section 5, numerical results are reported by focusing on the capital requirements derived by applying both the Internal Model and the market-wide approach of the Standard Formula. Main results have been extended in Section 6 to evaluate the effect of reinsurance. The conclusion follows.

2. A Brief Description of the Delegated Acts (DA) Standard Formula

We give a brief description of the main elements of Standard Formula for Premium and Reserve Risk defined by Delegated Acts (see [1]). Since Quantitative Impact Studies 3 (QIS3), a unique sub-module for the joined valuation of risks related both to future claims arising during and after the period until the one-year time horizon for the solvency assessment (Premium Risk) and the risk related to a non-sufficient amount of the technical provisions (Reserve Risk) has been introduced. The derived capital charge must be then aggregated to lapse and cat risk to quantify the capital requirement for Non-Life Underwriting Risk.

Focusing on Premium and Reserve risk, we have that the capital requirement SCR_{NL}^{SF} is equal to the following formula:

$$SCR_{NL}^{SF} = 3 \cdot \sigma_{NL} \cdot V_{NL} \qquad (1)$$

where V_{NL} is the volume measure net of reinsurance and σ_{NL} is the standard deviation for non-life premium and reserve. σ_{NL} can be described as the standard deviation of the ratio between the aggregate claims amount of premium and reserve risk and the volume measure, and it is then strictly related to the variability coefficient (CV) of aggregate claim amount.

In particular, Equation (1) assumes to measure the distance between the 99.5% quantile and the mean of the probability distribution of aggregate claims amount by using a fixed multiplier of the standard deviation equal to 3. This choice has replaced the $\rho(\sigma_{NL})$ function used since QIS5 [16], which was based on the assumption of a LogNormal distribution of total losses. From a practical point of view, skewness of distribution is not directly taken into account anymore. The drawback is

---

[1] For a frequency-severity approach see, for instance, [5–10].
[2] Analysis of effect of reinsurance on risk reserve are also in [11–14].
[3] See [15] for a detailed description of several alternatives to evaluate commissions that reinsurer pays to ceding company.

a potential underestimation of capital requirement for small insurers and an overestimation for big insurers. We have indeed found that the LogNormal assumption (and then $\rho(\sigma_{NL})$) returns a multiplier equal to 3 only when σ_{NL} is roughly 14.47%. For smaller volatilities coefficients (as it usually happens for big insurers), Equation (1) leads to a capital requirement that is larger than QIS5.

The net volume measure V_{NL} is equal to the sum of all the lines of business (LoBs) of net best estimate of claims reserve at the valuation date plus net premium volume. This volume is equal to the maximum between last year and next year earned premiums plus the expected present value of future premiums after one-year for existing contracts and contracts of the following year. Finally, in the valuation of V_{NL}, it is allowed to take into account a geographical diversification of business held in different macro-geographical regions of world, through the Herfindahl Index.

With regard to σ_{NL}, the overall volatility is derived by a double steps aggregation process based on an initial aggregation of standard deviation of premium and reserve risk of single LoB assuming a linear correlation coefficient equal to 0.5. Then, the standard deviation will be aggregated between different lines of business by using a given correlation matrix (see Annex IV of Delegated Acts [1] for details).

In order to quantify the standard deviation of premium or reserve risk of a single LoB, two different approaches are provided. The first one is based on fixed volatility factors and it is defined as a "market-wide approach", while the second one is based on methodologies (see Annex XVII of [1]) that take into account the specific technical data of the company ("undertaking-specific approach"). Adoption of the latter approach must be approved by the supervising authority. The differences between market-wide and the undertaking-specific approach may be noticeable in the single-LoB volatility valuation. The market approach is based on a market-wide estimate of the standard deviation for premium risk, determined by a specific volatility factor given as input (see Annex II and XIV of [1]). For instance, similarly to the main non-life LoB analyzed in the next, these factors for Premium risk are reported in Table 1.

Table 1. Volatility factor, $\sigma_{prem,lob}$ (DA—Premium Risk).

LoBs	Accident[4]	Motor Damages	Property	Motor Third-Party Liab.	General Third-Party Liab.
Volatility Factor	8.5%	8%	8%	10%	14%

Only for Premium Risk, values of $\sigma_{prem,lob}$ can be multiplied by a non-proportional factor NP_{lob} in order to take into account existing Excess of Loss treaties. This factor is set out at 80% for Property, Motor Third Party Liabilities (MTPL) and General Third Party Liabilities (GTPL) and at 100% for other LoBs.

It is, however, allowed to use an undertaking specific approach (see Annex XVII of [1]) to also derive an alternative estimate of NP_{lob} based on the valuation of the reducing effect of XL treaty on the variability coefficient of the aggregate claim amount. In this case, the final value of NP_{lob} will be a weighted average of fixed NP_{lob} and the corresponding estimate. The weight of the factor estimated by data is given by a fixed credibility factor increasing the larger the available time-series. For all LoBs, the weights are greater than zero if data of at least last five years are available and tend to one. MTPL, GTPL and Credit and Suretyship should have data over 15 years and other LoBs at least over 10 years.

3. General Framework

We present an Internal Model for Premium Risk for a multi-line Non-Life insurer to take into account the characteristics of each line of business (LoB) and the diversification effect due to the aggregation of them. To introduce the framework, let $\widetilde{Y}_{t+1}$ be the random variable (r.v.[5]) of a one-year technical result for the period $(t, t+1)$, evaluated at the end of time t, as the difference between earned premium of the total portfolio with $h = 1, \ldots, L$ LoBs and total amount of claims and expenses of the year. For the sake of simplicity, we will start by considering a gross of reinsurance technical result. Generalizations to also include the reinsurance effect are in the next Section[6].

By considering the main sources of risks, we may decompose $\widetilde{Y}_{t+1}$ as follows:

$$\widetilde{Y}_{t+1} = \sum_{h=1}^{L} \left(B_{t+1,h}^{writt} + V_{t,h}^{P} - \widetilde{V}_{t+1,h}^{P} - \widetilde{E}_{t+1,h} - \widetilde{X}_{t+1,h}^{paid,CY} - \widetilde{V}_{t+1,h}^{S,CY} \right) \quad (2)$$

Earned premiums of a single LoB are here described as the difference between written premium of the year $B_{t+1,h}^{writt}$ and the one-year change in premium reserve ($\widetilde{V}_{t+1,h}^{P} - V_{t,h}^{P}$) for unearned premiums and unexpired risks evaluated under Solvency II criteria. In the same way we take into account the claim cost of the year, by considering both payments ($\widetilde{X}$) for claims and the provisions for outstanding claims ($\widetilde{V}_{t+1}^{S}$). Regarding premium risk, we consider only payment for losses of claims incurred during the year $t+1$ ($\widetilde{X}_{t+1,h}^{paid,CY}$) and the reserve at the end of year $t+1$ for new claims ($\widetilde{V}_{t+1,h}^{S,CY}$). Both payments and reserves for claims incurred in previous years are necessarily covered by initial claims reserve and their volatility attains to reserve risk. Finally we assume random the expenses $\widetilde{E}_{t+1,h}$ too.

Formula (2) may be rewritten as follows:

$$\widetilde{Y}_{t+1} = \sum_{h=1}^{L} \left(P_{t+1,h} + \lambda_h P_{t+1,h} + c_h B_{t+1,h} + V_{t,h}^{P} - \widetilde{V}_{t+1,h}^{P} - \widetilde{E}_{t+1,h} - \widetilde{X}_{t+1,h}^{paid,CY} - \widetilde{V}_{t+1,h}^{S,CY} \right) \quad (3)$$

In Equation (3), gross premiums of the h-th LoB are represented by risk premiums split into three components: the expected amount for claims of current year $P_h = E\left(\widetilde{X}_h^{paid,CY} + \widetilde{V}_h^{S,CY} \right)$, the safety loadings ($\lambda_h \cdot P_h$) and the expense loading equal to the expected amount of expenses, i.e., $c_h B_{t+1,h} = E\left(\widetilde{E}_{t+1,h} \right)$.

For sake of simplicity, we can assume that earned premiums and written premiums are equal[7] and recalling a classical notation in Risk Theory, we can identify the aggregate claim amount by a generic random variable $\widetilde{X} = \widetilde{X}^{paid,CY} + \widetilde{V}^{S,CY}$ independent by paid or reserved claims:

$$\widetilde{Y}_{t+1} = \sum_{h=1}^{L} \left(P_{t+1,h} + \lambda_h P_{t+1,h} + c_h B_{t+1,h} - \widetilde{E}_{t+1,h} - \widetilde{X}_{t+1,h} \right) \quad (4)$$

where $\widetilde{X}_{t+1,h}$ describes the aggregate claim amount of next year related to new business.

To evaluate characteristics of $\widetilde{Y}_{t+1}$, we can make some assumptions about aggregate claim amounts and expenses. Following the collective approach (e.g., see [5,8,17]), for each LoB, the aggregate claims amount is given by a mixed compound process:

$$\widetilde{X}_{t+1,h} = \sum_{j=1}^{\widetilde{K}_{t+1,h}} \widetilde{Z}_{j,t+1,h}$$

where the number of claims distribution, $\widetilde{K}_{t+1,h}$, follows the Poisson law, with parameter, n, increasing year by year according to the real growth rate g (i.e., $n_{t+1,h} = n_{t,h}(1 + g_h)$). We are assuming that the

---

[5] From now on, tilde over a letter will indicate a random variable.
[6] In the next Section we add a second term that takes into account reinsurance treaties. It considers premium received and claims paid by the reinsurer and other amounts function of the reinsurance form (as commission for Quota Share treaties).
[7] See [18] for an analysis of this relation in order to consider the effect of premium reserve.

expected number of claims grows along with the number of contracts. Frequency is then constant in period $(t, t+1)$. In the present paper, trends as well as long-term cycles are not considered and only short-term fluctuations that may affect the volatility of the number of claims are taken into account. For this purpose, a structural variable $\widetilde{q}_h$ will be introduced to represent short-term fluctuations in the number of claims. Then we have that n turns out to be a stochastic parameter $(n_{t+1,h} \cdot \widetilde{q}_h)$ where $\widetilde{q}_h$ has its own probability distribution depending on the short-term fluctuations it is going to represent. In Section 5, we will assume that $\widetilde{q}_h$ is Gamma distributed with mean equal to one. Standard results from mathematical statistics imply that the mixture Poisson-Gamma leads to a Negative Binomial r.v. for the number of claims.

The claim size amounts $\widetilde{Z}_{j,t+1,h}$ are assumed i.i.d. and scaled by the claim inflation rate i_h. In other words, we have that simple moments of order r of severity distribution are equal to $E(\widetilde{Z}_{t+1,h}^r) = (1 + i_h)^r \cdot E(\widetilde{Z}_{t,h}^r)$. Different distributional assumptions (for details see [19]) may be considered for claim size but for sake of simplicity and without loss of generalization, only the results under LogNormal assumption will be reported below.

In order to take into account expense volatility, we will assume that acquisition and management expenses are described by two random variables with mean and standard deviation equal to $(c_h^A B_{t+1,h}, \sigma_h^A B_{t+1,h})$ and $(c_h^M B_{t+1,h}, \sigma_h^M B_{t+1,h})$ respectively, with $c_h^A + c_h^M = c_h$. The coefficients c_h^A and c_h^M represent the percentages of gross premiums used to cover respectively acquisition and management expenses. σ_h^A and σ_h^M describe the standard deviation of expense ratios considering only acquisition or management expenses.

To simulate expenses, a LogNormal distribution has been used in the next case study. It will be assumed that expenses are not correlated to the claim amount. However, the distributional and dependence assumptions do not have a great impact on the capital charge (except for specific lines as Credit and Suretyship or Financial Losses for some specialist insurers).

Under these assumptions, main cumulants of $\widetilde{X}_{t+1,h}$ and $\widetilde{E}_{t+1,h}$ may be derived to obtain exact formulae for cumulants of technical results of a single line of business.

The cumulant generating function (f.g.c.), $\Psi_{\widetilde{Y}_{t+1,h}}(s)$, of technical result of the h-th single LoB is:

$$\Psi_{\widetilde{Y}_{t+1,h}}(s) = s \cdot B_{t+1,h} - \Psi_{\widetilde{E}_{t+1,h}}(s) - \Psi_{\widetilde{X}_{t+1,h}}(s) =$$

where $M_{\widetilde{Z}_{t+1,h}}(s)$ is the moment generating function of claim-size.

Then, the mean, variance and skewness of $\widetilde{Y}_{h,t+1}$ are:

$$E(\widetilde{Y}_{h,t+1}) = \lambda_h P_{t+1,h}$$

$$\sigma^2(\widetilde{Y}_{t+1,h}) = \left((\sigma_h^A)^2 + (\sigma_h^M)^2\right) B_{t+1,h}^2 + n_{t+1,h} a_{2,\widetilde{Z}_{t+1,h}} + n_{t+1,h}^2 a_{1,\widetilde{Z}_{t+1,h}}^2 \sigma_{\widetilde{q}_h}^2$$

$$\gamma(\widetilde{Y}_{t+1,h}) =$$

$$= \frac{\mu_3(\widetilde{E}_{t+1,h}^A) + \mu_3(\widetilde{E}_{t+1,h}^M) + n_{t+1,h} a_{3,\widetilde{z}_{t+1,h}} + 3 n_{t+1,h}^2 a_{1,\widetilde{Z}_{t+1,h}} a_{2,\widetilde{Z}_{t+1,h}} \sigma_{\widetilde{q}_h}^2 + n_{t+1,h}^3 a_{1,\widetilde{Z}_{t+1,h}}^3 \mu_3(\widetilde{q}_h)}{\left(\left((\sigma_h^A)^2 + (\sigma_h^M)^2\right) B_{t+1,h}^2 + n_{t+1,h} a_{2,\widetilde{Z}_{t+1,h}} + n_{t+1,h} a_{1,\widetilde{Z}_{t+1,h}}^2 \sigma_{\widetilde{q}_h}^2\right)^{3/2}}$$

where $a_{r,\widetilde{Z}_{t+1,h}}$ are non-central moments of $\widetilde{Z}_{t+1,h}$ of order r and $\mu_3(\cdot)$ describes the central moment of order 3.

Aggregated technical results will depend instead on the dependence assumed between several lines of business. According to the VaR risk measure (see [20]) at confidence level α = 99.5% as defined by Solvency II ([1]), the capital requirement (SCR) for Premium could be derived as:

$$SCR_\alpha = -VaR_{1-\alpha}\left(\widetilde{Y}_{t+1}\right) = VaR_\alpha\left(\sum_{h=1}^{L} \widetilde{E}_{t+1,h} + \widetilde{X}_{t+1,h}\right) - \sum_{h=1}^{L} B_{t+1,h}$$

It is noteworthy that we recognize expected profits/losses in the capital requirement evaluation by considering safety loadings. From our point of view, safety loading should be regarded, but it is not clear if it will be allowed in Internal Model by the supervisor, because QIS5 [16] and Delegated Acts [1] Standard Formula do not mention it in the evaluation (see Section 2). This solution in the Standard Formula is coming from the QIS5 multiplier of standard deviation found as the distance between the desired quantile (at 99.5% level) and the expected losses. It is worth pointing out that this approach would be not conservative if underpricing was in force, and a negative technical result would be expected implying a consequent higher risk profile.

4. Reinsurance Effect

In order to consider the effect of reinsurance treaties, Formula (4) may be enriched as follows:

$$\widetilde{Y}_{t+1}^{net} = \sum_{h=1}^{L}\left[\left(P_{t+1,h} + \lambda_h P_{t+1,h} + c_h B_{t+1,h} - \widetilde{E}_{t+1,h} - \widetilde{X}_{t+1,h}\right) - \left(B_{t+1,h}^{RE} - \widetilde{X}_{t+1,h}^{RE} - \widetilde{C}_{t+1,h}^{RE}\right)\right]$$

where $B_{t+1,h}^{RE}$ describes premiums paid to the reinsurer, while $\widetilde{X}_{t+1,h}^{RE}$ is the amount of claims paid or reserved born by the reinsurer. Finally, we consider stochastic ceding commissions $\widetilde{C}_{t+1,h}^{RE}$ that the reinsurer usually pays in proportional treaties to the ceding company for the afforded commercial expenses.

We will consider in the next Section either the case of fixed commissions equal to a deterministic percentage of premiums or the case of "sliding scale" commissions. A sliding scale commission is a percent of premium paid by the reinsurer to the ceding company, which "slides" with the actual loss experience, usually subjected to minimum and maximum amounts.

We start by considering the effect of two global Quota Share treaties, with either fixed commissions or sliding commissions.

As is well known, in the case of a Quota Share reinsurance treaty, with an insurer's retention quota $\beta_h \in (0,1)$, the aggregate claim amount charged to reinsurer is equal to $\widetilde{X}_{t+1,h}^{RE} = (1-\beta_h)\widetilde{X}_{t+1,h}$. On the other hand, the gross premiums ceded to the reinsurer are:

$$B_{t+1,h}^{RE} = (1-\beta_h)B_{t+1,h}$$

In proportional treaties, the reinsurer pays the cedant a commission on the premiums it receives to compensate for the cost of acquiring the business and maintaining the portfolio. To describe commissions, we have assumed $\widetilde{C}_{t+1,h}^{RE} = \widetilde{c}_h^{RE} B_{t+1,h}^{RE}$. In this regard, we consider two alternative ways. On one hand we assume a fixed percentage of ceded premiums as commission: $C_{t+1,h}^{RE} = c_h^{RE} B_{t+1,h}^{RE}$ (i.e., $\widetilde{c}_h^{RE} = c_h^{RE}$). On the other hand, we consider a sliding commission that rewards or penalizes the insurer according to the quality of portfolio protected by the treaty. The system consists of a variable commission whose value depends by the observed loss ratio (see [15]).

We assume to describe the random commission rate according to the next formula:

$$\widetilde{c}_h^{RE} = c_h^{RE}\left[1 + \left(1 - \frac{\widetilde{LR}_{h,t+1}}{E\left(\widetilde{LR}_{h,t+1}\right)}\right)\right] \tag{5}$$

where $\widetilde{LR}_{h,t+1}$ is the loss ratio at time $t+1$. Sliding commissions are here assumed not subjected to minimum and maximum amounts. In Section 6, we will also test numerically the effect of a different structure where a minimum and maximum commission is provided when observed loss ratio falls out of a certain range. For each line of business, we can easily derive the characteristics of technical result net of reinsurance $\widetilde{Y}_{t+1,h}^{net}$ and of aggregate claim amount retained by ceding company.

We report exact cumulants of combined ratio net of reinsurance $\widetilde{CR}_{t+1,h}^{net}$ for both cases of fixed ($\widetilde{CR}_{t+1,h}^{net,QSF}$) and scaling commissions ($\widetilde{CR}_{t+1,h}^{net,QSS}$).

First of all, the expected combined ratio net of Quota Share treaty, $\widetilde{CR}_{t+1,h}^{net,QS}$, for both fixed and scaling commissions is:

$$E\left(\widetilde{CR}_{t+1,h}^{net,QS}\right) = E\left(\frac{\widetilde{E}_{t+1,h} + \widetilde{X}_{t+1,h} - \widetilde{C}_{t+1,h}^{RE} - \widetilde{X}_{t+1,h}^{RE}}{B_{t+1,h} - B_{t+1,h}^{RE}}\right) = \frac{1+c_h}{1-\lambda_h} + \frac{c_h - c_h^{RE}(1-\beta_h)}{\beta_h}$$

Note that the net combined ratio is equal to $E\left(\widetilde{CR}_{t+1,h}^{gross,QS}\right)$ when commission rate c_h^{RE} is equal to the expenses loading coefficient c_h.

Furthermore the standard deviation is:

$$\sigma(\widetilde{CR}_{t+1,h}^{net,QS})$$
$$= \sqrt{\frac{\sigma^2(\widetilde{E}_{t+1,h}) + \sigma^2(\widetilde{X}_{t+1,h} - \widetilde{X}_{t+1,h}^{RE}) + \sigma^2(\widetilde{C}_{t+1,h}^{RE}) + 2Cov(\widetilde{X}_{t+1,h} - \widetilde{X}_{t+1,h}^{RE}, -\widetilde{C}_{t+1,h}^{RE})}{\beta_h^2 B_{t+1,h}^2}}$$
$$= \sqrt{\frac{1}{\beta_h^2}\sigma^2(\widetilde{ER}_{t+1,h}^{gross}) + \sigma^2(\widetilde{LR}_{t+1,h}^{gross}) + \frac{\sigma^2(\widetilde{C}_{t+1,h}^{RE}) - 2\beta_h Cov(\widetilde{X}_{t+1,h}^{RE}, \widetilde{C}_{t+1,h}^{RE})}{\beta_h^2 B_{t+1,h}^2}}$$

where, in the case of fixed commissions, we have:

$$\sigma\left(\widetilde{CR}_{t+1,h}^{net,QSF}\right) = \sqrt{\frac{1}{\beta_h^2}\sigma^2\left(\widetilde{ER}_{t+1,h}^{gross}\right) + \sigma^2\left(\widetilde{LR}_{t+1,h}^{gross}\right)}$$

with variability greater than the corresponding value for the gross of reinsurance case because of a higher volatility of net expense ratio.

For sliding commissions, we have instead:

$$\sigma(\widetilde{CR}_{t+1,h}^{net,QS}) =$$
$$= \sqrt{\frac{1}{\beta_h^2}\sigma^2(\widetilde{ER}_{t+1,h}^{gross}) + \sigma^2(\widetilde{LR}_{t+1,h}^{gross}) + \frac{(c_h^{RE}B_{t+1,h}^{RE}CV(\widetilde{X}_{t+1,h}^{RE}))^2 - 2\beta_h Cov(\widetilde{X}_{t+1,h}^{RE}, -\frac{c_h^{RE} B_{t+1,h}^{RE}}{E(\widetilde{X}_{t+1,h}^{RE})}\widetilde{X}_{t+1,h}^{RE})}{\beta_h^2 B_{t+1,h}^2}}$$
$$= \sqrt{\frac{1}{\beta_h^2}\sigma^2(\widetilde{ER}_{t+1,h}^{gross}) + \sigma^2(\widetilde{LR}_{t+1,h}^{gross}) + \left(\frac{(1-\beta_h)}{\beta_h}c_h^{RE}CV(\widetilde{X}_{t+1,h})\right)^2 + 2\frac{c_h^{RE}B_{t+1,h}^{RE}}{\beta_h E(\widetilde{X}_{t+1,h})}\sigma^2(\widetilde{LR}_{t+1,h}^{gross})}$$

where we observe the effects of both variability of commissions and negative dependency between commissions and aggregate claims amount. We have indeed that the correlation coefficient is equal to:

$$\rho\left(\widetilde{X}_{t+1,h}^{RE}, \widetilde{C}_{t+1,h}^{RE}\right) = -\frac{\frac{(1-\beta_h)c_h^{RE}B_{t+1,h}^{RE}\sigma^2(\widetilde{X}_{t+1,h})}{E(\widetilde{X}_{t+1,h})}}{\sigma\left(\widetilde{X}_{t+1,h}^{RE}\right)\sigma\left(\widetilde{C}_{t+1,h}^{RE}\right)} = -1$$

and also $\rho\left(\widetilde{X}_{t+1,h}, \widetilde{C}_{t+1,h}^{RE}\right) = -1$, i.e., they are negatively linear dependent, where we remind that β_h denotes the insurer's retention quota for line h.

Furthermore, we will consider Excess of Loss treaty, with a retention for claim unit and no limit to reinsurer exposure. In the case of an Excess of Loss treaty, the stochastic claim amount charged to the reinsurer for year t is:

$$\widetilde{X}_{t+1,h}^{RE} = \sum_{j=1}^{\widetilde{K}_{t+1,h}} \widetilde{Z}_{j,t+1,h}^{RE} = \sum_{j=1}^{\widetilde{K}_{t+1,h}} Max(0, \widetilde{Z}_{j,t+1,h}^{RE} - M_{t+1,h})$$

having denoted by $M_{t+1,h}$ the insurer's retention limit for year $t+1$. The reinsurer risk premium $P_{t+1,h}^{RE}$ is given by the well-known relationship:

$$P_{t+1,h}^{RE} = E\left(\widetilde{X}_{t+1,h}^{RE}\right) = n_{t+1,h} E\left(\widetilde{Z}_{t+1,h}^{RE}\right)$$

No explicit commission and loss participations are usually provided in the case of the Excess of Loss coverage, so that we get: $B_{t+1,h}^{RE} = P_{t+1,h}^{RE}\left(1 + \lambda_h^{RE}\right)$ and $\widetilde{C}_{t+1,h}^{RE} = 0$, with λ_h^{RE} being the safety loading coefficient applied by reinsurer, usually greater than the safety loading coefficient λ_h, as increasing as the insurer's retention limit is growing up.

In general, the f.g.c. net of XL is equal to:

$$\Psi_{\widetilde{Y}_{t+1,h}^{net}}(s) = s \cdot \left(B_{t+1,h} - B_{t+1,h}^{RE}\right) - \Psi_{\widetilde{E}_{t+1,h}}(s) - \Psi_{\widetilde{X}_{t+1,h}^{net}}(s) =$$

from which we can derive cumulants of technical result net of XL in a similar way as the Quota Share case.

5. Numerical Analysis

To show the effect of an Internal Model (IM) based on a Collective Risk Model for Premium risk, two non-life insurance companies with a different dimension are considered (their figures are summed up in Table 2). It is assumed that both insurers underwrite business in the same five lines of business (Accident, Motor Other Damages (MOD), Property, Motor Third-Party Liability and General Third-Party Liability) with the same mix of portfolio (the proportions used resemble the real proportions in the Italian insurance market). The comparison of results will allow us to describe the effect of a different portfolio size on the aggregate claims amount distribution and on the capital requirements.

Table 2. Gross premium volumes of both insurers (amounts in mln of Euro).

LoBs	OMEGA		EPSILON		Both Insurers
	B_t	B_{t+1}	B_t	B_{t+1}	$B_{t,h}/\Sigma_h\, B_{t,h}$
Accident	100.0	105.0	10.0	10.5	10.0%
MOD	100.0	105.0	10.0	10.5	10.0%
Property	150.0	157.5	15.0	15.8	15.0%
MTPL	550.0	577.5	55.0	57.8	55.0%
GTPL	100.0	105.0	10.0	10.5	10.0%
TOTAL	1000.0	1050.0	100.0	105.0	100.0%

The main parameters of Collective Risk Model are in Table 3. As we can see, both insurers have the same characteristics apart from the expected number of claims. OMEGA is assumed to be ten times larger than EPSILON. Safety loading coefficient (λ) and the standard deviation of structure variable (σ_q) are obtained mainly by Italian market Loss Ratios and Combined Ratios. About λ, it depends by the mean of the empirical combined ratios. It shows a negative value for LoBs where the observed combined ratios are on average greater than one e.g., in GTPL. Furthermore, it is noteworthy to recall that the safety loading is here expressed as a percentage of risk premium. Expense parameters (see c^M, c^A, σ^M, σ^A defined in Section 3) have been calibrated by using the historical pattern of both management and acquisition expenses in the same period. The small values of σ^M and σ^A that will lead to a low variability of expenses producing a low additional capital requirement for expense risk could be noticed. The CV of claim size (c_Z) is fixed, for each LoB, and calibrated on the Italian market data. Moreover, the expected number of claims (n_t) and the expected claim cost (m_t) reported in Table 3 for each LoB are referred to the initial year t; they will increase in the examined year $t+1$ as described in the previous Section for the dynamic portfolio, according to the annual rate of real growth of portfolio (g) as well as to the number of claims and the annual claim inflation rate (i) and to claim size, assumed to be almost 2% and 3% respectively for all LoBs in the simulations.

Table 3. Parameters for premium risk.

Insurers	LoBs	n_t	σ_q	g	m_t	c_Z	i	λ	c^M,	c^A,	σ^M	σ^A
OMEGA	Accid.	16,428	15.2%	1.9%	3200	3	3%	27.7%	4.6%	28.2%	0.3%	0.8%
	MOD	25,900	11.1%	1.9%	2500	2	3%	13.9%	4.7%	21.5%	0.4%	1.4%
	Prop.	18,849	6.9%	1.9%	6000	8	3%	−6.4%	4.7%	24.8%	0.6%	0.6%
	MTPL	116,509	8.6%	1.9%	4000	4	3%	−4.0%	4.7%	14.0%	0.7%	0.8%
	GTPL	8225	12.8%	1.9%	10,000	12	3%	−13.1%	4.5%	24.0%	0.8%	1.5%
EPSILON	Accid.	1643	15.2%	1.9%	3200	3	3%	27.7%	4.6%	28.2%	0.3%	0.8%
	MOD	2590	11.1%	1.9%	2500	2	3%	13.9%	4.7%	21.5%	0.4%	1.4%
	Prop.	1885	6.9%	1.9%	6000	8	3%	−6.4%	4.7%	24.8%	0.6%	0.6%
	MTPL	11,651	8.6%	1.9%	4000	4	3%	−4.0%	4.7%	14.0%	0.7%	0.8%
	GTPL	823	12.8%	1.9%	10,000	12	3%	−13.1%	4.5%	24.0%	0.8%	1.5%

Characteristics of simulated distribution of losses for Premium risk and for each LoB are reported in Table 4. One million simulations have been applied in order to assure stable convergence. Premium risk, CV, and skewness of the Aggregate amount of next-year claims plus expenses ($\widetilde{X}_{t+1} + \widetilde{E}_{t+1}$) are figured out.

The high variability of GTPL because of a large variability coefficient of claim-size is noteworthy. Furthermore, the effect of non-pooling risk is significant for MOD and Property. As expected, we have indeed that the bigger insurer shows for several LoB a CV of $\widetilde{X}_{t+1}$ slightly greater than the value of the standard deviation of σ_q because of the relevant diversification effect. The effect of size is indeed noticeable for EPSILON company where LoBs with high c_Z as Property and GTPL show the greater increase of variability with respect to OMEGA.

Finally, the aggregate distribution has been derived by assuming a Gaussian Copula function whose parameters have been calibrated by using the correlation matrix proposed by the standard Formula in Technical Specifications of QIS5 (see [16]) and Delegated Acts [1]. We limited the analysis to this simple choice of copula having at its disposal correlation coefficient provided by the Standard Formula, but the evaluation may be properly extended in order to consider both a more significant tail dependency between several LoBs and hierarchical structure based on Archimedean Copulas to aggregate LoBs (see at this regard [21]). Despite the positive correlation provided by Solvency II, we observe in Table 4 a, diversification effect between LoBs.

Table 4. CV and skewness of simulated distribution for each LoB (Gross of Reinsurance).

LoBs	OMEGA						EPSILON					
	$\widetilde{X}_{t+1}$		$\widetilde{E}_{t+1}$		$\widetilde{X}_{t+1} + \widetilde{E}_{t+1}$		$\widetilde{X}_{t+1}$		$\widetilde{E}_{t+1}$		$\widetilde{X}_{t+1} + \widetilde{E}_{t+1}$	
	CV	Skew.	CV	Skew.	CV	Skew.	CV	Skew.	CV	Skew.	CV	Skew.
Accident	5.34%	0.30	2.53%	0.08	9.49%	0.30	17.01%	0.37	2.53%	0.08	10.52%	0.37
MOD	11.15%	0.22	5.45%	0.18	8.09%	0.21	11.89%	0.23	5.44%	0.18	8.60%	0.22
Property	9.00%	0.95	2.88%	0.15	6.52%	0.92	19.66%	6.56	2.88%	0.15	14.16%	6.52
MTPL	8.68%	0.18	5.40%	0.19	7.18%	0.17	9.39%	0.21	5.39%	0.20	7.76%	0.21
GTPL	18.26%	2.84	5.87%	0.18	13.65%	2.79	42.14%	12.87	5.87%	0.18	31.34%	12.82
Total	**5.87%**	**0.24**	**2.62%**	**0.15**	**4.55%**	**0.23**	**7.86%**	**2.73**	**2.62%**	**0.15**	**6.07%**	**2.69**

Table 5 shows SCR ratio obtained by IM as the capital requirement for Premium risk divided by initial gross premium volume. According to OMEGA, as expected, the highest ratios are registered for the line GTPL (65.3%) due mainly to its large variability (CV = 13.7%). Property and MTPL show high ratios too (respectively 26.7% and 24.8%). The large safety loadings lead to lower ratios for MOD (11.9%) and Accident (9.1%). Focusing on EPSILON, the effect of pooling risk is clearly noticeable on Premium risk capital charges.

Table 5. SCR ratio $\left(\frac{SCR_{99.5\%}}{B_t}\right)$ (Gross of Reinsurance).

LoBs	OMEGA				EPSILON			
	SCR Ratio	SCR Ratio (λ = 0)	SCR Ratio (No Exp. Risk)	SCR Ratio (SF)	SCR Ratio	SCR Ratio (λ = 0)	SCR Ratio (No Exp. Risk)	SCR Ratio (SF)
Accident	9.08%	24.4%	8.99%	26.78%	12.19%	27.5%	12.11%	26.78%
MOD	11.93%	21.4%	11.59%	25.20%	13.41%	22.9%	13.07%	25.20%
Property	26.65%	21.6%	26.53%	25.20%	66.58%	61.5%	66.50%	25.20%
MTPL	24.81%	21.3%	24.68%	31.50%	26.81%	23.3%	26.64%	31.50%
GTPL	65.32%	54.0%	65.27%	44.10%	168.82%	157.5%	168.79%	44.10%
Total	**19.35%**	**17.0%**	**19.25%**	**22.78%**	**30.76%**	**28.2%**	**30.66%**	**22.78%**

As expected, the effect of expenses is not significant on the capital requirement for Premium risk. Finally, neglecting safety loading (*i.e.*, assuming λ = 0), SCR is significantly greater for Accident and MOD (where λ > 0). By contrast, the choice of Standard Formula to not consider safety loading seems to be less prudential for most important LoBs, but it is influenced by the phase of the underwriting cycle. The SCR ratio for only Premium Risk, derived by applying the "market-wide approach" of the Standard Formula (SF) (see Section 2), is also reported in Table 5.

Both insurers have the same ratios for each LoB when SF is applied because of the lack of a size factor. The total SCR ratio, derived by the SF, is also equal for both insurers having assumed the same mix of portfolio. It is interesting to compare this ratio to the results obtained by the IM. A consistent comparison could be developed only by considering the case of λ = 0 because, as previously mentioned, the Standard Formula neglects safety loading in capital requirement evaluation. We observe a saving of capital by using the Internal Model for OMEGA, while a significant increase of capital is requested for the smaller insurer if IM is used.

Main differences are justified by considering that volatility factor used in the Standard Formula have been calibrated on the European market, while main parameters of the Internal Model have been derived by considering the risk profile of each specific insurer.

Exploring deeply the differences between IM and SF, some key points could be captured.

(a) In the Internal Model, we are considering also the volatility of expenses, neglected by the Standard Formula. Main results confirm that the effect of expenses is not very significant for the LoB analyzed.

(b) For OMEGA, the standard deviations of (X/B) of Accident (8.1%), MOD (7.2%), MTPL (7.4%) and Property (6.8%) are lower than volatility factors provided by the Standard Formula (see Table 1). A greater value is indeed observed for GTPL (15.1% against a volatility factor of 14%). For EPSILON, the high variability coefficient of severity distribution and a low expected number of claims lead to very high standard deviation of (X/B) for Property (15%) and GTPL (36%) when IM is applied.

(c) Because of the skewness of the overall aggregate distribution, for both insurers, the ratio between 99.5% quantile less the mean and the standard deviation is very far from the multiplier equal to 3 fixed by the Standard Formula. The implicit multiplier, derived by IM as $\frac{VaR_{0.995}\left(\sum_{h=1}^{L} \tilde{X}_{t+1,h}\right) - \sum_{h=1}^{L} P_{t+1,h}}{\sigma\left(\sum_{h=1}^{L} \tilde{X}_{t+1,h}\right)}$, is equal to 2.76 for OMEGA and to 3.15 for EPSILON.

6. The Effect of Alternative Reinsurance Strategies

The model has been also applied net of reinsurance in order to compare the effect on capital requirement of different reinsurance treaties. For each line of business, we assume evaluating the following reinsurance strategies:

- *QSF1*: Quota Share treaties with a retention β_h equal to 90% for Accident and MOD, 80% for Property, 95% for MTPL and 85% for GTPL and a fixed commission applied to reinsurer premiums and equal to the expected expense ratio. In this case we have $c_h = c_h^{RE}$.
- *QSF2*: Quota Share treaties with the same retentions β_h of *QSF1* and a fixed commission applied to reinsurer premiums and equal to 80% of the expected expense ratio. In this case we have $c_h^{RE} = 0.8\, c_h$.
- *QSS1*: Quota Share treaties with the same retentions β_h of *QSF1* and a sliding commission applied to reinsurer premiums. Provisional and expected commission rate is equal to 80% of the expected expense ratio $E(c_h^{RE}) = 0.8\, c_h$, while the effective percentage varies according to the observed loss experience as provided by Formula (5).
- *QSS2*: Quota Share treaties with the same retentions β_h of *QSF1* and a sliding commission applied to reinsurer premiums. Provisional and expected commission rate is equal to 80% of the expected expense ratio $E(c_h^{RE}) = 0.8\, c_h$. The commissions are adjusted also in this case according to the observed loss ratio. We build up five bins of width 10% and we modify the percentage according to the ratio between the average value of the classes where the observed loss ratio falls and the expected loss ratio. According to this classification, we assume a maximum value equal to the expected loss ratio plus 25% and a minimum value equal to the expected loss ratio less 25%. The excesses due to loss ratios outside the limits of the scale (above or below) are not taken into account in the calculation of commission rate. This structure implicitly defines a minimum and a maximum commission.
- *XL*: an XL treaty for each LoB with a retention limit equal to $M_{t+1,h} = E\left(\tilde{Z}_{t+1,h}\right) + 15\sigma\left(\tilde{Z}_{t+1,h}\right)$. Safety loading coefficient λ_h^{RE} of the reinsurer is equal to the safety loading coefficient of insurer, proportionally increased to take into account the savings of variability coefficient of the insurer because of reinsurance.
- *XLQS*: a QS treaty with retention and sliding commissions equal to *QSS2* for Accident, MOD and Property and a XL treaty with retention limit and safety loadings equal to XL1 for MTPL and GTPL.

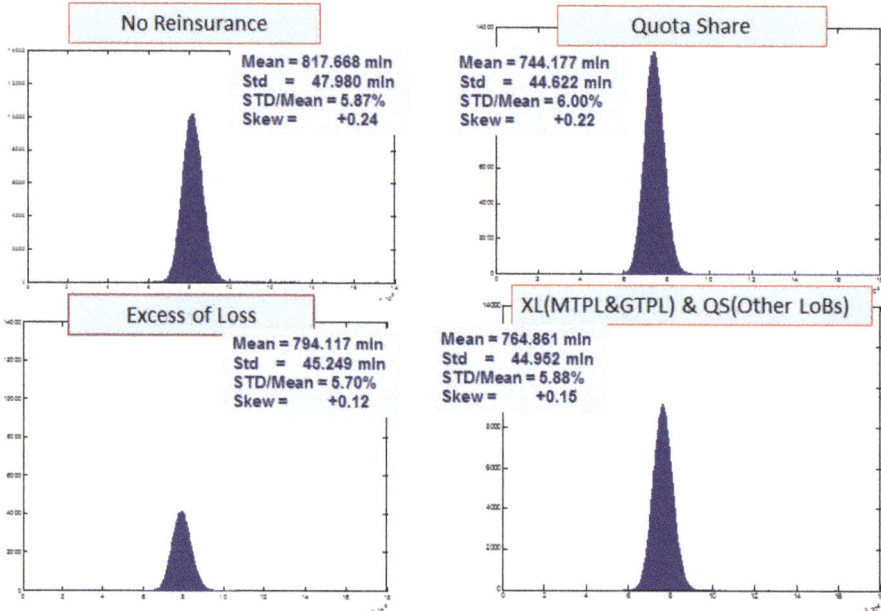

Figure 1. Distribution of aggregate claim amount of Total Portfolio for OMEGA according to different reinsurance strategies.

For the sake of simplicity, we report in Figures 1 and 2 only the aggregated distribution of aggregate claim amount of gross and net of reinsurance respectively in order to catch the effect of several treaties on the shape of distribution. Quota Share treaty intuitively leads to a variability coefficient and a skewness similar to the gross reinsurance case. We do not have the same CV because the different retentions between Lines of business lead to a different mix of portfolio with respect to reinsurance cases. We have instead a greater effect on CV and skewness when a XL treaty is used. Finally, the choice of different treaties between long-tail business and other LoBs leads to results similar to XL because of the high weight of MTPL on the total portfolio.

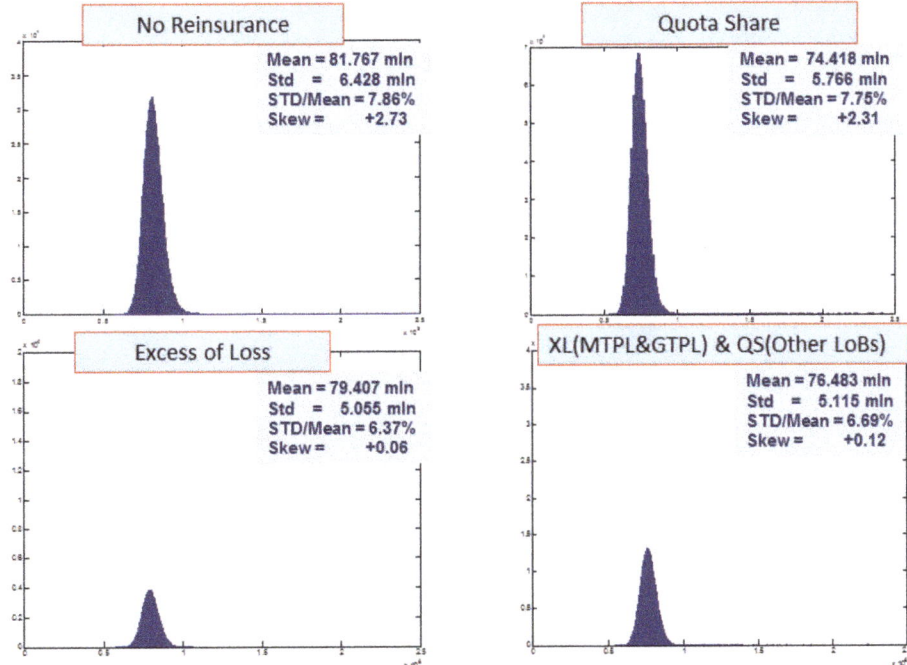

Figure 2. Distribution of aggregate claim amount of Total Portfolio for EPSILON according to different reinsurance strategies.

Table 6. CV and skewness of simulated distribution for each LoB (Gross and Net of Reinsurance).

LoBs	OMEGA							
	$CV(\tilde{X}_{t+1})$				$\gamma(\tilde{X}_{t+1})$			
	No Reins	QS	XL	XLQS	No Reins	QS	XL	XLQS
Accident	15.34%	15.34%	15.29%	15.34%	0.30	0.30	0.30	0.30
MOD	11.15%	11.15%	11.14%	11.15%	0.22	0.22	0.22	0.22
Property	9.00%	9.00%	7.69%	9.00%	0.95	0.95	0.17	0.95
MTPL	8.68%	8.68%	8.65%	8.65%	0.18	0.18	0.18	0.18
GTPL	18.26%	18.26%	14.27%	14.27%	2.84	2.84	0.18	0.18
Total	*5.87%*	*6.00%*	*5.70%*	*55.88%*	*0.24*	*0.22*	*0.12*	*0.15*
LoBs	EPSILON							
	$CV(\tilde{X}_{t+1})$				$\gamma(\tilde{X}_{t+1})$			
	No Reins	QS	XL	XLQS	No Reins	QS	XL	XLQS
Accident	17.01%	17.01%	16.54%	17.01%	0.37	0.37	0.32	0.37
MOD	11.89%	11.89%	11.79%	11.89%	0.23	0.23	0.22	0.23
Property	19.66%	19.66%	12.92%	19.66%	6.56	6.56	0.34	6.56
MTPL	9.39%	9.39%	9.09%	9.09%	0.21	0.21	0.17	0.17
GTPL	42.14%	42.14%	23.28%	23.28%	12.87	12.87	0.22	0.22
Total	*7.86%*	*7.75%*	*6.37%*	*6.69%*	*2.73*	*2.31*	*0.06*	*0.12*

Analyzing the effects on aggregate claim amount for each LoB (see Table 6), we observe a similar behavior of proportional and non-proportional treaties for Accident and MOD while a greater saving of variability and skewness is provided by XL for LoBs with a greater c_Z as MTPL, GTPL and Property. Because of a higher pooling risk, the relative effect of non-proportional treaties is higher for EPSILON. We have in this case that aggregated CV moves from 7.9% to 6.3% and aggregated skewness varies from 2.73 to 0.06 when a XL treaty is applied.

In order to consider the effect of pricing of the treaties, we evaluate the characteristics of Combined Ratio distribution. As previously described, several QS treaties are considered with the same retention and different commission rates. We report in Table 7 simulated characteristics of Combined Ratio (CR) of total portfolio for both insurers. It is noteworthy that the high number of simulations (1 million) assured a strong convergence of simulated moments to the exact ones. Some negligible differences are observed for high skewed LoB (as GTPL) of small companies.

Table 7. Characteristics of Combined Ratio distribution for both insurers (Total Portfolio—Gross and Net Reinsurance).

LoBs	Stats	No Reins	QSF1 $c^{re}=c$ Fixed Comm.	QSF2 $c^{re}=$ 0.8c Fixed Comm.	QSS1 $E(c^{re})=$ 0.8c Sliding Comm.	QSS2 $E(c^{re})=$ 0.8c Classes (Min, Max)	XL	QSXL
OMEGA	Mean	101.29%	101.24%	101.77%	101.77%	101.77%	101.81%	102.20%
	St. Dev.	4.61%	4.73%	4.73%	4.81%	4.80%	4.47%	4.67%
	Skew.	0.23	0.21	0.21	0.22	0.20	0.11	0.14
EPSILON	Mean	101.29%	101.24%	101.77%	101.77%	101.77%	102.21%	102.40%
	St. Dev.	6.15%	6.09%	6.09%	6.27%	6.20%	5.01%	5.33%
	Skew.	2.69	2.27	2.25	2.39	2.15	0.05	0.11

According to gross of reinsurance distribution, we observe an average CR on the portfolio greater than one because of negative safety loadings in Property, MTPL and GTPL. As already showed for aggregate claim amount characteristics, a higher variability and skewness for EPSILON is confirmed.

Furthermore, the different results related to simulated distribution of combined ratios net of reinsurance can be compared. In particular, in the case of XL strategy, the distribution is heavily affected by reinsurer pricing with a higher combined ratio. On the other hand, this treaty allows the highest reduction of variability and skewness. With regard to proportional treaties, we observe the greater CV in the case of sliding commissions (QSS1) because of both the variance of $\tilde{C}^{re}$ and the dependence with the aggregate claim amount. A very slight reduction of variability and skewness with respect to QSS1 is observed when the QSS2 methodology is considered. In this case, sliding commissions are based on fixed classes with a minimum and a maximum value where if the observed loss ratio falls outside the range, these excesses are not considered in the commissions. The effect is more noticeable for EPSILON because of the higher variability of the company.

Moving to SCR for Premium risk for OMEGA, we observe in Figure 3 how all strategies reduce the required capital, but they bring it into effect in a rather different way. In the case of the Quota Share, with fixed commissions equal to expenses loading, we have a reduction of required capital for each LoB equal to the quota to be reinsured $(1-\beta_h)$. Other Quota Share treaties are more realistic by assuming lower commission rates or variable commissions, but the unfavorable pricing and the greater variability lead to a reduced saving of capital requirement. The XL strategy is clearly depressing the expected technical results. The assumed XL coverage is indeed more expensive than QS coverage, but it is more effective on reducing the downside risk. In general, it provides a greater saving of capital except when compared to the Quota Share QSF1 with fixed commission rate so that $c^{re}=c$.

The ratio between total capital requirement for Premium Risk and gross premiums ranges indeed between 17.55% of *QSF1* Treaty to 19.35% of Gross of Reinsurance case. As expected for lines with high variability and skewness as GTPL, XL is the most efficient treaty, despite the high pricing. For this LoB, the SCR net XL is indeed 47% of gross premiums against a ratio of 65% evaluated gross reinsurance, while the reinsurer applies a safety loading coefficient λ^{RE} equal to roughly 54% of ceded risk premiums for GTPL.

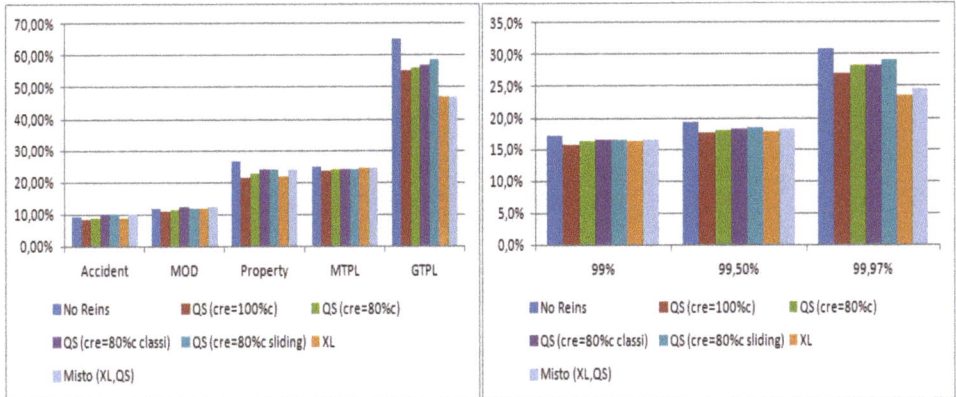

Figure 3. SCR ratio for each LoB and Total SCR ratio according to different reinsurance strategies (OMEGA insurer).

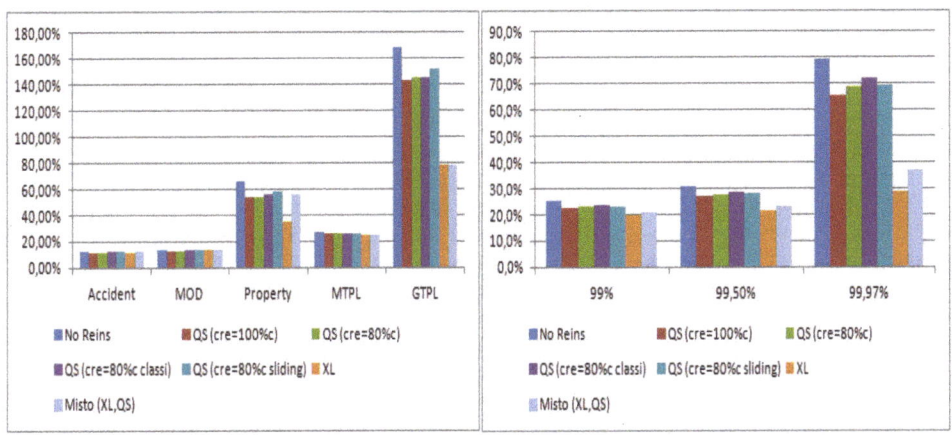

Figure 4. SCR ratio for each LoB and Total SCR ratio according to different reinsurance strategies (EPSILON insurer).

When the smaller company is considered (Figure 4), we have noticeable differences between proportional and non-proportional treaties. With respect to a capital ratio gross of reinsurance of roughly 31%, QS treaties settle around 27%–29%, while XL shows a ratio of 21.5%. In this treaty, despite the greater safety loading of reinsurer (λ^{RE}) for OMEGA, the higher the reduction of pooling risk, the greater is the saving of capital. We have indeed that in this case, not only GTPL but also Property shows a significant reduction of capital when XL is applied (78% and 35% of premiums for SCR^{net} against 169% and 67% gross of reinsurance).

Furthermore, we can observe how XL treaties appear very efficient when higher confidence levels are taken into account. For example, when a confidence level of 99.97% is considered, the gross SCR ratio is respectively 31% and 79% for OMEGA and EPSILON, while the ratio net of XL is equal to 23% and 29% a roughly 15% and 64% less for the two companies. It is clear how the different dimensions lead to different effects when non-proportional treaties are considered.

Finally the IM capital requirements can be compared with those obtained by the Standard Formula also for net of reinsurance cases (see Figure 5).

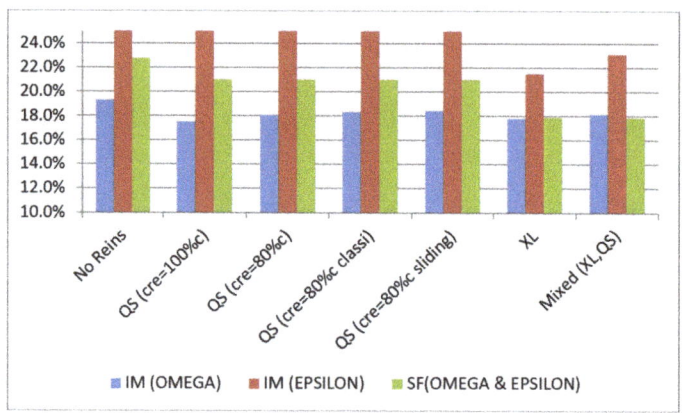

Figure 5. SCR ratios for both insurers derived by Internal Model and market-wide Standard Formula.

Both insurers show again the same ratio when SF is considered because of the same mix of portfolio and the same reinsurance strategies. This result emphasizes another pitfall of the market-wide formula that provides, through the fixed NP_{lob} factor, the same effect of non-proportional reinsurance despite a different size of portfolio. This factor, being independent by the characteristics of the XL treaty (as for example the attachment point of the layer), assumes for some LoBs a greater saving of variability with respect to the effective reduction obtained by analyzing the distribution of aggregate claim amount. We have indeed that the ratio between the variability coefficients net and gross of reinsurance for MTPL is equal to 99.6% for OMEGA and to 96.7% for EPSILON, while SF allows a NP_{lob} equal to 80% for this LoB. Considering instead the GTPL, we derive IM ratios equal to respectively 78% and 56% for the insurers because of the high variability of this LoB. This overestimation of the effect of XL, provided by the Standard Formula for MTPL, shows a poor convenience in the development of the Internal Model for OMEGA when this treaty is applied. On the other hand, the SF provides a significant underestimation of capital requirement when the small insurer is considered.

Moving to Quota Share treaties, the effect of different commission rates is not considered by the Standard Formula that leads to the same capital ratio for all proportional treaties here analyzed.

7. Conclusions

A reliable comparison of different reinsurance covers provided by the real market makes the insurer able to identify the most appropriate strategic planning. Starting from the Collective Risk Theory approach, we extend the relations in order to consider proportional or non-proportional reinsurance strategies. By considering several Quota-Share treaties scenarios, we derive the exact characteristics of combined ratio distribution by considering the effect of alternative methodology on providing ceding commissions.

Moreover, the Monte Carlo Simulation technique has allowed for the comparison of the effect on capital requirements of different strategies. This technique provides a useful insight of the whole complex risk process, with special advantages in cases of portfolios with a large skewness of the loss distribution, whereas the use of approximation formulas are not reliable.

The proposed theoretical model is clearly a simplified version of a more complex model that should be built up, but here suitable analyses about primary insurance aspects have been preferred. In particular, we have focused on the mitigation effect of reinsurance on underwriting Premium Risk, neglecting the additional capital requirement needed to cover the default risk of the reinsurer, since the latter depends clearly on reinsurer reliability as a risk factor and only in terms of volume on the ceded business.

The comparison with the Standard Formula, defined by Delegated Acts, has allowed us to emphasize some technical weaknesses of the market-wide approach, such as the lack of size factor, the use of a default value of the non-proportional factor and the replacement of the LogNormal assumption with a fixed multiplier.

Conflicts of Interest: The authors declare no conflict of interest.

References

1. European Commission. "Commission Delegated Regulation (EU) 2015/35 Supplementing Directive 2009/138/EC of the European Parliament and of the Council on the Taking-up and Pursuit of the Business of Insurance and Reinsurance (Solvency II), 10 of October 2014." *Off. J. EU*, 2015. Available online: http://eur-lex.europa.eu/legal-content/EN/TXT/?uri=CELEX:32015R0035 (accessed on 29 May 2015).
2. B. De Finetti. *Il Problema dei Pieni.* Roma, Italy: Giornale dell'Istituto Italiano degli Attuari, 1940.
3. W. Hurlimann. "Excess of loss reinsurance with reinstatements revisited." *Astin Bull.* 35 (2005): 211–238.
4. R. Phifer. *Reinsurance Fundamentals.* New York, NY, USA: John Wiley & Sons, 1996.
5. R.E. Beard, T. Pentikäinen, and E. Pesonen. *Risk Theory*, 3rd ed. London, UK: Chapman & Hall, 1984.
6. H. Bühlmann. *Mathematical Methods in Risk Theory.* New York, NY, USA: Springer-Verlag, 1970.
7. C.D. Daykin, and G.B. Hey. "Managing uncertainty in a general insurance company." *J. Inst. Actuar.* 117 (1990): 173–277. [CrossRef]
8. C. Daykin, T. Pentikäinen, and M. Pesonen. *Practical Risk Theory for Actuaries.* Monographs on Statistics and Applied Probability 53; London, UK: Chapman & Hall, 1994.
9. T. Pentikäinen, H. Bonsdorff, M. Pesonen, J. Rantala, and M. Ruohonen. *Insurance Solvency and Financial Strength.* Helsinki, Finland: Finnish Insurance Training and Publishing Company, 1989.
10. N. Savelli, and G.P. Clemente. "Modelling Aggregate Non-Life Underwriting Risk: Standard Formula vs Internal Model." *Giornale dell'Istituto Italiano degli Attuari* LXXII (2009): 301–338.
11. S.M. Coutts, and T. Thomas. "Modelling the impact of reinsurance on financial strength." *Br. Actuar. J.* 3 (1997): 583–653. [CrossRef]
12. S.M. Coutts, and T. Thomas. "Capital and risk and their relationship to reinsurance programmes." In Proceedings of the 5th International Conference on Insurance Solvency and Finance, London, UK, 17 June 1997.
13. M. De Lourdes Centeno. "The effect of the retention limit on risk reserve." *ASTIN Bull.* 25 (1995): 67–74. [CrossRef]
14. N. Savelli. "Risk analysis of a non-life insurer and traditional reinsurance effects on the solvency profile." In Proceedings of the 6th International Congress on "Insurance: Mathematics and Economics", Lisbon, Portugal, 15–17 July 2002.
15. D. Clark. "Basics of Reinsurance Pricing." *CAS Study Notes*, 1996. Available online: https://www.casact.org/library/studynotes/clark6.pdf (accessed on 29 May 2015).
16. European Commission. "Quantitative impact study 5—Technical specifications." Available online: https://eiopa.europa.eu/Pages/QIS/QIS5-Technical-Specifications.aspx (accessed on 29 May 2015).
17. T. Pentikäinen, and J. Rantala. *Solvency of Insurers and Equalization Reserves.* Helsinki, Finland: Insurance Publishing Company Ltd., 1982.
18. L. Ballotta, and N. Savelli. "Dynamic Financial Analysis and Risk-Based Capital for a General Insurer." In Proceedings of the Transactions XXVIII International Congress of Actuaries, Paris, France, 28 May–2 June 2006.

19. S. Klugman, H.H. Panjer, and G.E. Wilmot. *Loss Models: From Data to Decisions* Wiley Series in Probability and Statistics; 3rd ed. Hoboken, NJ, USA: John Wiley & Sons, 2008.
20. P. Artzner, F. Delbaen, J.M. Eber, and D. Heath. "Coherent Measures of Risk." *Math. Financ.* 9 (1999): 203–228. [CrossRef]
21. N. Savelli, and G.P. Clemente. "Hierarchical Structures in the aggregation of Premium Risk for Insurance Underwriting." *Scand. Actuar. J.* 3 (2011): 193–213. [CrossRef]

© 2015 by the authors. Licensee MDPI, Basel, Switzerland. This article is an open access article distributed under the terms and conditions of the Creative Commons Attribution (CC BY) license (http://creativecommons.org/licenses/by/4.0/).

Article

Optimal Dynamic Portfolio with Mean-CVaR Criterion

Jing Li [1] and Mingxin Xu [2,*]

[1] Federal Reserve Bank of New York, New York, NY 10045, USA; jing.li@ny.frb.org
[2] University of North Carolina at Charlotte, Department of Mathematics and Statistics, Charlotte, NC 28223, USA
* Author to whom correspondence should be addressed; mxu2@uncc.edu; Tel.: 704-340-4699.

Received: 6 August 2013; in revised form: 19 October 2013; Accepted: 4 November 2013; Published: 11 November 2013

Abstract: Value-at-risk (VaR) and conditional value-at-risk (CVaR) are popular risk measures from academic, industrial and regulatory perspectives. The problem of minimizing CVaR is theoretically known to be of a Neyman–Pearson type binary solution. We add a constraint on expected return to investigate the mean-CVaR portfolio selection problem in a dynamic setting: the investor is faced with a Markowitz type of risk reward problem at the final horizon, where variance as a measure of risk is replaced by CVaR. Based on the complete market assumption, we give an analytical solution in general. The novelty of our solution is that it is no longer the Neyman–Pearson type, in which the final optimal portfolio takes only two values. Instead, in the case in which the portfolio value is required to be bounded from above, the optimal solution takes three values; while in the case in which there is no upper bound, the optimal investment portfolio does not exist, though a three-level portfolio still provides a sub-optimal solution.

Keywords: conditional value-at-risk; mean-CVaR portfolio optimization; risk minimization; Neyman–Pearson problem; 91G10; 91B30; 90C46; G11; G32; C61

1. Introduction

The portfolio selection problem published by Markowitz [1] in 1952 is formulated as an optimization problem in a one-period static setting with the objective of maximizing expected return, subject to the constraint of variance being bounded from above. In 2005, Bielecki *et al.* [2] published the solution to this problem in a dynamic complete market setting. In both cases, the measure of risk of the portfolio is chosen as variance and the risk-reward problem is understood as the "mean-variance" problem.

Much research has been done in developing risk measures that focus on extreme events in the tail distribution where the portfolio loss occurs (variance does not differentiate loss or gain), and quantile-based models have thus far become the most popular choice. Among those, conditional value-at-risk (CVaR), developed by Rockafellar and Uryasev [3,4], also known as expected shortfall by Acerbi and Tasche [5], has become a prominent candidate to replace variance in the portfolio selection problem. On the theoretical side, CVaR is a "coherent risk measure", a term coined by Artzner *et al.* [6,7] in pursuit of an axiomatic approach for defining properties that a 'good' risk measure should possess. On the practical side, the convex representation of CVaR from Rockafellar and Uryasev [3] opened the door for convex optimization for the mean-CVaR problem and gave it vast advantage in implementation. In a one-period static setting, Rockafellar and Uryasev [3] demonstrated how linear programming can be used to solve the mean-CVaR problem, making it a convincing alternative to the Markowitz [1] mean-variance concept.

The work of Rockafellar and Uryasev [3] has raised huge interest for extending this approach. Acerbi and Simonetti [8] and Adam *et al.* [9] generalized CVaR to a spectral risk measure in a static setting. A spectral risk measure is also known as weighted value-at-risk (WVaR) by Cherny [10], who, in turn, studied its optimization problem. Ruszczynski and Shapiro [11] revised CVaR into a multi-step dynamic risk measure, namely the "conditional risk mapping for CVaR", and solved the corresponding mean-CVaR problem using Rockafellar and Uryasev's [3] technique for each time step. When expected return is replaced by expected utility, the utility-CVaR portfolio optimization problem is often studied in a continuous-time dynamic setting; see Gandy [12] and Zheng [13]. More recently, the issue of robust implementation is dealt with in Quaranta and Zaffaroni [14], Gotoh *et al.* [15], Huang *et al.* [16] and El Karoui *et al.* [17]. Research on systemic risk that involves CVaR can be found in Acharya *et al.* [18], Chen *et al.* [19] and Adrian and Brunnermeier [20].

To the best of our knowledge, no complete characterization of a solution has been done for the mean-CVaR problem in a continuous-time dynamic setting. Similar to Bielecki *et al.* [2], we reduce the problem to a combination of a static optimization problem and a hedging problem with the complete market assumption. Our main contribution is that in solving the static optimization problem, we find a complete characterization, whose nature is different than what is known in the literature. As a pure CVaR minimization problem without the expected return constraint, Sekine [21], Li and Xu [22] and Melnikov and Smirnov [23] found the optimal solution to be binary. This is confirmed to be true for more general law-invariant risk (preference) measure minimization by Schied [24] and He and Zhou [25]. The key to finding the solution that is binary is the association of the mean-CVaR problem with the Neyman–Pearson problem. We observe in Section 2.1 that the stochastic part of CVaR minimization can be transformed into shortfall risk minimization using the representation (CVaR is the Fenchel–Legendre dual of the expected shortfall) given by Rockafellar and Uryasev [3]. Föllmer and Leukert [26] characterized the solution to the latter problem in a general semimartingale complete market model to be binary, where they have demonstrated its close relationship to the Neyman–Pearson problem of hypothesis testing between the risk neutral probability measure, $\tilde{P}$, and the physical probability measure, P.

Adding the expected return constraint to WVaR minimization (CVaR is a particular case of WVaR), Cherny [10] found conditions under which the solution to the mean-WVaR problem was still binary and conditions under which the solution does not exist. In this paper, we discuss all cases for solving the mean-CVaR problem depending on a combination of two criteria: the level of the Radon–Nikodým derivative, $\frac{d\tilde{P}}{dP}$, relative to the confidence level of the risk measure; and the level of the return requirement. More specifically, when the portfolio is uniformly bounded from above and below, we find the optimal solution to be nonexistent or binary in some cases and, more interestingly, take three values in the most important case (see Case 4 of Theorem 3.15). When the portfolio is unbounded from above, in most cases (see Case 2 and 4 in Theorem 3.17), the solution is nonexistent, while portfolios of three levels still give sub-optimal solutions. Since the new solution we find can take not only the upper or the lower bound, but also a level in between, it can be viewed in part as a generalization of the binary solution for the Neyman–Pearson problem with an additional constraint on expectation.

This paper is organized as follows. Section 2 formulates the dynamic portfolio selection problem and compares the structure of the binary solution and the three-level solution, with an application of exact calculation in the Black–Scholes model. Section 3 details the analytic solution in general, where the proofs are delayed to the Appendix A. Section 4 lists possible future work.

2. The Structure of the Optimal Portfolio

2.1. Main Problem

Let $(\Omega, \mathcal{F}, (\mathcal{F})_{0 \leq t \leq T}, P)$ be a filtered probability space that satisfies the usual conditions, where $\mathcal{F}_0$ is trivial and $\mathcal{F}_T = \mathcal{F}$. The market model consists of $d + 1$ tradable assets: one riskless asset (money market account) and d risky assets (stock). Suppose the risk-free interest rate, r, is a constant and the stock, S_t, is a d-dimensional real-valued locally-bounded semimartingale process. Let the number of shares invested in the risky asset, ξ_t, be a d-dimensional predictable process, such that the stochastic integral with respect to S_t is well-defined. Then, the value of a self-financing portfolio, X_t, evolves according to the dynamics:

$$dX_t = \xi_t dS_t + r(X_t - \xi_t S_t)dt, X_0 = x_0$$

Here, $\xi_t dS_t$ and $\xi_t S_t$ are interpreted as inner products if the risky asset is multidimensional $d > 1$. The portfolio selection problem is to find the best strategy, $(\xi_t)_{0 \leq t \leq T}$, to minimize the conditional value-at-risk (CVaR) of the final portfolio value, X_T, at confidence level $0 < \lambda < 1$, while requiring the expected value to remain above a constant z.[1] In addition, we require uniform lower bound x_d and upper bound x_u on the value of the portfolio over time, such that $-\infty < x_d < x_0 < x_u \leq \infty$. Therefore, our main dynamic problem is:

$$\inf_{\xi_t} CVaR_\lambda(X_T) \tag{1}$$

$$\text{subject to } E[X_T] \geq z, x_d \leq X_t \leq x_u \text{ a.s.} \forall t \in [0, T]$$

Note that the no-bankruptcy condition can be imposed by setting the lower bound to be $x_d = 0$, and the portfolio value can be unbounded from above by taking the upper bound as $x_u = \infty$. Our solution will be based on the following complete market assumption.

Assumption 2.1 *There is no free lunch with vanishing risk (as defined in Delbaen and Schachermayer [27]), and the market model is complete with a unique equivalent local martingale measure, $\widetilde{P}$, such that the Radon–Nikodým derivative, $\frac{d\widetilde{P}}{dP}$, has a continuous distribution.*

Under the above assumption, any $\mathcal{F}$-measurable random variable can be replicated by a dynamic portfolio. Thus, the dynamic optimization problem Equation (1) can be reduced to: first, find the optimal solution, X^{**}, to the main static problem:

$$\inf_{X \in \mathcal{F}} CVaR_\lambda(X) \tag{2}$$

$$\text{subject to } E[X] \geq z, \widetilde{E}[X] = x_r, x_d \leq X \leq x_u \text{ a.s.}$$

if it exists, and then, find the dynamic strategy that replicates the $\mathcal{F}$-measurable random variable, X^{**}. Here, the expectations, E and $\widetilde{E}$, are taken under the physical probability measure, P, and the risk neutral probability measure, $\widetilde{P}$, respectively. Constant $x_r = x_0 e^{rT}$ is assumed to satisfy $-\infty < x_d < x_0 \leq x_r < x_u \leq \infty$, and the additional capital constraint $\widetilde{E}[X] = x_r$ is the key to making sure that the optimal solution can be replicated by a dynamic self-financing strategy with initial capital x_0.

Using the equivalence between the conditional value-at-risk and the Fenchel–Legendre dual of the expected shortfall derived in Rockafellar and Uryasev [3]:

$$CVaR_\lambda(X) = \frac{1}{\lambda} \inf_{x \in \mathbb{R}} \left(E\left[(x - X)^+\right] - \lambda x \right), \forall \lambda \in (0, 1) \tag{3}$$

the CVaR optimization problem Equation (2) can be reduced to an expected shortfall optimization problem, which we name the *two-constraint problem*:

---

[1] Krokhmal et al. [28] showed conditions under which the problem of maximizing expected return with the CVaR constraint is equivalent to the problem of minimizing CVaR with the expected return constraint. In this paper, we use the term mean-CVaR problem for both cases.

Step 1: minimization of expected shortfall

$$v(x) = \inf_{X \in \mathcal{F}} E\left[(x - X)^+\right] \quad (4)$$

subject to $E[X] \geq z$, (return constraint)

$\widetilde{E}[X] = x_r$, (capital constraint)

$x_d \leq X \leq x_u$ a.s.

Step 2: minimization of conditional value-at-risk

$$\inf_{X \in \mathcal{F}} CVaR_\lambda(X) = \frac{1}{\lambda} \inf_{x \in \mathbb{R}} (v(x) - \lambda x) \quad (5)$$

To compare our solution to existing ones in the literature, we also name an auxiliary problem, which simply minimizes the conditional value-at-risk without the return constraint, the *one-constraint problem*: Step 1 in Equation (4) is replaced by:

Step 1: minimization of expected shortfall

$$v(x) = \inf_{X \in \mathcal{F}} E\left[(x - X)^+\right] \quad (6)$$

subject to $\widetilde{E}[X] = x_r$, (capital constraint)

$x_d \leq X \leq x_u$ a.s.

Step 2 in Equation (5) remains the same.

2.2. Main Result

This subsection is devoted to a conceptual comparison between the solutions to the *one-constraint problem* and the *two-constraint problem*. The solution to the expected shortfall minimization problem in Step 1 of the one-constraint problem is found by Föllmer and Leukert [26] under Assumption 2.1 to be binary in nature:

$$X(x) = x_d \mathbb{I}_A + x \mathbb{I}_{A^c}, \text{ for } x_d < x < x_u \quad (7)$$

where $\mathbb{I}.(\omega)$ is the indicator function and set A is defined as the collection of states where the Radon–Nikodým derivative is above a threshold, $\left\{\omega \in \Omega : \frac{d\widetilde{P}}{dP}(\omega) > a\right\}$. This particular structure, in which the optimal solution, $X(x)$, takes only two values, namely, the lower bound, x_d, and x, is intuitively clear once the problems of minimizing expected shortfall and hypothesis testing between P and $\widetilde{P}$ are connected in Föllmer and Leukert [26], the later being well-known to possess a binary solution by the Neyman–Pearson Lemma. There are various ways to prove the optimality. Other than the Neyman–Pearson approach, it can be viewed as the solution from a convex duality perspective; see Theorem 1.19 in Xu [29]. In addition, a simplified version to the proof of Proposition 3.14 gives a direct method using the Lagrange multiplier for convex optimization.

The solution to Step 2 of one-constraint problem and, thus, to the main problems in Equations (1) and (2), as a pure risk minimization problem without the return constraint is given in Schied [24], Sekine [21] and Li and Xu [22]. Since Step 2 only involves minimization over a real-valued number, x, the binary structure is preserved through this step. Under some technical conditions, the solution to Step 2 of the one-constraint problem is shown by Li and Xu [22] (Theorem 2.10 and Remark 2.11) to be:

$$X^* = x_d \mathbb{I}_{A^*} + x^* \mathbb{I}_{A^{*c}}, \quad \text{(two-line configuration)} \quad (8)$$

$$CVaR_\lambda(X^*) = -x_r + \frac{1}{\lambda}(x^* - x_d)\left(P(A^*) - \lambda \widetilde{P}(A^*)\right) \qquad (9)$$

where (a^*, x^*) is the solution to the capital constraint $(\widetilde{E}[X(x)] = x_r)$ in Step 1 and the first order Euler condition $(v'(x) = 0)$ in Step 2:

$$x_d \widetilde{P}(A) + x\widetilde{P}(A^c) = x_r, \quad \text{(capitalconstraint)} \qquad (10)$$

$$P(A) + \frac{\widetilde{P}(A^c)}{a} - \lambda = 0. \quad \text{(firstorderEulercondition)} \qquad (11)$$

A static portfolio holding only the riskless asset will yield a constant portfolio value, $X \equiv x_r$, with $CVaR(X) = -x_r$. The diversification by dynamically managing the exposure to risky assets decreases the risk of the overall portfolio by an amount shown in Equation (9). One interesting observation is that the optimal portfolio exists regardless of whether the upper bound on the portfolio is finite $x_u < \infty$ or not $x_u = \infty$. This conclusion will change drastically as we add the return constraint to the optimization problem.

The main result of this paper is to show that the optimal solution to the two-constraint problem and, thus, main problem Equation (1) and Equation (2), does not have a Neyman–Pearson type of binary solution, which we call two-line configuration in Equation (8); instead, it has a three-line configuration. Proposition 3.14 and Theorem 3.15 prove that, when the upper bound is finite $x_u < \infty$, and under some technical conditions, the solution to Step 2 of the two-constraint problem turns out to be:

$$X^{**} = x_d \mathbb{I}_{A^{**}} + x^{**} \mathbb{I}_{B^{**}} + x_u \mathbb{I}_{D^{**}}, \quad \text{(three-lineconfiguration)} \qquad (12)$$

$$CVaR_\lambda(X_T^{**}) = \frac{1}{\lambda}((x^{**} - x_d)P(A^{**}) - \lambda x^{**}) \qquad (13)$$

where (a^{**}, b^{**}, x^{**}) is the solution to the capital constraint and the first order Euler condition, plus the additional return constraint $(E[X(x)] = z)$:

$$x_d P(A) + xP(B) + x_u P(D) = z, \quad \text{(returnconstraint)} \qquad (14)$$

$$x_d \widetilde{P}(A) + x\widetilde{P}(B) + x_u \widetilde{P}(D) = x_r, \quad \text{(capitalconstraint)} \qquad (15)$$

$$P(A) + \frac{\widetilde{P}(B) - bP(B)}{a-b} - \lambda = 0. \quad \text{(firstorderEulercondition)} \qquad (16)$$

The sets in Equations (14)–(16) are defined by different levels of the Radon–Nikodým derivative:

$$A = \left\{\omega \in \Omega : \frac{d\widetilde{P}}{dP}(\omega) > a\right\}, B = \left\{\omega \in \Omega : b \le \frac{d\widetilde{P}}{dP}(\omega) \le a\right\}, D = \left\{\omega \in \Omega : \frac{d\widetilde{P}}{dP}(\omega) < b\right\}$$

When the upper bound is infinite $x_u = \infty$, Theorem 3.17 shows that the solution for the optimal portfolio is no longer a three-line configuration. It can be pure money market account investment (one-line), binary (two-line) or very likely nonexistent. In the last case, the infimum of the CVaR can still be computed, and a sequence of three-line configuration portfolios can be found with their CVaR converging to the infimum.

2.3. Example: Exact Calculation in the Black–Scholes Model

We show the closed-form calculation of the three-line configuration presented in Equations (12)–(16), as well as the corresponding optimal dynamic strategy in the benchmark Black–Scholes Model. Suppose an agent is trading between a money market account with interest rate r and one stock[2] that follows geometric Brownian motion $dS_t = \mu S_t dt + \sigma S_t dW_t$ with instantaneous rate of return μ, volatility σ and initial stock price S_0. The endowment starts at x_0, and bankruptcy is prohibited at any time, $x_d = 0$, before the final horizon, T. The optimal portfolio, X^*, in Equation (8) for the one constraint problem is a binary option $X^* = x^* \mathbb{I}_{A^{*c}}$ with expected return $z^* \stackrel{\Delta}{=} E[X^*]$. The expected terminal value, $E[X_T]$, is required to be above a fixed level z to satisfy the return constraint. When z is low, namely, $z \leq z^*$, the return constraint is non-binding, and obviously the two-line configuration, X^*, is optimal. Let $\bar{z}$ be the highest expected value achievable by any self-financing portfolio starting with initial capital x_0 (see Definition 3.2 and Lemma 3.3). When the return requirement becomes meaningful, i.e., $z \in (z^*, \bar{z}]$, the three-line configuration, X^{**}, provided by Equation (12), becomes optimal.

Since the Radon–Nikodým derivative, $\frac{d\widetilde{P}}{dP}$, is a scaled power function of the final stock price, which has a log-normal distribution, the probabilities in Equations (14)–(16) can be computed in closed-form:

$$P(A) = N\left(-\frac{\theta\sqrt{T}}{2} - \frac{\ln a}{\theta\sqrt{T}}\right), \quad P(D) = 1 - N\left(-\frac{\theta\sqrt{T}}{2} - \frac{\ln b}{\theta\sqrt{T}}\right), \quad P(B) = 1 - P(A) - P(D)$$
$$\widetilde{P}(A) = N\left(\frac{\theta\sqrt{T}}{2} - \frac{\ln a}{\theta\sqrt{T}}\right), \quad \widetilde{P}(D) = 1 - N\left(\frac{\theta\sqrt{T}}{2} - \frac{\ln b}{\theta\sqrt{T}}\right), \quad \widetilde{P}(B) = 1 - \widetilde{P}(A) - \widetilde{P}(D)$$

where $\theta = \frac{\mu - r}{\sigma}$ and $N(\cdot)$ is the cumulative distribution function of a standard normal random variable. From these, the solution, (a^{**}, b^{**}, x^{**}), to Equations (15) and (16) can be found numerically and, thus, the X^{**} from Equation (12). The formulae[3] for the dynamic value of the optimal portfolio, X_t^{**}, the corresponding dynamic hedging strategy, ξ_t^{**}[4], and the associated final minimal risk, $CVaR_\lambda(X_T^{**})$, are:

$$X_t^{**} = e^{-r(T-t)}[x^{**}N(d_+(a^{**}, S_t, t)) + x_d N(d_-(a^{**}, S_t, t))]$$
$$+ e^{-r(T-t)}[x^{**}N(d_-(b^{**}, S_t, t)) + x_u N(d_+(b^{**}, S_t, t))] - e^{r(T-t)}x^{**}$$
$$\xi_t^{**} = \frac{x^{**} - x_d}{\sigma S_t \sqrt{2\pi(T-t)}} e^{-r(T-t) - \frac{d_-^2(a^{**}, S_t, t)}{2}} + \frac{x^{**} - x_u}{\sigma S_t \sqrt{2\pi(T-t)}} e^{-r(T-t) - \frac{d_+^2(b^{**}, S_t, t)}{2}}$$
$$CVaR_\lambda(X_T^{**}) = \tfrac{1}{\lambda}((x^{**} - x_d)P(A^{**}) - \lambda x^{**})$$

where we define: $d_-(a, s, t) = \frac{1}{\theta\sqrt{T-t}}\left[-\ln a + \frac{\theta}{\sigma}\left(\frac{\mu + r - \sigma^2}{2}t - \ln \frac{s}{S_0}\right) + \frac{\theta^2}{2}(T-t)\right]$ and $d_+(a, s, t) = -d_-(a, s, t)$.

Numerical results comparing the minimal risk for various levels of upper-bound x_u and return constraint z are summarized in Table 1. As expected, the upper bound on the portfolio value, x_u, has no impact on the one-constraint problem, as (x^*, a^*) and $CVaR_\lambda(X_T^*)$ are optimal whenever $x_u \geq x^*$. On the contrary, in the two-constraint problem, the stricter the return requirement, z, the more the three-line configuration, X^{**}, deviates from the two-line configuration, X^*. Stricter return requirement (higher z) implies higher minimal risk $CVaR_\lambda(X_T^{**})$; while a less strict upper bound (higher x_u) decreases minimal risk $CVaR_\lambda(X_T^{**})$. Notably, under certain conditions in Theorem 3.17, for all levels of return $z \in (z^*, \bar{z}]$, when $x_u \to \infty$, $CVaR_\lambda(X_T^{**})$ approaches $CVaR_\lambda(X_T^*)$, as the optimal solution ceases to exist in the limiting case.

---

[2] It is straight-forward to generalize the calculation to the multi-dimensional Black–Scholes Model. Since we provide in this paper an analytical solution to the static CVaR minimization problem, calculation in other complete market models can be carried out as long as the dynamic hedge can be expressed in a simple manner.

[3] X_t^{**} coincides with the dynamic value of a European option with payoff X^{**}, and ξ_t^{**} coincides with its delta-hedge.

[4] Note that since the solution, X^*, is binary and the solution, X^{**}, takes three values, they share the practical difficulty as all digital options do near expiration, namely, the hedge ratio can be very big in magnitude at the boundary near expiration, which makes it impractical to do the hedging properly. We point out that this property is not shared by the optimal solution to the mean-variance type of problems.

Table 1. Black–Scholes example for one-constraint (pure CVaR minimization) and two-constraint (mean-CVaR optimization) problems with parameters: $r = 5\%$, $\mu = 0.2$, $\sigma = 0.1$, $S_0 = 10$, $T = 2$, $x_0 = 10$, $x_d = 0$, $\lambda = 5\%$. Consequently, $z^* = 18.8742$ and $\bar{z} = 28.8866$.

One-Constraint Problem			Two-Constraint Problem			
x_u	30	50	x_u	30	30	50
			z	20	25	25
x^*	19.0670	19.0670	x^{**}	19.1258	19.5734	19.1434
a^*	14.5304	14.5304	a^{**}	14.3765	12.5785	14.1677
			b^{**}	0.0068	0.1326	0.0172
$CVaR_{5\%}(X_T^*)$	−15.2118	−15.2118	$CVaR_{5\%}(X_T^{**})$	−15.2067	−14.8405	−15.1483

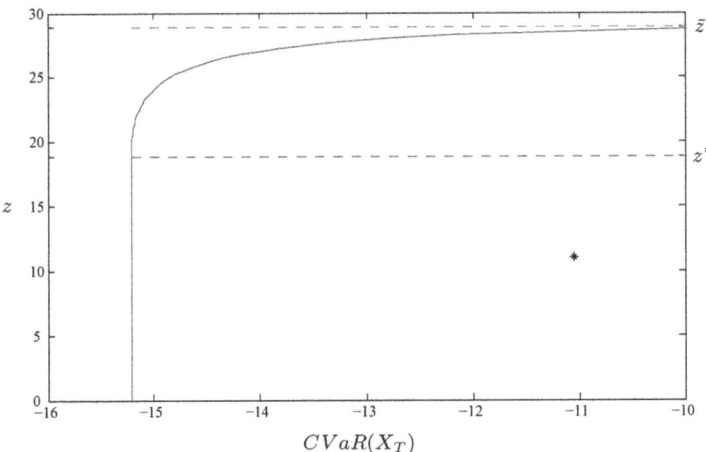

Figure 1. Efficient frontier for mean-CVaR portfolio selection.

Figure 1 plots the efficient frontier of the above mean-CVaR portfolio selection problem with fixed upper bound $x_u = 30$. The curve between return level z^* and $\bar{z}$ are the mean-CVaR efficient portfolio from various three-line configurations, while the straight line is the same mean-CVaR efficient two-line configuration when the return constraint is non-binding. The star positioned at $(-x_r, x_r) = (-11.0517, 11.0517)$, where $x_r = x_0 e^{rT}$, corresponds to the portfolio that invests purely in the money market account. In contrast to its position on the traditional capital market Line (the efficient frontier for a mean-variance portfolio selection problem), the pure money market account portfolio is no longer efficient in the mean-CVaR portfolio selection problem.

3. Analytical Solution to the Portfolio Selection Problem

Under Assumption 2.1, the solution to the main mean-CVaR optimization problem Equation (2), i.e., the two-constraint problem Equations (4) and (5), will be discussed in two separate cases where the upper bound for the portfolio value is finite or infinite. The main results are stated in Theorem 3.15 and Theorem 3.17, respectively. To create a flow showing clearly how the optimal solutions are related to the two-line and three-line configurations, all proofs will be delayed to the Appendix A.

3.1. Case $x_u < \infty$: Finite Upper Bound

We first define the general three-line configuration and its degenerate two-line configurations. Recall from Section 2.2 the definitions of the sets, A, B, D, are:

$$A = \left\{\omega \in \Omega : \frac{d\widetilde{P}}{dP}(\omega) > a\right\}, B = \left\{\omega \in \Omega : b \leq \frac{d\widetilde{P}}{dP}(\omega) \leq a\right\}, D = \left\{\omega \in \Omega : \frac{d\widetilde{P}}{dP}(\omega) < b\right\} \quad (17)$$

Definition 3.1 *Suppose $x \in [x_d, x_u]$.*

1. Any three-line configuration has the structure $X = x_d \mathbb{I}_A + x \mathbb{I}_B + x_u \mathbb{I}_D$.
2. The two-line configuration $X = x \mathbb{I}_B + x_u \mathbb{I}_D$ is associated with the above definition in the case $a = \infty$, $B = \left\{\omega \in \Omega : \frac{d\widetilde{P}}{dP}(\omega) \geq b\right\}$ and $D = \left\{\omega \in \Omega : \frac{d\widetilde{P}}{dP}(\omega) < b\right\}$.

    The two-line configuration $X = x_d \mathbb{I}_A + x \mathbb{I}_B$ s associated with the above definition in the case $b = 0$, $A = \left\{\omega \in \Omega : \frac{d\widetilde{P}}{dP}(\omega) > a\right\}$, and $B = \left\{\omega \in \Omega : \frac{d\widetilde{P}}{dP}(\omega) \leq a\right\}$.

    The two-line configuration $X = x_d \mathbb{I}_A + x_u \mathbb{I}_D$ is associated with the above definition in the case $a = b$, $A = \left\{\omega \in \Omega : \frac{d\widetilde{P}}{dP}(\omega) > a\right\}$, and $D = \left\{\omega \in \Omega : \frac{d\widetilde{P}}{dP}(\omega) < a\right\}$.

Moreover:

1. General constraints are the capital constraint and the equality part of the expected return constraint for a three-line configuration $X = x_d \mathbb{I}_A + x \mathbb{I}_B + x_u \mathbb{I}_D$:

$$E[X] = x_d P(A) + x P(B) + x_u P(D) = z$$
$$\widetilde{E}[X] = x_d \widetilde{P}(A) + x \widetilde{P}(B) + x_u \widetilde{P}(D) = x_r$$

2. Degenerated Constraints 1 are the capital constraint and the equality part of the expected return constraint for a two-line configuration $X = x \mathbb{I}_B + x_u \mathbb{I}_D$:

$$E[X] = x P(B) + x_u P(D) = z$$
$$\widetilde{E}[X] = x \widetilde{P}(B) + x_u \widetilde{P}(D) = x_r$$

Degenerated Constraints 2 are the capital constraint and the equality part of the expected return constraint for a two-line configuration $X = x_d \mathbb{I}_A + x \mathbb{I}_B$:

$$E[X] = x_d P(A) + x P(B) = z$$
$$\widetilde{E}[X] = x_d \widetilde{P}(A) + x \widetilde{P}(B) = x_r$$

Degenerated Constraints 3 are the capital constraint and the equality part of the expected return constraint for a two-line configuration $X = x_d \mathbb{I}_A + x_u \mathbb{I}_D$:

$$E[X] = x_d P(A) + x_u P(D) = z$$
$$\widetilde{E}[X] = x_d \widetilde{P}(A) + x_u \widetilde{P}(D) = x_r$$

Note that Degenerated Constraints 1 correspond to the general constraints when $a = \infty$; Degenerated Constraints 2 correspond to the general constraints when $b = 0$; and Degenerated Constraints 3 correspond to the general constraints when $a = b$.

We use the two-line configuration $X = x_d \mathbb{I}_A + x_u \mathbb{I}_D$, where the value of the random variable, X, takes either the upper or the lower bound, as well as its capital constraint to define the 'bar-system' from which we calculate the highest achievable return.

Definition 3.2 (The bar-system) *For fixed $-\infty < x_d < x_r < x_u < \infty$, let $\bar{a}$ be a solution to the capital constraint $\widetilde{E}[X] = x_d \widetilde{P}(A) + x_u \widetilde{P}(D) = x_r$ in Degenerated Constraints 3 for the two-line configuration $X =*

$x_d \mathbb{I}_A + x_u \mathbb{I}_D$. In the bar-system, $\overline{A}, \overline{D}$ and $\overline{X}$ are associated with the constant, $\overline{a}$, in the sense $\overline{X} = x_d \mathbb{I}_{\overline{A}} + x_u \mathbb{I}_{\overline{D}}$, where $\overline{A} = \left\{ \omega \in \Omega : \frac{d\widetilde{P}}{dP}(\omega) > \overline{a} \right\}$ and $\overline{D} = \left\{ \omega \in \Omega : \frac{d\widetilde{P}}{dP}(\omega) < \overline{a} \right\}$. Define the expected return of the bar-system as $\overline{z} = E[\overline{X}] = x_d P(\overline{A}) + x_u P(\overline{D})$.

Lemma 3.3 $\overline{z}$ *is the highest expected return that can be obtained by a self-financing portfolio with initial capital x_0, whose value is bounded between x_d and x_u:*

$$\overline{z} = \max_{X \in \mathcal{F}} E[X] \text{ s.t. } \widetilde{E}[X] = x_r = x_0 e^{rT}, x_d \leq X \leq x_u \text{ a.s.}$$

In the following lemma, we vary the x value in the two-line configurations $X = x \mathbb{I}_B + x_u \mathbb{I}_D$ and $X = x_d \mathbb{I}_A + x \mathbb{I}_B$, while maintaining the capital constraints, respectively. We observe their expected returns to vary between values x_r and $\overline{z}$ in a monotone and continuous fashion.

Lemma 3.4 *For fixed $-\infty < x_d < x_r < x_u < \infty$.*

1. *Given any $x \in [x_d, x_r]$, let b be a solution to the capital constraint $\widetilde{E}[X] = x\widetilde{P}(B) + x_u \widetilde{P}(D) = x_r$ in Degenerated Constraints 1 for the two-line configuration $X = x \mathbb{I}_B + x_u \mathbb{I}_D$. Define the expected return of the resulting two-line configuration as $z(x) = E[X] = xP(B) + x_u P(D)$.[5] Then $z(x)$ is a continuous function of x and decreases from $\overline{z}$ to x_r as x increases from x_d to x_r.*

2. *Given any $x \in [x_r, x_u]$, let a be a solution to the capital constraint $\widetilde{E}[X] = x_d \widetilde{P}(A) + x\widetilde{P}(B) = x_r$ in Degenerated Constraints 2 for the two-line configuration $X = x_d \mathbb{I}_A + x \mathbb{I}_B$. Define the expected return of the resulting two-line configuration as $z(x) = E[X] = x_d P(A) + xP(B)$. Then, $z(x)$ is a continuous function of x and increases from x_r to $\overline{z}$ as x increases from x_r to x_u.*

From now on, we will concern ourselves with requirements on the expected return in the interval, $z \in [x_r, \overline{z}]$, because, on one side, Lemma 3.3 ensures that there are no feasible solutions to main problem Equation (2) if we require an expected return higher than $\overline{z}$. On the other side, Lemma 3.3, Lemma 3.4 and Theorem 3.11 lead to the conclusion that a return constraint where $z \in (-\infty, x_r)$ is too weak to differentiate the two-constraint problem from the one-constraint problem, as their optimal solutions concur.

Definition 3.5 *For fixed $-\infty < x_d < x_r < x_u < \infty$ and a fixed level $z \in [x_r, \overline{z}]$, define x_{z1} and x_{z2} to be the corresponding x value for two-line configurations $X = x \mathbb{I}_B + x_u \mathbb{I}_D$ and $X = x_d \mathbb{I}_A + x \mathbb{I}_B$ that satisfy Degenerated Constraints 1 and Degenerated Constraints 2, respectively.*

Definition 3.5 implies when we fix the level of expected return, z, we can find two particular feasible solutions: $X = x_{z1} \mathbb{I}_B + x_u \mathbb{I}_D$, satisfying $\widetilde{E}[X] = x_{z1} \widetilde{P}(B) + x_u \widetilde{P}(D) = x_r$ and $E[X] = x_{z1} P(B) + x_u P(D) = z$; and $X = x_d \mathbb{I}_A + x_{z2} \mathbb{I}_B$, satisfying $\widetilde{E}[X] = x_d \widetilde{P}(A) + x_{z2} \widetilde{P}(B) = x_r$ and $E[X] = x_d P(A) + x_{z2} P(B) = z$. The values, x_{z1} and x_{z2}, are well defined, because Lemma 3.4 guarantees $z(x)$ to be an invertible function in both cases. We summarize in the following lemma whether the two-line configurations satisfying the capital constraints meet or fail the return constraint as x ranges over its domain, $[x_d, x_u]$, for the two-line and three-line configurations in Definition 3.1.

Lemma 3.6 *For fixed $-\infty < x_d < x_r < x_u < \infty$ and a fixed level $z \in [x_r, \overline{z}]$.*

1. *If we fix $x \in [x_d, x_{z1}]$, the two-line configuration $X = x \mathbb{I}_B + x_u \mathbb{I}_D$, which satisfies the capital constraint $\widetilde{E}[X] = x\widetilde{P}(B) + x_u \widetilde{P}(D) = x_r$ in Degenerated Constraints 1, satisfies the expected return constraint: $E[X] = xP(B) + x_u P(D) \geq z$;*

2. *If we fix $x \in (x_{z1}, x_r]$, the two-line configuration $X = x \mathbb{I}_B + x_u \mathbb{I}_D$, which satisfies the capital constraint $\widetilde{E}[X] = x\widetilde{P}(B) + x_u \widetilde{P}(D) = x_r$ in Degenerated Constraints 1, fails the expected return constraint: $E[X] = xP(B) + x_u P(D) < z$;*

---

[5] Threshold b and, consequently, sets B and D are all dependent on x through the capital constraint; therefore, $z(x)$ is not a linear function of x.

3. If we fix $x \in [x_r, x_{z2}]$, the two-line configuration $X = x_d \mathbb{I}_A + x\mathbb{I}_B$, which satisfies the capital constraint $\widetilde{E}[X] = x_d \widetilde{P}(A) + x\widetilde{P}(B) = x_r$ in Degenerated Constraints 2, fails the expected return constraint: $E[X] = xP(B) + x_u P(D) < z$;

4. If we fix $x \in [x_{z2}, x_u]$, the two-line configuration $X = x_d \mathbb{I}_A + x\mathbb{I}_B$, which satisfies the capital constraint $\widetilde{E}[X] = x_d \widetilde{P}(A) + x\widetilde{P}(B) = x_r$ in Degenerated Constraints 2, satisfies the expected return constraint: $E[X] = xP(B) + x_u P(D) \geq z$.

We turn our attention to solving Step 1 of the two-constraint problem (4):
Step 1: minimization of expected shortfall:

$$v(x) = \inf_{X \in \mathcal{F}} E\left[(x - X)^+\right]$$

subject to
$$E[X] \geq z, \quad \text{(return constraint)}$$
$$\widetilde{E}[X] = x_r, \quad \text{(capital constraint)}$$
$$x_d \leq X \leq x_u \text{ a.s.}$$

Notice that a solution is called for any given real number, x, independent of the return level, z, or capital level x_r. From Lemma 3.6 and the fact that the two-line configurations are optimal solutions to Step 1 of the one-constraint problem (see Theorem 3.11), we can immediately draw the following conclusion.

Proposition 3.7 *For fixed $-\infty < x_d < x_r < x_u < \infty$ and a fixed level $z \in [x_r, \bar{z}]$.*

1. *If we fix $x \in [x_d, x_{z1}]$, then there exists a two-line configuration $X = x\mathbb{I}_B + x_u \mathbb{I}_D$ which is the optimal solution to Step 1 of the two-constraint problem;*
2. *If we fix $x \in [x_{z2}, x_u]$, then there exists a two-line configuration $X = x_d \mathbb{I}_A + x\mathbb{I}_B$, which is the optimal solution to Step 1 of the two-constraint problem.*

When $x \in (x_{z1}, x_{z2})$, Lemma 3.6 shows that the two-line configurations, which satisfy the capital constraints ($\widetilde{E}[X] = x_r$) do not generate high enough expected return ($E[X] < z$) to be feasible anymore. It turns out that a novel solution of the three-line configuration is the answer: it can be shown to be both feasible and optimal.

Lemma 3.8 *For fixed $-\infty < x_d < x_r < x_u < \infty$ and a fixed level $z \in [x_r, \bar{z}]$. Given any $x \in (x_{z1}, x_{z2})$, let the pair of numbers, $(a, b) \in \mathbb{R}^2$ ($b \leq a$), be a solution to the capital constraint $\widetilde{E}[X] = x_d \widetilde{P}(A) + x\widetilde{P}(B) + x_u \widetilde{P}(D) = x_r$ in the general constraints for the three-line configuration $X = x_d \mathbb{I}_A + x\mathbb{I}_B + x_u \mathbb{I}_D$. Define the expected return of the resulting three-line configuration as $z(a, b) = E[X] = x_d P(A) + xP(B) + x_u P(D)$. Then, $z(a, b)$ is a continuous function, which decreases from $\bar{z}$ to a number below z:*

1. *When $a = b = \bar{a}$ from Definition 3.2 of a bar-system, the three-line configuration degenerates to $X = \overline{X}$ and $z(\bar{a}, \bar{a}) = E\left[\overline{X}\right] = \bar{z}$.*
2. *When $b < \bar{a}$ and $a > \bar{a}$, $z(a, b)$ decreases continuously as b decreases and a increases.*
3. *In the extreme case when $a = \infty$, the three-line configuration becomes the two-line configuration $X = x\mathbb{I}_B + x_u \mathbb{I}_D$; in the extreme case when $b = 0$, the three-line configuration becomes the two-line configuration $X = x_d \mathbb{I}_A + x\mathbb{I}_B$. In either case, the expected value is below z by Lemma 3.6.*

Proposition 3.9 *For fixed $-\infty < x_d < x_r < x_u < \infty$ and a fixed level $z \in [x_r, \bar{z}]$. If we fix $x \in (x_{z1}, x_{z2})$, then there exists a three-line configuration $X = x_d \mathbb{I}_A + x\mathbb{I}_B + x_u \mathbb{I}_D$ that satisfies the general constraints, which is the optimal solution to Step 1 of the two-constraint problem.*

Combining Proposition 3.7 and Proposition 3.9, we arrive at the following result on the optimality of the three-line configuration.

Theorem 3.10 (Solution to Step 1: Minimization of Expected Shortfall)

For fixed $-\infty < x_d < x_r < x_u < \infty$ and a fixed level $z \in [x_r, \bar{z}]$. $X(x)$ and the corresponding value function, $v(x)$, described below, are optimal solutions to Step 1: minimization of expected shortfall of the two-constraint problem:

- $x \in (-\infty, x_d]$: $X(x) =$ any random variable with values in $[x_d, x_u]$ satisfying both the capital constraint $\widetilde{E}[X(x)] = x_r$ and the return constraint $E[X(x)] \geq z$. $v(x) = 0$.
- $x \in [x_d, x_{z1}]$: $X(x) =$ any random variable with values in $[x, x_u]$ satisfying both the capital constraint $\widetilde{E}[X(x)] = x_r$ and the return constraint $E[X(x)] \geq z$. $v(x) = 0$.
- $x \in (x_{z1}, x_{z2})$: $X(x) = x_d \mathbb{I}_{A_x} + x \mathbb{I}_{B_x} + x_u \mathbb{I}_{D_x}$, where A_x, B_x, D_x are determined by a_x and b_x as in (17) satisfying the general constraints: $\widetilde{E}[X(x)] = x_r$ and $E[X(x)] = z$. $v(x) = (x - x_d)P(A_x)$.
- $x \in [x_{z2}, x_u]$: $X(x) = x_d \mathbb{I}_{A_x} + x \mathbb{I}_{B_x}$, where A_x, B_x are determined by a_x as in Definition 3.1 satisfying both the capital constraint $\widetilde{E}[X(x)] = x_r$ and the return constraint $E[X(x)] \geq z$. $v(x) = (x - x_d)P(A_x)$.
- $x \in [x_u, \infty)$: $X(x) = x_d \mathbb{I}_{\overline{A}} + x_u \mathbb{I}_{\overline{B}} = \overline{X}$, where $\overline{A}, \overline{B}$ are associated to $\overline{a}$ as in Definition 3.2 satisfying both the capital constraint $\widetilde{E}[X(x)] = x_r$ and the return constraint $E[X(x)] = \overline{z} \geq z$. $v(x) = (x - x_d)P(\overline{A}) + (x - x_u)P(\overline{B})$.

To solve Step 2 of the two-constraint problem Equation (5) and, thus, the main problem Equation (2), we need to minimize

$$\frac{1}{\lambda} \inf_{x \in \mathbb{R}} (v(x) - \lambda x),$$

where $v(x)$ has been computed in Theorem 3.10. Depending on the z level in the return constraint being lenient or strict, the solution is sometimes obtained by the two-line configuration, which is optimal to the one-constraint problem and other times obtained by a true three-line configuration. To proceed in this direction, we recall the solution to the one-constraint problem from Li and Xu [22].

Theorem 3.11 (Theorem 2.10 and Remark 2.11 in Li and Xu [22] when $x_u < \infty$)

1. Suppose ess sup $\frac{d\widetilde{P}}{dP} \leq \frac{1}{\lambda}$. $X = x_r$ is the optimal solution to Step 2: minimization of conditional value-at-risk of the one-constraint problem, and the associated minimal risk is:

$$CVaR(X) = -x_r$$

2 Suppose ess sup $\frac{d\widetilde{P}}{dP} > \frac{1}{\lambda}$.

- If $\frac{1}{\overline{a}} \leq \frac{\lambda - P(\overline{A})}{1 - \widetilde{P}(\overline{A})}$ (see Definition 3.2 for the bar-system), then $\overline{X} = x_d \mathbb{I}_{\overline{A}} + x_u \mathbb{I}_{\overline{D}}$ is the optimal solution to Step 2: minimization of conditional value-at-risk of the one-constraint problem, and the associated minimal risk is:

$$CVaR(\overline{X}) = -x_r + \frac{1}{\lambda}(x_u - x_d)\left(P(\overline{A}) - \lambda \widetilde{P}(\overline{A})\right)$$

- Otherwise, let a^* be the solution to the equation $\frac{1}{a} = \frac{\lambda - P(A)}{1 - \widetilde{P}(A)}$. Associate sets $A^* = \left\{\omega \in \Omega : \frac{d\widetilde{P}}{dP}(\omega) > a^*\right\}$ and $B^* = \left\{\omega \in \Omega : \frac{d\widetilde{P}}{dP}(\omega) \leq a^*\right\}$ to level a^*. Define $x^* = \frac{x_r - x_d \widetilde{P}(A^*)}{1 - \widetilde{P}(A^*)}$, so that configuration

$$X^* = x_d \mathbb{I}_{A^*} + x^* \mathbb{I}_{B^*}$$

satisfies the capital constraint $\widetilde{E}[X^*] = x_d \widetilde{P}(A^*) + x^* \widetilde{P}(B^*) = x_r$.[6], and the associated minimal risk is:

$$CVaR(X^*) = -x_r + \frac{1}{\lambda}(x^* - x_d)\left(P(A^*) - \lambda \widetilde{P}(A^*)\right)$$

---

[6] Equivalently, (a^*, x^*) can be viewed as the solution to the capital constraint and the first order Euler condition in Equation (10) and (11). Then, X^* (what we call the 'star-system') is the optimal solution to Step 2: minimization of conditional value-at-risk of the one-constraint problem

Definition 3.12 In part 2 of Theorem 3.11, define $z^* = \bar{z}$ in the first case when $\frac{1}{a} \leq \frac{\lambda - P(\overline{A})}{1 - \widetilde{P}(\overline{A})}$; define $z^* = E[X^*]$ in the second case when $\frac{1}{a} > \frac{\lambda - P(\overline{A})}{1 - \widetilde{P}(\overline{A})}$.

We see that when z is smaller than z^*, the binary solutions, X^* and $\overline{X}$, provided in Theorem 3.11 are indeed the optimal solutions to Step 2 of the two-constraint problem. However, when z is greater than z^*, these two-line configurations are no longer feasible in the two-constraint problem. We now show that the three-line configuration is not only feasible, but also optimal. First, we establish the convexity of the objective function and its continuity in a Lemma.

Lemma 3.13 $v(x)$ is a convex function for $x \in \mathbb{R}$ and, thus, continuous.

Proposition 3.14 For fixed $-\infty < x_d < x_r < x_u < \infty$ and a fixed level $z \in (z^*, \bar{z}]$.

Suppose ess sup $\frac{d\widetilde{P}}{dP} > \frac{1}{\lambda}$. The solution, (a^{**}, b^{**}, x^{**}) (and, consequently, A^{**}, B^{**} and D^{**}), to the equations:

$$x_d P(A) + x P(B) + x_u P(D) = z, \quad \text{(returnconstraint)}$$
$$x_d \widetilde{P}(A) + x \widetilde{P}(B) + x_u \widetilde{P}(D) = x_r, \quad \text{(capitalconstraint)}$$
$$P(A) + \frac{\widetilde{P}(B) - bP(B)}{a - b} - \lambda = 0, \quad \text{(firstorderEulercondition)}$$

exists. $X^{**} = x_d \mathbb{I}_{A^{**}} + x^{**} \mathbb{I}_{B^{**}} + x_u \mathbb{I}_{D^{**}}$ (what we call the 'double-star system') is the optimal solution to Step 2: minimization of conditional value-at-risk of the two-constraint problem, and the associated minimal risk is:

$$CVaR(X^{**}) = \frac{1}{\lambda}((x^{**} - x_d)P(A^{**}) - \lambda x^{**})$$

Putting together Proposition 3.14 with Theorem 3.11, we arrive at the main theorem of this paper.

Theorem 3.15 (Minimization of conditional value-at-risk when $x_u < \infty$)
For fixed $-\infty < x_d < x_r < x_u < \infty$.

1. Suppose ess sup $\frac{d\widetilde{P}}{dP} \leq \frac{1}{\lambda}$ and $z = x_r$. The pure money market account investment $X = x_r$ is the optimal solution to Step 2: minimization of conditional value-at-risk of the two-constraint problem, and the associated minimal risk is:

$$CVaR(X) = -x_r$$

2. Suppose ess sup $\frac{d\widetilde{P}}{dP} \leq \frac{1}{\lambda}$ and $z \in (x_r, \bar{z}]$. The optimal solution to Step 2: minimization of conditional value-at-risk of the two-constraint problem does not exist, and the minimal risk is:

$$CVaR(X) = -x_r$$

3. Suppose ess sup $\frac{d\widetilde{P}}{dP} > \frac{1}{\lambda}$ and $z \in [x_r, z^*]$ (see Definition 3.12 for z^*).

   - If $\frac{1}{a} \leq \frac{\lambda - P(\overline{A})}{1 - \widetilde{P}(\overline{A})}$ (see Definition 3.2), then the bar-system $\overline{X} = x_d \mathbb{I}_{\overline{A}} + x_u \mathbb{I}_{\overline{D}}$ is the optimal solution to Step 2: minimization of conditional value-at-risk of the two-constraint problem, and the associated minimal risk is:

   $$CVaR(\overline{X}) = -x_r + \frac{1}{\lambda}(x_u - x_d)\left(P(\overline{A}) - \lambda \widetilde{P}(\overline{A})\right)$$

   - Otherwise, the star-system $X^* = x_d \mathbb{I}_{A^*} + x^* \mathbb{I}_{B^*}$ defined in Theorem 3.11 is the optimal solution to Step 2: minimization of conditional value-at-risk of the two-constraint problem, and the associated minimal risk is:

   $$CVaR(X^*) = -x_r + \frac{1}{\lambda}(x^* - x_d)\left(P(A^*) - \lambda \widetilde{P}(A^*)\right)$$

(4) Suppose ess sup $\frac{d\widetilde{P}}{dP} > \frac{1}{\lambda}$ and $z \in (z^*, \bar{z}]$. The double-star-system $X^{**} = x_d \mathbb{I}_{A^{**}} + x^{**} \mathbb{I}_{B^{**}} + x_u \mathbb{I}_{D^{**}}$ defined in Proposition 3.14 is the optimal solution to Step 2: minimization of conditional value-at-risk of the two-constraint problem, and the associated minimal risk is:

$$CVaR(X^{**}) = \frac{1}{\lambda}((x^{**} - x_d)P(A^{**}) - \lambda x^{**})$$

We observe that the pure money market account investment is rarely optimal. When the Radon–Nikodým derivative is bounded above by the reciprocal of the confidence level of the risk measure (ess sup $\frac{d\widetilde{P}}{dP} \leq \frac{1}{\lambda}$), a condition not satisfied in the Black–Scholes Model, the solution does not exist unless the return requirement coincides with the risk-free rate. When the Radon–Nikodým derivative exceeds $\frac{1}{\lambda}$ with positive probability and the return constraint is low, $z \in [x_r, z^*]$, the two-line configuration, which is optimal to the *CVaR* minimization problem without the return constraint, is also the optimal to the mean-*CVaR* problem. However, in the more interesting case in which the return constraint is materially high, $z \in (z^*, \bar{z}]$, the optimal three-line-configuration sometimes takes the value of the upper bound, x_u, to raise the expected return at the cost of the minimal risk, which will be at a higher level. This analysis complies with the numerical example shown in Section 2.3.

3.2. *Case $x_u = \infty$: No Upper Bound*

We first restate the solution to the one-constraint problem from Li and Xu [22] in the current context: when $x_u = \infty$, where we interpret $\bar{A} = \Omega$ and $\bar{z} = \infty$.

Theorem 3.16 (Theorem 2.10 and Remark 2.11 in Li and Xu [22] when $x_u = \infty$)

1. Suppose ess sup $\frac{d\widetilde{P}}{dP} \leq \frac{1}{\lambda}$. *The pure money market account investment $X = x_r$ is the optimal solution to Step 2: minimization of conditional value-at-risk of the one-constraint problem, and the associated minimal risk is:*

$$CVaR(X) = -x_r$$

2. Suppose ess sup $\frac{d\widetilde{P}}{dP} > \frac{1}{\lambda}$. *The star-system $X^* = x_d \mathbb{I}_{A^*} + x^* \mathbb{I}_{B^*}$ defined in Theorem 3.11 is the optimal solution to Step 2: minimization of conditional value-at-risk of the one-constraint problem, and the associated minimal risk is:*

$$CVaR(X^*) = -x_r + \frac{1}{\lambda}(x^* - x_d)\left(P(A^*) - \lambda \widetilde{P}(A^*)\right)$$

We observe that although there is no upper bound for the portfolio value, the optimal solution remains bounded from above, and the minimal *CVaR* is bounded from below. The problem of purely minimizing *CVaR* risk of a self-financing portfolio (bounded below by x_d to exclude arbitrage) from initial capital, x_0, is feasible in the sense that the risk will not approach $-\infty$, and the minimal risk is achieved by an optimal portfolio. When we add substantial return constraint to the *CVaR* minimization problem, although the minimal risk can still be calculated in the most important case (Case 4 in Theorem 3.17), it is truly an infimum and not a minimum, thus it can be approximated closely by a sub-optimal portfolio, but not achieved by an optimal portfolio.

Theorem 3.17 (Minimization of Conditional Value-At-Risk When $x_u = \infty$)

For fixed $-\infty < x_d < x_r < x_u = \infty$.

1. Suppose ess sup $\frac{d\widetilde{P}}{dP} \leq \frac{1}{\lambda}$ and $z = x_r$. *The pure money market account investment $X = x_r$ is the optimal solution to Step 2: minimization of conditional value-at-risk of the two-constraint problem, and the associated minimal risk is:*

$$CVaR(X) = -x_r$$

2. Suppose ess sup $\frac{d\widetilde{P}}{dP} \leq \frac{1}{\lambda}$ and $z \in (x_r, \infty)$. The optimal solution to Step 2: minimization of conditional value-at-risk of the two-constraint problem does not exist, and the minimal risk is:

$$CVaR(X) = -x_r$$

3. Suppose ess sup $\frac{d\widetilde{P}}{dP} > \frac{1}{\lambda}$ and $z \in [x_r, z^*]$. The star-system $X^* = x_d \mathbb{I}_{A^*} + x^* \mathbb{I}_{B^*}$ defined in Theorem 3.11 is the optimal solution to Step 2: minimization of conditional value-at-risk of the two-constraint problem, and the associated minimal risk is:

$$CVaR(X^*) = -x_r + \frac{1}{\lambda}(x^* - x_d)\Big(P(A^*) - \lambda\widetilde{P}(A^*)\Big)$$

4. Suppose ess sup $\frac{d\widetilde{P}}{dP} > \frac{1}{\lambda}$ and $z \in (z^*, \infty)$. The optimal solution to Step 2: minimization of conditional value-at-risk of the two-constraint problem does not exist, and the minimal risk is:

$$CVaR(X^*) = -x_r + \frac{1}{\lambda}(x^* - x_d)\Big(P(A^*) - \lambda\widetilde{P}(A^*)\Big)$$

Remark 3.18 *From the proof of the above theorem in the Appendix A, we note that in Case 4, we can always find a three-line configuration as a sub-optimal solution, i.e., there exists for every $\epsilon > 0$ a corresponding portfolio $X_\epsilon = x_d \mathbb{I}_{A_\epsilon} + x_\epsilon \mathbb{I}_{B_\epsilon} + \alpha_\epsilon \mathbb{I}_{D_\epsilon}$, which satisfies the general constraints and produces a CVaR level close to the lower bound: $CVaR(X_\epsilon) \leq CVaR(X^*) + \epsilon$.*

4. Future Work

The second part of Assumption 2.1, namely the Radon–Nikodým derivative, $\frac{d\widetilde{P}}{dP}$, having a continuous distribution, is imposed for the simplification it brings to the presentation in the main theorems. Further work can be done when this assumption is weakened. We expect that the main results should still hold, albeit in a more complicated form.[7] It will also be interesting to extend the closed-form solution for mean-CVaR minimization by replacing CVaR with law-invariant convex risk measures in general. Another direction will be to employ dynamic risk measures into the current setting.

Although in this paper we focus on the complete market solution, to solve the problem in an incomplete market setting, which includes stochastic volatility or jump models, the exact hedging argument via the martingale representation theorem that translates the dynamic problem Equation (??) into the static problem Equation (2) has to be replaced by a super-hedging argument via the optional decomposition developed by Kramkov [30] and Föllmer and Kabanov [31]. The detail is similar to the process carried out for shortfall risk minimization in Föllmer and Leukert [26], convex risk minimization in Rudloff [32] and law-invariant risk preference in He and Zhou [25]. The curious question is: Will the three-line configuration remain optimal?

Acknowledgments: The findings and conclusions expressed are solely those of the author and do not represent views of the Federal Reserve Bank of New York or the staff of the Federal Reserve System.

Conflicts of Interest: The authors declare no conflict of interest.

---

[7] The outcome in its format resembles techniques employed in Föllmer and Leukert [26] and Li and Xu [22], where the point masses on the thresholds for the Radon–Nikodým derivative in Equation (17) have to be dealt with carefully.

Appendix A. Appendix

A.1. Proof of Lemma 3.3

The problem of

$$\bar{z} = \max_{X \in \mathcal{F}} E[X] \text{ s.t. } \widetilde{E}[X] = x_r, x_d \leq X \leq x_u \text{ a.s.}$$

is equivalent to the expected shortfall problem:

$$\bar{z} = - \min_{X \in \mathcal{F}} E\left[(x_u - X)^+\right] \text{ s.t. } \widetilde{E}[X] = x_r, X \geq x_d \text{ a.s.}$$

Therefore, the answer is immediate. ◇

A.2. Proof of Lemma 3.4

Choose $x_d \leq x_1 < x_2 \leq x_r$. Let $X_1 = x_1 \mathbb{I}_{B_1} + x_u \mathbb{I}_{D_1}$, where $B_1 = \left\{\omega \in \Omega : \frac{d\widetilde{P}}{dP}(\omega) \geq b_1\right\}$ and $D_1 = \left\{\omega \in \Omega : \frac{d\widetilde{P}}{dP}(\omega) < b_1\right\}$. Choose b_1 such that $\widetilde{E}[X_1] = x_r$. This capital constraint means $x_1 \widetilde{P}(B_1) + x_u \widetilde{P}(D_1) = x_r$. Since $\widetilde{P}(B_1) + \widetilde{P}(D_1) = 1$, $\widetilde{P}(B_1) = \frac{x_u - x_r}{x_u - x_1}$ and $\widetilde{P}(D_1) = \frac{x_r - x_1}{x_u - x_1}$. Define $z_1 = E[X_1]$. Similarly, z_2, X_2, B_2, D_2, b_2 corresponds to x_2, where $b_1 > b_2$ and $\widetilde{P}(B_2) = \frac{x_u - x_r}{x_u - x_2}$ and $\widetilde{P}(D_2) = \frac{x_r - x_2}{x_u - x_2}$. Note that $D_2 \subset D_1$, $B_1 \subset B_2$ and $D_1 \setminus D_2 = B_2 \setminus B_1$. We have:

$$\begin{aligned}
z_1 - z_2 &= x_1 P(B_1) + x_u P(D_1) - x_2 P(B_2) - x_u P(D_2) \\
&= (x_u - x_2) P(B_2 \setminus B_1) - (x_2 - x_1) P(B_1) \\
&= (x_u - x_2) P\left(b_2 < \tfrac{d\widetilde{P}}{dP}(\omega) < b_1\right) - (x_2 - x_1) P\left(\tfrac{d\widetilde{P}}{dP}(\omega) \geq b_1\right) \\
&= (x_u - x_2) \int_{\{b_2 < \frac{d\widetilde{P}}{dP}(\omega) < b_1\}} \tfrac{dP}{d\widetilde{P}}(\omega) d\widetilde{P}(\omega) - (x_2 - x_1) \int_{\{\frac{d\widetilde{P}}{dP}(\omega) \geq b_1\}} \tfrac{dP}{d\widetilde{P}}(\omega) d\widetilde{P}(\omega) \\
&> (x_u - x_2) \tfrac{1}{b_1} \widetilde{P}(B_2 \setminus B_1) - (x_2 - x_1) \tfrac{1}{b_1} \widetilde{P}(B_1) \\
&= (x_u - x_2) \tfrac{1}{b_1} \left(\tfrac{x_u - x_r}{x_u - x_2} - \tfrac{x_u - x_r}{x_u - x_1}\right) - (x_2 - x_1) \tfrac{1}{b_1} \tfrac{x_u - x_r}{x_u - x_1} = 0
\end{aligned}$$

For any given $\epsilon > 0$, choose $x_2 - x_1 \leq \epsilon$; then:

$$\begin{aligned}
z_1 - z_2 &= (x_u - x_1) P(B_2 \setminus B_1) - (x_2 - x_1) P(B_2) \\
&\leq (x_u - x_1) P(B_2 \setminus B_1) \\
&\leq (x_u - x_1) \left(\tfrac{x_u - x_r}{x_u - x_2} - \tfrac{x_u - x_r}{x_u - x_1}\right) \\
&\leq \tfrac{(x_2 - x_1)(x_u - x_r)}{x_u - x_2} \leq x_2 - x_1 \leq \epsilon
\end{aligned}$$

Therefore, z decreases continuously as x increases when $x \in [x_d, x_r]$. When $x = x_d$, $z = \bar{z}$ from Definition 3.2. When $x = x_r$, $X \equiv x_r$ and $z = E[X] = x_r$. Similarly, we can show that z increases continuously from x_r to $\bar{z}$ as x increases from x_r to x_u. ◇

Lemma 3.6 is a logical consequence of Lemma 3.4 and Definition 3.5; Proposition 3.7 follows from Lemma 3.6; so their proofs will be skipped.

A.3. Proof of Lemma 3.8

Choose $-\infty < b_1 < b_2 \leq \bar{b} = \bar{a} \leq a_2 < a_1 < \infty$. Let configuration $X_1 = x_d \mathbb{I}_{A_1} + x \mathbb{I}_{B_1} + x_u \mathbb{I}_{D_1}$ correspond to the pair, (a_1, b_1), where $A_1 = \left\{\omega \in \Omega : \frac{d\widetilde{P}}{dP}(\omega) > a_1\right\}$, $B_1 = \left\{\omega \in \Omega : b_1 \leq \frac{d\widetilde{P}}{dP}(\omega) \leq a_1\right\}$, $D_1 = \left\{\omega \in \Omega : \frac{d\widetilde{P}}{dP}(\omega) < b_1\right\}$. Similarly, let configuration $X_2 = x_d \mathbb{I}_{A_2} + x \mathbb{I}_{B_2} + x_u \mathbb{I}_{D_2}$ correspond to the pair, (a_2, b_2). Define $z_1 = E[X_1]$ and $z_2 = E[X_2]$. Since both X_1 and X_2 satisfy the capital constraint, we have:

$$x_d \widetilde{P}(A_1) + x \widetilde{P}(B_1) + x_u \widetilde{P}(D_1) = x_r = x_d \widetilde{P}(A_2) + x \widetilde{P}(B_2) + x_u \widetilde{P}(D_2)$$

This simplifies to the equation:

$$(x - x_d)\widetilde{P}(A_2 \smallsetminus A_1) = (x_u - x)\widetilde{P}(D_2 \smallsetminus D_1) \tag{18}$$

Then:

$$
\begin{aligned}
z_2 - z_1 &= x_d P(A_2) + x P(B_2) + x_u P(D_2) - x_d P(A_1) - x P(B_1) - x_u P(D_1) \\
&= (x_u - x)P(D_2 \smallsetminus D_1) - (x - x_d)P(A_2 \smallsetminus A_1) \\
&= (x_u - x)P(D_2 \smallsetminus D_1) - (x_u - x)\frac{\widetilde{P}(D_2 \smallsetminus D_1)}{\widetilde{P}(A_2 \smallsetminus A_1)} P(A_2 \smallsetminus A_1) \\
&= (x_u - x)\widetilde{P}(D_2 \smallsetminus D_1)\left(\frac{P(D_2 \smallsetminus D_1)}{\widetilde{P}(D_2 \smallsetminus D_1)} - \frac{P(A_2 \smallsetminus A_1)}{\widetilde{P}(A_2 \smallsetminus A_1)}\right) \\
&= (x_u - x)\widetilde{P}(D_2 \smallsetminus D_1)\left(\frac{\int_{\{b_1 \leq \frac{d\widetilde{P}}{dP}(\omega) < b_2\}} \frac{dP}{d\widetilde{P}}(\omega)d\widetilde{P}(\omega)}{\widetilde{P}(D_2 \smallsetminus D_1)} - \frac{\int_{\{a_2 < \frac{d\widetilde{P}}{dP}(\omega) \leq a_1\}} \frac{dP}{d\widetilde{P}}(\omega)d\widetilde{P}(\omega)}{\widetilde{P}(A_2 \smallsetminus A_1)}\right) \\
&\geq (x_u - x)\widetilde{P}(D_2 \smallsetminus D_1)\left(\frac{1}{b_2} - \frac{1}{a_2}\right) > 0
\end{aligned}
$$

Suppose the pair, (a_1, b_1), is chosen, so that X_1 satisfies the budget constraint $\widetilde{E}[X_1] = x_r$. For any given $\epsilon > 0$, choose $b_2 - b_1$ small enough such that $P(D_2 \smallsetminus D_1) \leq \frac{\epsilon}{x_u - x}$. Now choose a_2, such that $a_2 < a_1$, and Equation (18) is satisfied. Then, X_2 also satisfies the budget constraint $\widetilde{E}[X_2] = x_r$, and:

$$z_2 - z_1 = (x_u - x)P(D_2 \smallsetminus D_1) - (x - x_d)P(A_2 \smallsetminus A_1) \leq (x_u - x)P(D_2 \smallsetminus D_1) \leq \epsilon$$

We conclude that the expected value of the three-line configuration decreases continuously as b decreases and a increases. ◇

In the following, we provide the main proof of the paper: the optimality of the three-line configuration.

A.4. Proof of Proposition 3.9

Denote $\rho = \frac{d\widetilde{P}}{dP}$. According to Lemma 3.8, there exists a three-line configuration $\hat{X} = x_d \mathbb{I}_A + x \mathbb{I}_B + x_u \mathbb{I}_D$ that satisfies the general constraints:

$$
\begin{aligned}
E[X] &= x_d P(A) + x P(B) + x_u P(D) = z \\
\widetilde{E}[X] &= x_d \widetilde{P}(A) + x \widetilde{P}(B) + x_u \widetilde{P}(D) = x_r
\end{aligned}
$$

where:

$$A = \{\omega \in \Omega : \rho(\omega) > \hat{a}\}, B = \{\omega \in \Omega : \hat{b} \leq \rho(\omega) \leq \hat{a}\}, D = \{\omega \in \Omega : \rho(\omega) < \hat{b}\}$$

As standard for convex optimization problems, if we can find a pair of Lagrange multipliers, $\lambda \geq 0$ and $\mu \in \mathbb{R}$, such that $\hat{X}$ is the solution to the minimization problem:

$$\inf_{X \in \mathcal{F}, \, x_d \leq X \leq x_u} E\left[(x - X)^+ - \lambda X - \mu \rho X\right] = E\left[(x - \hat{X})^+ - \lambda \hat{X} - \mu \rho \hat{X}\right] \tag{19}$$

then $\hat{X}$ is the solution to the constrained problem:

$$\inf_{X \in \mathcal{F}, \, x_d \leq X \leq x_u} E\left[(x - X)^+\right], \, s.t. E[X] \geq z, \widetilde{E}[X] = x_r$$

Define

$$\lambda = \frac{\hat{b}}{\hat{a} - \hat{b}}, \mu = -\frac{1}{\hat{a} - \hat{b}}$$

Then, Equation (19) becomes:

$$\inf_{X\in\mathcal{F},\, x_d\leq X\leq x_u} E\left[(x-X)^+ + \frac{\rho-\hat{b}}{\hat{a}-\hat{b}}X\right]$$

Choose any $X \in \mathcal{F}$, where $x_d \leq X \leq x_u$, and denote $G = \{\omega \in \Omega : X(\omega) \geq x\}$ and $L = \{\omega \in \Omega : X(\omega) < x\}$. Note that $\frac{\rho-\hat{b}}{\hat{a}-\hat{b}} > 1$ on set A, $0 \leq \frac{\rho-\hat{b}}{\hat{a}-\hat{b}} \leq 1$ on set B and $\frac{\rho-\hat{b}}{\hat{a}-\hat{b}} < 0$ on set D. Then, the difference:

$$E\left[(x-X)^+ + \frac{\rho-\hat{b}}{\hat{a}-\hat{b}}X\right] - E\left[(x-\hat{X})^+ + \frac{\rho-\hat{b}}{\hat{a}-\hat{b}}\hat{X}\right]$$
$$= E\left[(x-X)\mathbb{I}_L + \frac{\rho-\hat{b}}{\hat{a}-\hat{b}}X(\mathbb{I}_A + \mathbb{I}_B + \mathbb{I}_D)\right] - E\left[(x-x_d)\mathbb{I}_A + \frac{\rho-\hat{b}}{\hat{a}-\hat{b}}(x_d\mathbb{I}_A + x\mathbb{I}_B + x_u\mathbb{I}_D)\right]$$
$$= E\left[(x-X)\mathbb{I}_L + \left(\frac{\rho-\hat{b}}{\hat{a}-\hat{b}}(X-x_d) - (x-x_d)\right)\mathbb{I}_A + \frac{\rho-\hat{b}}{\hat{a}-\hat{b}}(X-x)\mathbb{I}_B + \frac{\rho-\hat{b}}{\hat{a}-\hat{b}}(X-x_u)\mathbb{I}_D\right]$$
$$\geq E\left[(x-X)\mathbb{I}_L + (X-x)\mathbb{I}_A + \frac{\rho-\hat{b}}{\hat{a}-\hat{b}}(X-x)\mathbb{I}_B + \frac{\rho-\hat{b}}{\hat{a}-\hat{b}}(X-x_u)\mathbb{I}_D\right]$$
$$= E\left[(x-X)(\mathbb{I}_{L\cap A} + \mathbb{I}_{L\cap B} + \mathbb{I}_{L\cap D}) + (X-x)(\mathbb{I}_{A\cap G} + \mathbb{I}_{A\cap L}) + \frac{\rho-\hat{b}}{\hat{a}-\hat{b}}(X-x)\mathbb{I}_B + \frac{\rho-\hat{b}}{\hat{a}-\hat{b}}(X-x_u)\mathbb{I}_D\right]$$
$$= E\left[(x-X)(\mathbb{I}_{L\cap B} + \mathbb{I}_{L\cap D}) + (X-x)\mathbb{I}_{A\cap G} + \frac{\rho-\hat{b}}{\hat{a}-\hat{b}}(X-x)\mathbb{I}_B + \frac{\rho-\hat{b}}{\hat{a}-\hat{b}}(X-x_u)\mathbb{I}_D\right]$$
$$= E\left[(x-X)(\mathbb{I}_{L\cap B} + \mathbb{I}_{L\cap D}) + (X-x)\mathbb{I}_{A\cap G} + \frac{\rho-\hat{b}}{\hat{a}-\hat{b}}(X-x)(\mathbb{I}_{B\cap G} + \mathbb{I}_{B\cap L}) + \frac{\rho-\hat{b}}{\hat{a}-\hat{b}}(X-x_u)(\mathbb{I}_{D\cap G} + \mathbb{I}_{D\cap L})\right]$$
$$= E\left[(x-X)\left(1 - \frac{\rho-\hat{b}}{\hat{a}-\hat{b}}\right)\mathbb{I}_{B\cap L} + \left(x - X + \frac{\rho-\hat{b}}{\hat{a}-\hat{b}}(X-x_u)\right)\mathbb{I}_{D\cap L} + (X-x)\mathbb{I}_{A\cap G}\right.$$
$$\left. + \frac{\rho-\hat{b}}{\hat{a}-\hat{b}}(X-x)\mathbb{I}_{B\cap G} + \frac{\rho-\hat{b}}{\hat{a}-\hat{b}}(X-x_u)\mathbb{I}_{D\cap G}\right] \geq 0$$

The last inequality holds because each term inside the expectation is greater than or equal to zero. ◊

Theorem 3.10 is a direct consequence of Lemma 3.6, Proposition 3.7 and Proposition 3.9.

A.5. Proof of Lemma 3.13

The convexity of $v(x)$ is a simple consequence of its definition (4). Real-valued convex functions on $\mathbb{R}$ are continuous on its interior of the domain, so $v(x)$ is continuous on $\mathbb{R}$. ◊

A.6. Proof of Proposition 3.14

For $z \in (z^*, \bar{z}]$, Step 2 of the two-constraint problem

$$\frac{1}{\lambda} \inf_{x \in \mathbb{R}} (v(x) - \lambda x)$$

is the minimum of the following five sub-problems after applying Theorem 3.10:

Case 1
$$\frac{1}{\lambda} \inf_{(-\infty, x_d]} (v(x) - \lambda x) = \frac{1}{\lambda} \inf_{(-\infty, x_d]} (-\lambda x) = -x_d$$

Case 2
$$\frac{1}{\lambda} \inf_{[x_d, x_{z1}]} (v(x) - \lambda x) = \frac{1}{\lambda} \inf_{[x_d, x_{z1}]} (-\lambda x) = -x_{z1} \leq -x_d$$

Case 3
$$\frac{1}{\lambda} \inf_{(x_{z1}, x_{z2})} (v(x) - \lambda x) = \frac{1}{\lambda} \inf_{(x_{z1}, x_{z2})} ((x - x_d) P(A_x) - \lambda x)$$

Case 4
$$\frac{1}{\lambda} \inf_{[x_{z2}, x_u]} (v(x) - \lambda x) = \frac{1}{\lambda} \inf_{[x_{z2}, x_u]} ((x - x_d) P(A_x) - \lambda x)$$

Case 5

$$\frac{1}{\lambda}\inf_{[x_u,\infty)}(v(x)-\lambda x)=\frac{1}{\lambda}\inf_{[x_u,\infty)}((x-x_d)P(\overline{A})+(x-x_u)P(\overline{B})-\lambda x)$$

Obviously, Case 2 dominates Case 1 in the sense that its minimum is lower. In Case 3, by the continuity of $v(x)$, we have:

$$\frac{1}{\lambda}\inf_{(x_{z1},x_{z2})}((x-x_d)P(A_x)-\lambda x)\leq\frac{1}{\lambda}((x_{z1}-x_d)P(A_{x_{z1}})-\lambda x_{z1})=-x_{z1}$$

The last equality comes from the fact $P(A_{x_{z1}})=0$: As in Lemma 3.8, we know that when $x=x_{z1}$, the three-line configuration $X=x_d\mathbb{I}_A+x\mathbb{I}_B+x_u\mathbb{I}_D$ degenerates to the two-line configuration $X=x_{z1}\mathbb{I}_B+x_u\mathbb{I}_D$, where $a_{x_{z1}}=\infty$. Therefore, Case 3 dominates Case 2. In Case 5:

$$\begin{aligned}\frac{1}{\lambda}\inf_{[x_u,\infty)}(v(x)-\lambda x)&=\frac{1}{\lambda}\inf_{[x_u,\infty)}((x-x_d)P(\overline{A})+(x-x_u)P(\overline{B})-\lambda x)\\&=\frac{1}{\lambda}\inf_{[x_u,\infty)}((1-\lambda)x-x_dP(\overline{A})-x_uP(\overline{B}))\\&=\frac{1}{\lambda}((1-\lambda)x_u-x_dP(\overline{A})-x_uP(\overline{B}))\\&=\frac{1}{\lambda}((x_u-x_d)P(\overline{A})-\lambda x_u)\\&\geq\frac{1}{\lambda}\inf_{[x_{z2},x_u]}((x-x_d)P(A_x)-\lambda x)\end{aligned}$$

Therefore, Case 4 dominates Case 5. When $x\in[x_{z2},x_u]$ and ess sup $\frac{d\widetilde{P}}{dP}>\frac{1}{\lambda}$, Theorem 3.10 and Theorem 3.11 imply that the infimum in Case 4 is achieved either by $\overline{X}$ or X^*. Since we restrict $z\in(z^*,\overline{z}]$ where $z^*=\overline{z}$ by Definition 3.12 in the first case, we need not consider this case in the current proposition. In the second case, Lemma 3.4 implies that $x^*<x_{z2}$ (because $z>z^*$). By the convexity of $v(x)$, and then the continuity of $v(x)$:

$$\begin{aligned}\frac{1}{\lambda}\inf_{[x_{z2},x_u]}((x-x_d)P(A_x)-\lambda x)&=\frac{1}{\lambda}((x_{z2}-x_d)P(A_{x_{z2}})-\lambda x_{z2})\\&\geq\frac{1}{\lambda}\inf_{(x_{z1},x_{z2})}((x-x_d)P(A_x)-\lambda x)\end{aligned}$$

Therefore, Case 3 dominates Case 4. We have shown that Case 3 actually provides the global infimum:

$$\frac{1}{\lambda}\inf_{x\in\mathbb{R}}(v(x)-\lambda x)=\frac{1}{\lambda}\inf_{(x_{z1},x_{z2})}(v(x)-\lambda x)$$

Now, we focus on $x\in(x_{z1},x_{z2})$, where $X(x)=x_d\mathbb{I}_{A_x}+x\mathbb{I}_{B_x}+x_u\mathbb{I}_{D_x}$ satisfies the general constraints:

$$E[X(x)]=x_dP(A_x)+xP(B_x)+x_uP(D_x)=z$$
$$\widetilde{E}[X(x)]=x_d\widetilde{P}(A_x)+x\widetilde{P}(B_x)+x_u\widetilde{P}(D_x)=x_r$$

and the definition for sets A_x, B_x and D_x are:

$$A_x=\left\{\omega\in\Omega:\frac{d\widetilde{P}}{dP}(\omega)>a_x\right\},B_x=\left\{\omega\in\Omega:b_x\leq\frac{d\widetilde{P}}{dP}(\omega)\leq a_x\right\},D_x=\left\{\omega\in\Omega:\frac{d\widetilde{P}}{dP}(\omega)<b_x\right\}$$

Note that $v(x)=(x-x_d)P(A_x)$ (see Theorem 3.10). Since $P(A_x)+P(B_x)+P(D_x)=1$ and $\widetilde{P}(A_x)+\widetilde{P}(B_x)+\widetilde{P}(D_x)=1$, we rewrite the capital and return constraints as:

$$x-z=(x-x_d)P(A_x)+(x-x_u)P(D_x)$$
$$x-x_r=(x-x_d)\widetilde{P}(A_x)+(x-x_u)\widetilde{P}(D_x)$$

Differentiating both sides with respect to x, we get:

$$P(B_x) = (x - x_d)\frac{dP(A_x)}{dx} + (x - x_u)\frac{dP(D_x)}{dx}$$
$$\widetilde{P}(B_x) = (x - x_d)\frac{d\widetilde{P}(A_x)}{dx} + (x - x_u)\frac{d\widetilde{P}(D_x)}{dx}$$

Since:

$$\frac{d\widetilde{P}(A_x)}{dx} = a_x \frac{dP(A_x)}{dx}, \quad \frac{d\widetilde{P}(D_x)}{dx} = b_x \frac{dP(D_x)}{dx}$$

we get:

$$\frac{dP(A_x)}{dx} = \frac{\widetilde{P}(B_x) - bP(B_x)}{(x - x_d)(a - b)}$$

Therefore:

$$\begin{aligned}(v(x) - \lambda x)' &= P(A_x) + (x - x_d)\frac{dP(A_x)}{dx} - \lambda \\ &= P(A_x) + \frac{\widetilde{P}(B_x) - bP(B_x)}{a - b} - \lambda\end{aligned}$$

When the above derivative is zero, we arrive at the first order Euler condition:

$$P(A_x) + \frac{\widetilde{P}(B_x) - bP(B_x)}{a - b} - \lambda = 0$$

To be precise, the above differentiation should be replaced by left-hand and right-hand derivatives, as detailed in the Proof for Corollary 2.8 in Li and Xu [22]. However, the first order Euler condition will turn out to be the same, because we have assumed that the Radon–Nikodým derivative, $\frac{d\widetilde{P}}{dP}$, has continuous distribution.

To finish this proof, we need to show that there exists an $x \in (x_{z1}, x_{z2})$ where the first order Euler condition is satisfied. From Lemma 3.8, we know that as $x \searrow x_{z1}$, $a_x \nearrow \infty$ and $P(A_x) \searrow 0$. Therefore:

$$\lim_{x \searrow x_{z1}} (v(x) - \lambda x)' = -\lambda < 0$$

As $x \nearrow x_{z2}$, $b_x \searrow 0$ and $P(D_x) \searrow 0$. Therefore:

$$\lim_{x \nearrow x_{z2}} (v(x) - \lambda x)' = P(A_{x_{z2}}) - \frac{\widetilde{P}(A^c_{x_{z2}})}{a_{x_{z2}}} - \lambda$$

This derivative coincides with the derivative of the value function of the two-line configuration that is optimal on the interval, $x \in [x_{z2}, x_u]$, provided in Theorem 3.10 (see Proof for Corollary 2.8 in Li and Xu [22]). Again, when $x \in [x_{z2}, x_u]$ and ess sup $\frac{d\widetilde{P}}{dP} > \frac{1}{\lambda}$, Theorem 3.10 and Theorem 3.11 imply that the infimum of $v(x) - \lambda x$ is achieved either by $\overline{X}$ or X^*. Since we restrict $z \in (z^*, \overline{z}]$ where $z^* = \overline{z}$ by Definition 3.12 in the first case, we need not consider this case in the current proposition. In the second case, Lemma 3.4 implies that $x^* < x_{z2}$ (because $z > z^*$). This, in turn, implies:

$$P(A_{x_{z2}}) - \frac{\widetilde{P}(A^c_{x_{z2}})}{a_{x_{z2}}} - \lambda < 0$$

We have just shown that there exist some $x^{**} \in (x_{z1}, x_{z2})$, such that $(v(x) - \lambda x)'|_{x=x^{**}} = 0$. By the convexity of $v(x) - \lambda x$, this is the point where it obtains the minimum value. Now:

$$\begin{aligned}CVaR(X^{**}) &= \tfrac{1}{\lambda}(v(x^{**}) - \lambda x^{**}) \\ &= \tfrac{1}{\lambda}((x^{**} - x_d)P(A^{**}) - \lambda x^{**})\end{aligned}$$

◇

A.7. Proof of Theorem 3.15

Case 3 and 4 are already proven in Theorem 3.11 and Proposition 3.14. In Case 1, where ess sup $\frac{d\tilde{P}}{dP} \le \frac{1}{\lambda}$ and $z = x_r$, $X = x_r$ is both feasible and optimal by Theorem 3.11. In Case 2, fix arbitrary $\epsilon > 0$. We will look for a two-line solution $X_\epsilon = x_\epsilon \mathbb{I}_{A_\epsilon} + \alpha_\epsilon \mathbb{I}_{B_\epsilon}$ with the right parameters, $a_\epsilon, x_\epsilon, \alpha_\epsilon$, which satisfies both the capital constraint and return constraint:

$$E[X_\epsilon] = x_\epsilon P(A_\epsilon) + \alpha_\epsilon P(B_\epsilon) = z \tag{20}$$

$$\tilde{E}[X_\epsilon] = x_\epsilon \tilde{P}(A_\epsilon) + \alpha_\epsilon \tilde{P}(B_\epsilon) = x_r \tag{21}$$

where:

$$A_\epsilon = \left\{ \omega \in \Omega : \frac{d\tilde{P}}{dP}(\omega) > a_\epsilon \right\}, B_\epsilon = \left\{ \omega \in \Omega : \frac{d\tilde{P}}{dP}(\omega) \le a_\epsilon \right\}$$

and produces a CVaR level close to the lower bound:

$$CVaR(X_\epsilon) \le CVaR(x_r) + \epsilon = -x_r + \epsilon.$$

First, we choose $x_\epsilon = x_r - \epsilon$. To find the remaining two parameters, a_ϵ and α_ϵ, so that Equations (20) and (21) are satisfied, we note:

$$x_r P(A_\epsilon) + x_r P(B_\epsilon) = x_r$$
$$x_r \tilde{P}(A_\epsilon) + x_r \tilde{P}(B_\epsilon) = x_r$$

and conclude that it is equivalent to finding a pair of a_ϵ and α_ϵ, such that the following two equalities are satisfied:

$$-\epsilon P(A_\epsilon) + (\alpha_\epsilon - x_r) P(B_\epsilon) = \gamma$$
$$-\epsilon \tilde{P}(A_\epsilon) + (\alpha_\epsilon - x_r) \tilde{P}(B_\epsilon) = 0$$

where we denote $\gamma = z - x_r$. If we can find a solution, a_ϵ, to the equation:

$$\frac{\tilde{P}(B_\epsilon)}{P(B_\epsilon)} = \frac{\epsilon}{\gamma + \epsilon} \tag{22}$$

then:

$$\alpha_\epsilon = x_r + \frac{\tilde{P}(A_\epsilon)}{\tilde{P}(B_\epsilon)} \epsilon$$

and we have the solutions for Equations (20) and (21). It is not difficult to prove that the fraction, $\frac{\tilde{P}(B)}{P(B)}$, increases continuously from zero to one as a increases from zero to $\frac{1}{\lambda}$. Therefore, we can find a solution, $a_\epsilon \in \left(0, \frac{1}{\lambda}\right)$, where Equation (22) is satisfied. By definition Equation (3):

$$CVaR_\lambda(X_\epsilon) = \frac{1}{\lambda} \inf_{x \in \mathbb{R}} \left(E\left[(x - X_\epsilon)^+\right] - \lambda x \right) \le \frac{1}{\lambda} \left(E\left[(x_\epsilon - X_\epsilon)^+\right] - \lambda x_\epsilon \right) = -x_\epsilon$$

The difference:

$$CVaR_\lambda(X_\epsilon) - CVaR(x_r) \le -x_\epsilon + x_r = \epsilon$$

Under Assumption 2.1, the solution in Case 2 is almost surely unique; the result is proven. ⋄

Proof of Theorem 3.17. Case 1 and 3 are obviously true in light of Theorem 3.16. The proof for Case 2 is similar to that in the Proof of Theorem 3.15, so we will not repeat it here. Since $E[X^*] = z^* < z$ in Case 4, $CVaR(X^*)$ is only a lower bound in this case. We first show that it is the true infimum obtained in Case 4. Fix arbitrary $\epsilon > 0$. We will look for a three-line solution $X_\epsilon = x_d \mathbb{I}_{A_\epsilon} + x_\epsilon \mathbb{I}_{B_\epsilon} + \alpha_\epsilon \mathbb{I}_{D_\epsilon}$ with the right parameters $a_\epsilon, b_\epsilon, x_\epsilon, \alpha_\epsilon$, which satisfies the general constraints:

$$E[X_\epsilon] = x_d P(A_\epsilon) + x_\epsilon P(B_\epsilon) + \alpha_\epsilon P(D_\epsilon) = z \tag{23}$$

$$\widetilde{E}[X_\epsilon] = x_d \widetilde{P}(A_\epsilon) + x_\epsilon \widetilde{P}(B_\epsilon) + \alpha_\epsilon \widetilde{P}(D_\epsilon) = x_r \tag{24}$$

where:

$$A_\epsilon = \left\{ \omega \in \Omega : \frac{d\widetilde{P}}{dP}(\omega) > a_\epsilon \right\}, B_\epsilon = \left\{ \omega \in \Omega : b_\epsilon \le \frac{d\widetilde{P}}{dP}(\omega) \le a_\epsilon \right\}, D_\epsilon = \left\{ \omega \in \Omega : \frac{d\widetilde{P}}{dP}(\omega) < b_\epsilon \right\}$$

and produces a CVaR level close to the lower bound:

$$CVaR(X_\epsilon) \le CVaR(X^*) + \epsilon$$

First, we choose $a_\epsilon = a^*$, $A_\epsilon = A^*$, $x_\epsilon = x^* - \delta$, where we define $\delta = \frac{\lambda}{\lambda - P(A^*)} \epsilon$. To find the remaining two parameters, b_ϵ and α_ϵ, so that Equation (23) and (24) are satisfied, we note:

$$E[X^*] = x_d P(A^*) + x^* P(B^*) = z^*$$
$$\widetilde{E}[X^*] = x_d \widetilde{P}(A^*) + x^* \widetilde{P}(B^*) = x_r$$

and conclude that it is equivalent to finding a pair of b_ϵ and α_ϵ, such that the following two equalities are satisfied:

$$-\delta(P(B^*) - P(D_\epsilon)) + (\alpha_\epsilon - x^*) P(D_\epsilon) = \gamma$$
$$-\delta\left(\widetilde{P}(B^*) - \widetilde{P}(D_\epsilon)\right) + (\alpha_\epsilon - x^*) \widetilde{P}(D_\epsilon) = 0$$

where we denote $\gamma = z - z^*$. If we can find a solution, b_ϵ, to the equation:

$$\frac{\widetilde{P}(D_\epsilon)}{P(D_\epsilon)} = \frac{\widetilde{P}(B^*)}{\frac{\gamma}{\delta} + P(B^*)} \tag{25}$$

then:

$$\alpha_\epsilon = x^* + \left(\frac{\widetilde{P}(B^*)}{\widetilde{P}(D_\epsilon)} - 1 \right) \delta$$

and we have the solutions for Equations (23) and (24). It is not difficult to prove that the fraction, $\frac{\widetilde{P}(D)}{P(D)}$, increases continuously from zero to $\frac{\widetilde{P}(B^*)}{P(B^*)}$ as b increases from zero to a^*. Therefore, we can find a solution, $b_\epsilon \in (0, a^*)$, where Equation (25) is satisfied. By definition Equation (3):

$$\begin{aligned} CVaR_\lambda(X_\epsilon) &= \tfrac{1}{\lambda} \inf_{x \in \mathbb{R}} \left(E\left[(x - X_\epsilon)^+\right] - \lambda x \right) \\ &\le \tfrac{1}{\lambda} \left(E\left[(x_\epsilon - X_\epsilon)^+\right] - \lambda x_\epsilon \right) \\ &= \tfrac{1}{\lambda} (x_\epsilon - x_d) P(A_\epsilon) - x_\epsilon \end{aligned}$$

The difference:

$$\begin{aligned} CVaR_\lambda(X_\epsilon) - CVaR(X^*) &\le \tfrac{1}{\lambda}(x_\epsilon - x_d) P(A_\epsilon) - x_\epsilon - \tfrac{1}{\lambda}(x^* - x_d) P(A^*) + x^* \\ &= \tfrac{1}{\lambda}(x^* - x_d)(P(A_\epsilon) - P(A^*)) + \left(1 - \tfrac{P(A_\epsilon)}{\lambda}\right)(x^* - x_\epsilon) = \epsilon \end{aligned}$$

Under Assumption 2.1, the solution in Case 4 is almost surely unique; the result is proven. ◊

References

1. H. Markowitz. "Portfolio selection." *J. Financ.* 7 (1952): 77–91.

2. T. Bielecki, H. Jin, S.R. Pliska, and X.Y. Zhou. "Continuous-time mean-variance portfolio selection with bankruptcy prohibition." *Math. Financ.* 15 (2005): 213–244. [CrossRef]
3. R.T. Rockafellar, and S. Uryasev. "Optimization of conditional value-at-risk." *J. Risk* 2 (2000): 21–51.
4. R.T. Rockafellar, and S. Uryasev. "Conditional value-at-risk for general loss distributions." *J. Bank. Financ.* 26 (2002): 1443–1471. [CrossRef]
5. C. Acerbi, and D. Tasche. "On the coherence of expected shortfall." *J. Bank. Financ.* 26 (2002): 1487–1503. [CrossRef]
6. P. Artzner, F. Delbaen, J.-M. Eber, and D. Heath. "Thinking coherently." *Risk* 10 (1997): 68–71.
7. P. Artzner, F. Delbaen, J.-M. Eber, and D. Heath. "Coherent measures of risk." *Math. Financ.* 9 (1999): 203–228. [CrossRef]
8. C. Acerbi, and P. Simonetti. *Portfolio Optimization with Spectral Measures of Risk*. Working Paper; Milan, Italy: Abaxbank, 2002.
9. A. Adam, M. Houkari, and J.P. Laurent. "Spectral risk measures and portfolio selection." *J. Bank. Financ.* 32 (2008): 1870–1882. [CrossRef]
10. A.S. Cherny. "Weighted V@R and its properties." *Financ. Stoch.* 10 (2006): 367–393. [CrossRef]
11. A. Ruszczyński, and A. Shapiro. "Conditional risk mapping." *Math. Oper. Res.* 31 (2006): 544–561. [CrossRef]
12. R. Gandy. "Portfolio Optimization With Risk Constraints." Ph.D. Thesis, University of Ulm, Ulm, Germany, July 2005.
13. H. Zheng. "Efficient frontier of utility and CVaR." *Math. Methods Oper. Res.* 70 (2009): 129–148. [CrossRef]
14. A.G. Quaranta, and A. Zaffaroni. "Robust optimization of conditional value at risk and portfolio selection." *J. Bank. Financ.* 32 (2008): 2046–2056. [CrossRef]
15. J.Y. Gotoh, K. Shinozaki, and A. Takeda. "Robust portfolio techniques for mitigating the fragility of CVaR minimization and generalization to coherent risk measures." *Quant. Financ.* 13 (2013): 1621–1635. [CrossRef]
16. D. Huang, S. Zhu, F.J. Fabozzi, and M. Fukushima. "Portfolio selection under distributional uncertainty: A relative robust CVaR approach." *Eur. J. Oper. Res.* 203 (2010): 185–194. [CrossRef]
17. N. El Karoui, A.E.B. Lim, and G.Y. Vahn. "Performance-Based Regularization in Mean-CVaR Portfolio Optimization." Working Paper. 2012. Available online: http://arxiv.org/abs/1111.2091 (accessed on 6 August 2013).
18. V. Acharya, L. Pedersen, T. Philippon, and M. Richardson. *Measuring Systemic Risk*. Working Paper; Cleveland, OH, U.S.A.: Federal Reserve Bank of Cleveland, 2010.
19. C. Chen, G. Iyengar, and C.C. Moallemi. "An axiomatic approach to systemic risk." *Manag. Sci.* 59 (2013): 1373–1388. [CrossRef]
20. T. Adrian, and M.K. Brunnermeier. *CoVaR*. Working Paper No. w17454; Princeton, NJ, USA: National Bureau of Economic Research, 2011.
21. J. Sekine. "Dynamic minimization of worst conditional expectation of shortfall." *Math. Financ.* 14 (2004): 605–618. [CrossRef]
22. J. Li, and M. Xu. "Risk minimizing portfolio optimization and hedging with conditional value-at-risk." *Rev. Futures Mark.* 16 (2008): 471–506.
23. A. Melnikov, and I. Smirnov. "Dynamic hedging of conditional value-at-risk." *Insur.: Math. Econ.* 51 (2012): 182–190. [CrossRef]
24. A. Schied. "On the Neyman–Pearson problem for law-invariant risk measures and robust utility functionals." *Ann. Appl. Probab.* 14 (2004): 1398–1423. [CrossRef]
25. X.D. He, and X.Y. Zhou. "Portfolio choice via quantiles." *Eur. J. Oper. Res.* 203 (2011): 185–194. [CrossRef]
26. H. Föllmer, and P. Leukert. "Efficient hedging: Cost versus shortfall risk." *Financ. Stoch.* 4 (2000): 117–146.
27. F. Delbaen, and W. Schachermayer. "A general version of the fundamental theorem of asset pricing." *Math. Ann.* 300 (1994): 463–520. [CrossRef]
28. P. Krokhmal, J. Palmquist, and S. Uryasev. "Portfolio optimization with CVaR objective and constraints." *J. Risk* 4 (2001): 43–68.
29. M. Xu. "Minimizing shortfall risk using duality approach—An application to partial hedging in incomplete markets." Ph.D. Thesis, Carnegie Mellon University, Pittsburgh, PA, USA, April 2004.
30. D. Kramkov. "Optional decomposition of supermartingales and hedging contingent claims in incomplete security markets." *Probab. Theory Relat. Fields* 105 (1996): 459–479. [CrossRef]

31. H. Föllmer, and Y.M. Kabanov. "Optional decomposition and Lagrange multipliers." *Financ. Stoch.* 2 (1998): 69–81.
32. B. Rudloff. "Convex hedging in incomplete markets." *Appl. Math. Financ.* 14 (2007): 437–452. [CrossRef]

 © 2013 by the authors. Licensee MDPI, Basel, Switzerland. This article is an open access article distributed under the terms and conditions of the Creative Commons Attribution (CC BY) license (http://creativecommons.org/licenses/by/4.0/).

Article
A Welfare Analysis of Capital Insurance

Ekaterina Panttser and Weidong Tian *

Belk College of Business, University of North Carolina at Charlotte, Charlotte, NC 28223, USA; epanttse@uncc.edu (E.P.)
* Author to whom correspondence should be addressed; wtian1@uncc.edu; Tel.:(1)-704-687-7702; Fax.: (1)-704-687-6987.

Received: 26 July 2013; in revised form: 29 August 2013; Accepted: 6 September 2013; Published: 17 September 2013

Abstract: This paper presents a welfare analysis of several capital insurance programs in a rational expectation equilibrium setting. We first explicitly characterize the equilibrium of each capital insurance program. Then, we demonstrate that a capital insurance program based on aggregate loss is better than classical insurance, when big financial institutions have similar expected loss exposures. By contrast, classical insurance is more desirable when the bank's individual risk is consistent with the expected loss in a precise way. Our analysis shows that a capital insurance program is a useful tool to hedge systemic risk from the regulatory perspective.

Keywords: capital insurance; welfare; equilibrium

1. Introduction

This paper presents a welfare analysis of recently proposed capital insurance programs in a rational expected equilibrium setting. The idea of capital insurance is motivated by the desire to resolve "too big to fail" issues. As those "too big to fail" banks or companies that are "financial in nature" (hereafter, banks)[1] expect capital injection from the central bank in times of financial distress, the banks might act in a risk-taking manner and put the central bank, the regulator and all taxpayers in a fragile financial position. In a capital insurance program (see [11]), the bank pays some amount as a premium or reserve to the central bank, which, in turn, would inject funds into the banks during future financial failures. A capital insurance program is motivated by the desire to protect taxpayers and the economy as a whole in the presence of a big financial predicament. Our purpose is to study whether this capital insurance idea works or not from the perspective of its welfare.

Capital insurance is very different from the current capital regulation implemented in BASEL II and BASEL III. It is also different from the Dodd-Frank Act, which posits several prudential standards and new stringent capital requirements to banks with systemic risks. According to the capital regulation requirement, the amount of capital reserve or the economic capital amount depends on the risk of the loss portfolio and the riskiness of the bank itself. The riskier the bank, the higher the economic capital; the economic capital is higher for a bank with a weak credit situation than for a strong counterpart, while assuming the portfolio to be identically the same. Therefore, the economic capital idea depends on both the individual bank's riskiness and the individual loss portfolio.

By contrast, capital insurance, in essence, is an insurance contract, and the capital insurance idea casts all banks together at the market level. On the one side, the central bank is an insurer of

---

[1] Under the standards set forth in section 113 of the Dodd-Frank Act, a bank holding company or "non-bank financial company" poses a potential systemic risk if "material financial distress at the company, or the nature, scope, size, scale, concentration, interconnectedness, or mix of the activities of the company, could pose a threat to the financial stability of the United States." Therefore, we focus only on these companies with systemic risks (too big to fail).

the contract and receives an insurance premium with the obligation to inject funds to save the bank in financial distress. On the other side, the bank is an insured in this contract agreement. As the central bank represents the taxpayer in this structure, the insurer of the contract is a taxpayer, and the premium represents a special purpose tax in the sense described by Acharya et al. [1]. In contrast to the traditional insurance contract, the contract redemption is contingent on the aggregate loss, and the insured event is contingent on a systematic event in the economy.

The rational expected equilibrium of the capital insurance program is explained as follows. The central bank issues insurance contracts to the banks, and the banks purchase these contracts, which are placed on the market. The central bank predicts the correct optimal demand from the banks with a given premium structure, so the central bank maximizes the welfare with the premium structure as characterized. Consequently, both the demand (from the banks) and the supply (from the central bank) are determined uniquely in a rational expectation equilibrium.

In this paper, we assume that the insurance contract payout has been placed as proposed by the capital insurance program. Therefore, we do not address the optimal capital insurance design problem. Instead, we consider two capital insurance programs. In the first one, the insurance contract insures the *aggregate loss* of all banks. In the second one, each bank buys insurance that depends on the aggregate loss of all banks, except for the insured bank's own loss portfolio. For comparison purposes, we further consider the situation in which each bank purchases insurance that relies on its own loss portfolio. This is "classical insurance" by the terminology in this paper, and it has the same indemnity as the traditional coinsurance contract. As the premium structure depends on all the loss portfolios of the banks, those loss portfolios together affect each bank's coinsurance demand. Therefore, classical insurance in our setting is different from the traditional coinsurance contract in equilibrium.

We demonstrate that many factors affect the welfare analysis and the chosen capital insurance program. *First*, the proposed two capital insurance programs are distinguished from each other by the correlation structure. A low correlation environment ensures the low welfare of the contract based on the aggregate loss, except for the individual bank's loss. Therefore, the aggregate insurance is better than the other one. In fact, when each loss portfolio can be observed completely by all banks and the central bank and the bank does not manipulate the book loss, aggregate insurance ensures a higher welfare than another one, in general.

Second, both the specific risk and the systematic risk components of the individual loss are important ingredients for comparing the classical insurance and the aggregate insurance contracts. These two components play a crucial role in the classical demand analysis of the coinsurance contract (for the mean-variance insured); see [9]. We demonstrate that the way in which each bank's specific risk and systematic risk components behave together in the market has a significant effect on the comparison analysis. When a higher individual risk corresponds to a higher expected loss per each volatility unit, we say that the market displays an *ordering loss market*. Otherwise, the market is a *disordering loss market*.[2] We show that classical insurance works better in the ordering loss market, while aggregate insurance is more beneficial to the central bank in the disordering loss market. Hence, our result is significantly disparate from the optimal sharing rules in a pure exchange market.[3] The optimal insuring rule, in our equilibrium, relies on the aggregate loss portfolio in a more complicated way. Literally, the way in which the loss portfolios are connected to each other implies a different welfare outcome of the insurance program.

Third, the way in which the systematic risk is distributed among each bank is also captious for a comparative welfare analysis of the insurance contracts. If each bank contributes equally or

---

[2] Precisely, when a risk-adjusted covariance of the loss portfolio is co-monotonic to the Sharpe ratio of the loss portfolio, we say it is an ordering loss market. If both of these sequences are counter-monotonic to each other, we say that the market is a disordering loss market. See Propositions 4, 6 and 7 below.

[3] By [4], the optimal sharing rules must increase with respect to the aggregate endowment. Our setting is different from Borch's equilibrium setting in the presence of the central bank.

very closely to each other in the total systematic risk, we show that aggregate insurance ensures a higher welfare. Therefore, it is a more desirable insurance program than the classical insurance one. Wagner [14] shows that diversification might enhance systemic risk, while it reduces each institution's individual probability of failure; so, a full diversification is not always beneficial from the systemic perspective. According to our result, aggregate insurance offers a solution in a full diversification situation to reduce the systemic risk.

The remainder of the paper is organized as follows. Section 2 introduces the setting and characterizes the equilibrium. Section 3 presents the comparison of three types of capital insurance programs by the welfare analysis developed in the equilibrium. Section 4 offers a discussion and the implications of our theoretical results. Moreover, we explain how to implement the capital insurance program in practice and how to identify the "too big to fail" banks from the regulatory perspective. Section 5 briefly describes the conclusions of the analysis conducted. All proofs are stated in Appendix A, and Appendix B presents the equilibrium in a general situation and identifies these "too big to fail" banks by using this capital insurance program.

2. The Model

There are N big banks indexed by $i = 1, \cdots, N$ in a one-period economic world. Each bank is endowed with a loss portfolio, $X_1, \cdots, X_N$, respectively. These loss portfolios are defined on the same state space Ω, and all banks have the same beliefs on the nature of state. This common belief is represented by one probability measure, P, on the state space. However, these bank's loss portfolios can be significantly different. We assume that each bank is risk-averse, and the preference of risk is interpreted by a utility function, $U_i(\cdot)$. The bank's initial wealth is given by W_0^i for each bank, $i = 1, \cdots, N$, respectively.

There is a government entity, such as the Financial Stability Oversight Council (FSOC) in the Dodd-Frank Act or a central bank, which sells the insurance contract to each bank. Each bank is either voluntarily or enforced to purchase the insurance contract by paying a particular amount as a premium, and a fund commitment is guaranteed by a central bank in a bad business situation in the future. The premium amount can be treated as a special tax purpose rate for each bank as suggested by Acharya et al. [1]. The fund commitment offered by the government entity is the indemnity of the insurance. Alternatively, these insurance contracts can be issued by a reinsurance company which is able to diversify the reinsurance risk. For simplicity, we name the insurer as a *regulator*.

The prototype insurance structure has the indemnity, $I_i(X, X_i)$, which depends on the individual book loss, X_i, and the aggregate loss, X. The aggregate loss $X = \sum_{i=1}^{N} X_i$. This insurance contract is called "capital insurance", as it depends on the aggregate loss being realized in the future. The capital insurance contract is different from the classical contracts in which $I_i(X, X_i)$ is irrelevant to the aggregate loss, X, and, instead, depends on the individual loss, X_i. Following the classical insurance literature ([2,13]), we assume that the insurance premium is determined by $(1 + \rho)\mathbb{E}[I(X, X_i)]$, where ρ is a load factor. For simplicity, we assume that the loss factor is the same across the bank industry, but it is possible to consider a bank-specific premium structure in the extended analysis. The loss factor is characterized by the regulator in equilibrium, which will be explained shortly.

Given a load factor, ρ, each bank chooses the best available insurance contract to maximize the expected utility (see [2]):

$$\mathbb{E}\left[U_i(W^i)\right] = \mathbb{E}\left[U_i\left(W_0^i - X_i + I_i(X, X_i) - (1+\rho)\mathbb{E}[I_i(X, X_i)]\right)\right] \tag{1}$$

The regulator is risk-neutral and receives the premium for each contract. The welfare of the regulator is:

$$W^r = \sum_i (1+\rho)\mathbb{E}[I_i(X, X_i)] - \sum_i I_i(X, X_i) - \sum_i c(I_i(X, X_i)) \tag{2}$$

where $c(I_i(X, X_i))$ represents the cost for the regulator to issue the contract, $I_i(X, X_i)$. The cost can be fixed, a constant percentage of the indemnity or can depend on a drastic market event. To focus on the analysis of the insurance program, we assume that the cost structure is a constant for each bank. The regulator's objective is to determine the best premium structure given the optimal demand for each bank (with any, a given load structure, ρ), as well as to maximize the expected welfare. Clearly, the insurance $I_i^*(X, X_i)$ in equilibrium depends on both the demand (from all banks) and the supply (from the regulator) and relies on the load factor, ρ^*, proposed by the regulator. We do not distinguish between the welfare and the expected welfare when there is no confusion in the rest of this paper.

In this paper, we focus on the following three capital insurance programs:

- *Aggregate Insurance*: $I_i(X, X_i) = \beta_i X$, where $\beta_i \geq 0$.
- *Classical Insurance*: $I_i(X, X_i) = \beta_i X_i$, where $\beta_i \geq 0$.
- *Aggregate-Cross Insurance*: $I_i(X, X_i) = \beta_i \hat{X}_i$, where $\hat{X}_i = \sum_{j \neq i} X_j$ is the total loss, except for the insured bank's loss, and $\beta_i \geq 0$.

In each case, bank i chooses the best coinsurance parameter, β_i. The optimal β is written as $\beta(\rho)$ to highlight its dependence on the load factor. The first insurance contract depends solely on the aggregate loss, X, so it is called "aggregate insurance". The coinsurance parameter, β_i, represents the percentage of the aggregate loss that is insured for the bank, i. Clearly, this coinsurance parameter depends on how much the individual bank's loss risk contributes to the aggregate loss, as will be seen later. The second insurance contract is a standard one, initiated by [2], and is termed "classical insurance". However, the premium structure in the traditional insurance contract is either given exogenously or depends on the specific loss portfolio in equilibrium. Therefore, our classical insurance is different from those traditional insurance contracts in a rational expectation equilibrium. The last insurance contract is motivated differently. Because of the possibility of the bank's manipulation of the loss report on X_i, as discussed in [6] in a similar context, there is a moral hazard issue in case $I_i(X, X_i)$ is related to X_i. To resolve it, Kashyap et al. [11] introduces the aggregate-cross insurance idea in which the bank insures the total risks of all banks, except for the bank's own risk. The aggregate-cross insurance contract is inspired by the idea outlined in [11].

In what follows, we impose two assumptions to simplify the discussions.

Assumption I: Each bank is a mean-variance agent with the reciprocal of the risk aversion parameter, $\gamma_i > 0$. We also assume zero (or constant) cost structure for each contract.[4]

Assumption II: There exists no asymmetric information between each bank and the regulator. The loss portfolio, X_i, is equivalently identified by the bank and the regulator, and both the bank and the regulator make a decision based on the same interpretation of the loss portfolio.

We now move to present our equilibrium analysis on each capital insurance program. We also examine how these loss portfolios affect each insurance contract, as well as the welfare. Moreover, we examine which insurance contract is desirable from the perspectives of the regulator and the bank.

2.1. Aggregate Insurance

We characterize the equilibrium precisely for the aggregate insurance. We start with the bank i's rational decision by assuming that the insurance contract has been placed on the market.

2.1.1. Optimal Load for Bank i

Bank i's objective is to find suitable coinsurance parameter β_i to maximize:

$$\max_{\beta_i \geq 0} \mathbb{E}\left[W^i\right] - \frac{1}{2\gamma_i} Var(W^i) \qquad (3)$$

---

[4] We follow the same mean-variance setting as in [12], in which the aggregate uncertainty insurance is considered, as we focus on the aggregate or systematic risk.

where $W^i = W_0^i - X_i + \beta_i X - (1+\rho)\mathbb{E}[\beta_i X]$ is the terminal wealth for the bank, i. Given the load factor, ρ, the optimal β_i for the bank, i, is[5]:

$$\beta^{i,a}(\rho) = \frac{Cov(X_i, X) - \rho \mathbb{E}(X)\gamma_i}{Var(X)} \tag{4}$$

if $Cov(X_i, X) - \rho \mathbb{E}(X)\gamma_i \geq 0$; otherwise, $\beta^{i,a}(\rho) = 0$. The symbol, "a", represents the "aggregate insurance". We use $\beta^{i,a}(\rho)$ to highlight the effect of the load factor, ρ, for the bank, i.

2.1.2. Optimal Load Factor for the Regulator

The regulator predicates the demand from the bank, i, as $\beta^{i,a}(\rho)X$ correctly for each bank, $i = 1, \cdots, N$. Therefore, by plugging Equation (??) into Equation (??) and assuming that $Cov(X_i, X) \geq \rho \mathbb{E}(X)\gamma_i$, the welfare is:

$$\mathbb{E}(W^r) = \rho \mathbb{E}(X) - \rho^2 \sum_i \frac{\gamma_i \mathbb{E}(X)^2}{Var(X)}. \tag{5}$$

By using Formula (??) and its first-order condition, the best load factor is determined by the regulator as:

$$\rho^{*,a} = \frac{1}{2\sum_i \gamma_i} \frac{Var(X)}{\mathbb{E}(X)}. \tag{6}$$

Consequently, under this premium structure, we obtain the following characterization of the equilibrium.

Proposition 1 *Assume for each* $i = 1, \cdots, N$,

$$\frac{Cov(X_i, X)}{Var(X)} \geq \frac{1}{2} \frac{\gamma_i}{\sum_i \gamma_i}, \tag{7}$$

then, the optimal load factor, $\rho^{*,a}$, is given by Equation (??); the welfare for the aggregate insurance is:

$$\mathbb{E}(W^{*,a}) = \frac{1}{4\sum_i \gamma_i} Var(X) \tag{8}$$

and the best coinsurance parameter for the bank, i, in this aggregate insurance contract is:

$$\beta^{i,a} = \frac{Cov(X_i, X)}{Var(X)} - \frac{1}{2} \frac{\gamma_i}{\sum_i \gamma_i}. \tag{9}$$

Proof: Under Condition Equation (??) and the choice of $\rho^{*,a}$ by Equation (??), we observe that $Cov(X_i, X) \geq \rho \gamma_i E[X]$. Therefore, $\beta^{i,a}(\rho)$ is given by Equation (??), and the equilibrium welfare is obtained in Equation (??). Then, the equilibrium follows from the standard first-order condition. In general, if condition (??) does not hold for each $i = 1, \cdots, N$, it means that $\beta^{i,a}(\rho)$ is a "corner solution", and the equilibrium welfare is changed accordingly. A general solution is presented in Appendix B. □

There are several remarkable points about aggregate insurance by using Proposition 1. *First*, the welfare estimated by the regulator depends on the *variability* of the aggregate loss, the systematic risk. The higher the variability, the higher the expected welfare. The smaller the variability, or alternatively,

---

[5] It is easy to see that $Var(W^i) = Var(X_i) + \beta_i^2 Var(X) - 2\beta_i Cov(X_i, X)$. Then, $\beta^{i,a}(\rho)$ follows from the first-order condition in Equation (??).

the more stable the aggregate loss is, the smaller the welfare. More interestingly, the welfare does not depend on the expected aggregate loss, $\mathbb{E}[X]$. Therefore, only the aggregative risk variability contributes to the welfare. Hence, Proposition 1 supports the aggregate insurance idea to reduce the systemic risk.

Second, the optimal coinsurance parameter, $\beta^{i,a}$, for bank i is the difference between the "beta", $\frac{Cov(X_i,X)}{Var(X)}$,[6] and the individual risk aversion parameter, γ_i, comparing with the total risk aversion among the banks, $\sum_i \gamma_i$. The higher the beta, the larger $\beta^{i,a}$; so the bank, i purchases insurance proportional to the systematic risk. It is intuitively appealing, because a higher beta implies a larger contribution of the bank, i, to the systematic risk or the bank, i, has a higher systemic risk. To hedge the systemic risk, the bank needs to insure a larger amount of the systematic risk. Moreover, the relationship between the bank i's risk aversion and the other bank's risk preferences is also important for the aggregate insurance. Higher $\frac{\gamma_i}{\sum_i \gamma_i}$ implies less risk aversion of the bank, i, and, thus, a smaller β_i.

Third, note that[7]:

$$\sum_i \beta^{i,a} = \tfrac{1}{2}, \tag{10}$$

the total aggregate insurance indemnity for the regulator, is $\sum_i I_i(X, X_i) = \tfrac{1}{2} X$. This states that exactly half of the systematic risk is insured in this program. The number $1/2$ comes from the mean-variance setting and does not have any specific meaning. However, a crucial insight at this point is that the aggregate loss is not fully insured in this equilibrium insurance market, which is similar to the classical result for the standard coinsurance contract.

2.2. Classical Insurance

For comparative purposes, we next consider the classical insurance, $I_i(X, X_i) = \beta_i X_i$. By the same idea, we characterize $\beta^{i,c}(\rho)$, ρ^* and the welfare sequentially. The equilibrium is summarized as follows.

2.2.1. Optimal Load for Bank i

$$\beta^{i,c}(\rho) = \max\left\{1 - \frac{\rho \mathbb{E}(X_i)\gamma_i}{Var(X_i)}, 0\right\} \tag{11}$$

where the symbol, "c", represents "classical insurance".

2.2.2. Optimal Load Factor for the Regulator

Given the above optimal load factor, $\beta^{i,c}(\rho)$, and assuming $\frac{\rho \mathbb{E}(X_i)\gamma_i}{Var(X_i)} \leq 1, i = 1, \cdots, N$, the welfare is obtained as follows.

$$\mathbb{E}(W^r) = \rho \mathbb{E}(X) - \rho^2 \sum_i \frac{\gamma_i \mathbb{E}(X_i)^2}{Var(X_i)} \tag{12}$$

Therefore, the optimal load factor from the regulator's perspective is:

$$\rho^{*,c} = \frac{1}{2} \frac{\mathbb{E}(X)}{\sum_i \frac{\gamma_i (\mathbb{E}(X_i))^2}{Var(X_i)}} \tag{13}$$

We have the following result.

---

[6] It is the beta in the capital asset pricing model when the loss variable is replaced by the return variable.
[7] Since $X = \sum_i X_i$, $\sum_i Cov(X_i, X) = Var(X)$.

Proposition 2 *Assume that for each $i = 1, \cdots, N$:*

$$\frac{\mathbb{E}(X)}{\sum_i \frac{\gamma_i(\mathbb{E}(X_i))^2}{Var(X_i)}} \frac{\gamma_i \mathbb{E}(X_i)}{Var(X_i)} \leq 2, \tag{14}$$

then, the optimal load factor is determined in Equation (??). The welfare of the classical insurance is:

$$\mathbb{E}(W^{*,c}) = \frac{1}{4} \frac{\mathbb{E}(X)^2}{\sum_i \frac{\gamma_i \mathbb{E}(X_i)^2}{Var(X_i)}} \tag{15}$$

and the best coinsurance parameter for the bank, i, in this classical insurance contract is:

$$\beta^{i,c} = 1 - \frac{1}{2} \frac{\mathbb{E}(X)}{\sum_i \frac{\gamma_i(\mathbb{E}(X_i))^2}{Var(X_i)}} \frac{\gamma_i \mathbb{E}(X_i)}{Var(X_i)} \tag{16}$$

Proof: The same as the proof of Proposition 2. □

According to Proposition 2, the welfare estimated by the regulator in classical insurance depends on both the expectation and the variance of individual loss, as well as the expectation of the aggregate loss, whereas the variability of the aggregate loss does not contribute to the estimated welfare directly. In fact, the correlation structure of the loss portfolios, $(X_1, \cdots, X_n)$, is not involved in the insurance contract at all. Therefore, the welfare depends only on the marginal distribution, but not on the joint distribution of the loss portfolios. Obviously, this should be seen as a limitation of classical insurance to address systemic risk. We will compare classical insurance with aggregate insurance in detail in the next section.

It is interesting to look at the optimal coinsurance parameter, β_i, for the bank, i, in the classical insurance contract. While keeping the risks on other banks fixed, the higher $Var(X_i)$, the higher β_i. More insurance is required for a higher individual risk. It is straightforward to verify that for large values of $\mathbb{E}[X_i]$, the optimal coinsurance parameter is increasing with respect to the increase of $\mathbb{E}[X_i]$. As the premium structure depends on all loss portfolios, $\{X_1, \cdots, X_n\}$, the risks of other banks affect the classical insurance demand in this setting[8].

2.3. Aggregate-Cross Insurance

At last, we consider the aggregate-cross insurance $I_i(X, X_i) = \beta_i \hat{X}_i$. By definition, it focuses on the insurance of all banks, except the insured bank in the market.

2.3.1. Optimal Load for Bank i

It is easy to derive $\beta^{i,ac}(\rho)$ in this situation as:

$$\beta^{i,ac}(\rho) = \max\left\{\frac{Cov(X_i, \hat{X}_i) - \rho\mathbb{E}(\hat{X}_i)\gamma_i}{Var(\hat{X}_i)}, 0\right\} \tag{17}$$

where the symbol, "ac", represents "aggregate-cross insurance".

---

[8] It is different from a traditional insurance contract on individual loss exposure. The load factor for a traditional insurance contract is either given exogenously or depends on the specific loss vector in equilibrium. Classical insurance in our setting, however, is characterized in a rational expectation equilibrium with banks and a regulator

2.3.2. Optimal Load Factor for the Regulator

By plugging Formula Equation (??) into Formula (??) and assuming that $Cov(X_i, \hat{X}_i) \geq \rho \mathbb{E}(\hat{X}_i)\gamma_i$, we have:

$$\mathbb{E}(W^r) = \rho \sum_i \mathbb{E}(\hat{X}_i) \frac{Cov(X_i, \hat{X}_i) - \rho \mathbb{E}(\hat{X}_i)\gamma_i}{Var(\hat{X}_i)} \tag{18}$$

and:

$$\rho^{*,ac} = \frac{1}{2} \frac{\sum_i \mathbb{E}(\hat{X}_i) \frac{Cov(X_i, \hat{X}_i)}{Var(\hat{X}_i)}}{\sum_i \frac{\gamma_i \mathbb{E}(\hat{X}_i)^2}{Var(\hat{X}_i)}}. \tag{19}$$

Therefore, we obtain the following proposition, the proof of which is similar to Propositions 1 and 2.

Proposition 3 *Assume for each* $i = 1, \cdots, N$:

$$\frac{\sum_i \mathbb{E}(\hat{X}_i) \frac{Cov(X_i, \hat{X}_i)}{Var(\hat{X}_i)}}{\sum_i \frac{\gamma_i \mathbb{E}(\hat{X}_i)^2}{Var(\hat{X}_i)}} \mathbb{E}(\hat{X}_i)\gamma_i \leq 2 Cov(X_i, \hat{X}_i). \tag{20}$$

Then, the welfare of the aggregate-cross insurance is:

$$\mathbb{E}(W^{*,ac}) = \frac{1}{4} \frac{\left(\sum_i \mathbb{E}(\hat{X}_i) \frac{Cov(X_i, \hat{X}_i)}{Var(\hat{X}_i)}\right)^2}{\sum_i \gamma_i \frac{\mathbb{E}(\hat{X}_i)^2}{Var(\hat{X}_i)}} \tag{21}$$

and the best coinsurance parameter for the bank, i, *in this aggregate-cross insurance contract is:*

$$\beta^{i,ac} = \frac{Cov(X_i, \hat{X}_i)}{Var(\hat{X}_i)} - \frac{1}{2} \frac{\sum_i \mathbb{E}(\hat{X}_i) \frac{Cov(X_i, \hat{X}_i)}{Var(\hat{X}_i)}}{\sum_i \frac{\gamma_i \mathbb{E}(\hat{X}_i)^2}{Var(\hat{X}_i)}} \frac{\mathbb{E}(\hat{X}_i)\gamma_i}{Var(\hat{X}_i)}. \tag{22}$$

By Proposition 3, the expected welfare in an aggregate-cross insurance contract depends positively on the covariance between the individual bank's loss, X_i, and the aggregate loss, except for the insured bank's loss, $\hat{X}_i$, for each bank, i. The intuition is simple: higher correlation coefficient $corr(X_i, \hat{X}_i)$ results in higher expected welfare from the regulator's perspective.

In contrast to classical insurance, aggregate-cross insurance depends on the correlation structure of the loss portfolios. We see easily that when X_i and $\hat{X}_i$ are uncorrelated for each i, both the estimated welfare and the optimal coinsurance β for bank i in this aggregate-cross insurance contract are equal to zero. In particular, when all banks' loss portfolios are independent, there is no necessity to buy the aggregate-cross insurance.

The next result illustrates the main insights of these three insurance contracts when the loss risk factors are uncorrelated. We say one contract is *preferred* to another one, as long as the former has higher welfare than the latter.

Proposition 4 *Assume that the loss portfolios are uncorrelated, i.e.,* $Cov(X_i, X_j) = 0$ $\forall i \neq j$. *Then, both the aggregate insurance and the classical insurance are preferred to the aggregate-cross insurance. Moreover:*

1. If the risk-adjusted variance vector, $\left(\frac{Var(X_i)}{\gamma_i}\right)$, and the Sharpe ratio vector, $\left(\frac{\mathbb{E}[X_i]}{\sqrt{Var(X_i)}}\right)$, are co-monotonic[9], then the classical insurance is preferred to the aggregate insurance.

2. If the risk-adjusted variance vector, $\left(\frac{Var(X_i)}{\gamma_i}\right)$, and the Sharpe ratio vector, $\left(\frac{\mathbb{E}[X_i]}{\sqrt{Var(X_i)}}\right)$, are counter-monotonic, and there exists one "too big to fail" bank in the sense that $\mathbb{E}[X]^2$ is close to $\sum_i \mathbb{E}[X_i]^2$, then the aggregate insurance is preferred to the classical insurance.

Proof: See Appendix A. □

There are several points in Proposition 4. First of all, the relationship between the risk-adjusted variance and the Sharpe ratio across the banks plays a crucial role in comparing classical insurance and aggregate insurance. As each X_i represents the loss portfolio, we assume a positive expected loss in our analysis. Its variance, $Var(X_i)$, represents the individual risk of the bank, i. Similarly, we use the terminology "Sharpe ratio" to represent the expected loss per each volatility unit. Both the risk-adjusted variance, $\frac{Var(X_i)}{\gamma_i}$, and the Sharpe ratio represent two important factors to characterize the loss risk for bank i.

Secondly, when these individual banks' risk-adjusted variance has the same order as the Sharpe ratio, i.e., a higher risk-adjusted variance is consistent with a higher Sharpe ratio, we say that the risk-adjusted variance is co-monotonic to the Sharpe ratio. In this case, the bank sector is in an ordering loss market, because a higher expected loss ensures a higher variance. Proposition 4 states that classical insurance is a better contract from the regulator's perspective in the ordering loss market.

Thirdly, in the disordering loss market in which a higher risk-adjusted variance is always linked to a smaller Sharpe ratio, in the presence of a few banks with very large expected loss, Proposition 4 ensures that aggregate insurance is the more beneficial insurance contract. To explain this, say bank 1 is big enough, such that $\mathbb{E}[X_1] \gg \mathbb{E}[X_2], \cdots, \mathbb{E}[X_n]$[10]. In this case, bank 1's expected loss is so big that the total expected systematic loss, $\mathbb{E}[X]$, is close to $\mathbb{E}[X_1]$; then, $\mathbb{E}[X]^2$ is close enough to $\sum \mathbb{E}[X_i]^2$. Therefore, the aggregate insurance issued to other banks with small losses together would benefit the regulator.

We next move to the more interesting situation in which each loss contributes to the systematic risk, so that these loss portfolios are correlated.

3. Systemic Risk and Comparative Analysis

In this section, we examine closely which insurance contract should be preferred to another one from the perspective of the regulator, as well as the bank. For this purpose, we assume that the contribution of each bank to the market risk is given exogenously. It is natural to examine the question in a one-factor model. A multi-factor model shares the same insights as a one-factor model.

Suppose $X_i = \alpha_i Y + \epsilon_i$, where ϵ_i is white noise with zero mean and variance σ_i^2. Y represents a market (or systematic) risk factor, and each ϵ_i represents the specific risk of bank i. The aggregate loss $X = \sum_i \alpha_i Y + \sum_i \epsilon_i = \alpha Y + \epsilon$, where $\alpha = \sum_{i=1}^n \alpha_i$. Write $\hat{X}_i = \hat{\alpha}_i Y + \hat{\epsilon}_i$, where $\epsilon = \sum_{i=1}^n \epsilon_i, \hat{\alpha}_i = \sum_{j=1, j \neq i}^n \alpha_j, \hat{\epsilon}_i = \sum_{j=1, j \neq i}^n \epsilon_j$.

We first consider one special case for which specific risks equal zero. By using Equations (??), (??) and (??), we have the following result.

---

[9] Given two vectors $a = (a_1, \cdots, a_n), b = (b_1, \cdots, b_n)$, a and b are counter-monotonic if $(a_i - a_j)(b_i - b_j) \leq 0, \forall i, j$, and at least one inequality is strict; a and b are co-monotonic if $(a_i - a_j)(b_i - b_j) \geq 0, \forall i, j$, and at least one inequality is strict.

[10] We write $x \gg y$ to denote $y/x \to 0$.

Proposition 5 *If there is no specific risk in the market, then the welfare is equivalent for all three types of insurance contracts. Precisely, if each $\sigma_i = 0$, then:*

$$\mathbb{E}(W^{*,a}) = \mathbb{E}(W^{*,c}) = \mathbb{E}(W^{*,ac}) = \frac{Var(Y)}{4\sum_i \gamma_i}\alpha^2 > 0 \qquad (23)$$

In general, when the systematic risk factor is highly volatile, that is, $Var(Y)$ is high, then these three contracts offer the same welfare asymptotically. Precisely, when $Var(Y) \to \infty$[11]:

$$\mathbb{E}(W^{*,a}) \sim \mathbb{E}(W^{*,c}) \sim \mathbb{E}(W^{*,ac}) \sim \frac{Var(Y)}{4\sum_i \gamma_i}\alpha^2. \qquad (24)$$

Proof: See Appendix A. □

Proposition 5 states that if $Var(Y)$ is extremely large relative to a company's specific risk, then from the regulator's perspective, the welfare of all three types of insurance contracts is almost identical and positively depends on both $Var(Y)$ and the aggregate contribution of all banks to the market risk, $\sum_i \alpha_i$. Alternatively, when the individual risks are immaterial compared to the systematic risk, these three contracts, in essence, provide the same welfare. Therefore, the capital insurance idea does not work particularly well under some circumstances with an extremely high systematic risk factor or extremely small specific risks.

Proposition 6 *If the risk-adjusted individual risk vector, $\left(\frac{Var(X_i)}{\gamma_i}\right)$, is co-monotonic to the Sharpe ratio vector, $\left(\frac{\mathbb{E}[X_i]}{\sqrt{Var(X_i)}}\right)$, then the classical insurance is preferred to the aggregate insurance in the sense that $\mathbb{E}[W^{*,a}] < \mathbb{E}[W^{*,c}]$.*

If the risk-adjusted individual risk vector, $\left(\frac{Var(X_i)}{\gamma_i}\right)$, is counter-monotonic to the Sharpe ratio vector, $\left(\frac{\mathbb{E}[X_i]}{\sqrt{Var(X_i)}}\right)$, and the expected aggregate loss, $\mathbb{E}[X]$, is large enough, then the aggregate insurance is preferred to the classical insurance in the sense that $\mathbb{E}[W^{*,c}] < \mathbb{E}[W^{*,a}]$.

Proof: See Appendix A. □

Proposition 6 has the same insight as Proposition 4, but Proposition 6 holds in a general correlated market environment. In the ordering loss market, such that a higher risk-adjusted variance corresponds to a Sharpe ratio, classical insurance works better. In the disordering loss market, however, the aggregate insurance contract should be preferred to the classical one when the expected total risk, $\mathbb{E}[X]$, is a big concern. Indeed, both Proposition 4 and Proposition 6 demonstrate in different market situations that aggregate insurance is a good design when the individual risk and the Sharpe ratio display a negative relationship for each bank.

To finish this section, we compare aggregate-cross insurance with classical insurance.

Proposition 7 *If the expected losses across the banks are fairly close, the risk-adjusted variance is co-monotonic to the Sharpe ratio, and the risk-adjusted correlated variance, $\rho_i^2 \frac{Var(X_i)}{\gamma}$, is co-monotonic to the Sharpe ratio of its dual risk, $\frac{\mathbb{E}[\hat{X}_i]}{\sqrt{Var(\hat{X}_i)}}$, where ρ_i is the correlation coefficient between X_i and $\hat{X}_i$ for each $i = 1, \cdots, N$; then $\mathbb{E}[W^{*,ac}] < \mathbb{E}[W^{*,c}]$.*

---

[11] By two functions, $f \sim g$, we mean that $\lim_{Var(Y) \to \infty} \frac{f}{g} = 1$.

Proof: See Appendix A. □

As shown in Proposition 6, the classical insurance is preferred to the aggregative insurance when risk-adjusted variance is co-monotonic to the Sharpe ratio. Therefore, Proposition 7 shows us that both the aggregative-type of insurances (i.e., aggregate and aggregate-cross insurance contracts) are not supportive under the situations described in Proposition 7.

4. Discussion

Under what circumstance should capital insurance programs be implemented and how? In this section, we show several important insights based on our theoretical results.

4.1. Disordering Loss Market and Ordering Loss Market

According to Proposition 4 and Proposition 6, based on our welfare analysis, the aggregate insurance contract should be insured by the regulator in the disordering loss market. When the individual risk of loss, $Var(X_i)$, is mismatched with the expected loss per unit, the loss in each bank displays the disordering loss market.

There are two important situations in which the disordering loss market occurs. The *first* situation is when the contribution to the aggregate loss of each back is fairly close, and each bank has a fairly close preference for risk. In other words, when the aggregate loss is almost equally distributed among the banks, it is a disordering loss market. To see this, we assume $\gamma_i = \gamma$ for all i. Clearly, the risk-adjusted variance, $\frac{Var(X_i)}{\gamma_i}$, is counter-monotonic to $\frac{\mathbb{E}[X_i]}{\sqrt{Var(X_i)}}$. Therefore, both Proposition 4 and Proposition 6 ensure that aggregate insurance is better than the classical insurance contract.

We describe the *second* situation in a one-factor model. We argue that when the individual risk mainly comes from the specific risk in each bank, this is another example of the disordering loss market. Write $X_i = \alpha_i Y + \epsilon_i, i = 1, \cdots, N$. When a higher individual risk, $Var(X_i)$, corresponds to a higher $\frac{Var(\epsilon_i)}{Var(X_i)}$, the market can be described as the *"disordering loss market"*. To demonstrate, we assume, again, $\gamma_i = \gamma$ for all i. Note that $\frac{Var(X_i)}{\mathbb{E}[X_i]^2} = Var(Y) + \left(\frac{\sigma_i}{\alpha_i}\right)^2$, and $\frac{Var(\epsilon_i)}{Var(X_i)}$ is increasing with respect to $\frac{\sigma_i}{\alpha_i}$. Then, under this assumption, $\frac{Var(X_i)}{\gamma_i}$ is co-monotonic to $\frac{Var(X_i)}{\mathbb{E}[X_i]^2}$ and, thus, counter-monotonic to $\frac{\mathbb{E}[X_i]}{\sqrt{Var(X_i)}}$; this is a disordering loss market. Hence, aggregate insurance is a better insurance program when specific risk plays a dominate role inside individual risk.

Table 1 demonstrates the first situation as described. There are 10 big banks in the market, and each bank has the same expected loss as $\alpha_i = 0.1$ for all $i = 1, \cdots, 10$. For simplicity, we assume that the variance of the systematic risk factor, Y, equals one and each $\gamma_i = 1$. However, the specific risk in each bank varies from 10% to 40%. Table 1 displays the negative relationship between the risk-adjusted variance and the Sharpe ratio of the loss portfolios among these 10 banks. Therefore, Table 1 shows one example of the disordering loss market, and we know that aggregate insurance is a preferred program by Proposition 6. Moreover, by numerical computations, $\frac{Cov(X_i, X)}{Var(X)} > 0.06 > \frac{1}{2N}$ for each $i = 1, \cdots, N$. Hence, the equilibrium of the aggregate insurance is given explicitly in Proposition 1.

The second situation is shown in Table 2, in which $\frac{\alpha}{\sigma}$ is increasing with respect to α. In this case, these banks have different expected loss, ranging from $0.1\mathbb{E}[Y]$ to $0.55\mathbb{E}[Y]$. As shown, there is a negative relationship between the risk-adjusted variance and the Sharpe ratio of the loss portfolios among these 10 banks; hence, Table 2 shows another example of the disordering loss market. By numerical computations, $\frac{Cov(X_i, X)}{Var(X)} > 0.08 > \frac{1}{2N}$ for each $i = 1, \cdots, N$. Hence, the equilibrium of the aggregate insurance is given explicitly in Proposition 1.

Table 1. Example 1 of a disordering loss market. This table displays a disordering loss market when each bank has the same expected loss in a one-factor model. Therefore, aggregate insurance is a better capital insurance program by Proposition 6. It can be checked that the condition in Proposition 1 is satisfied, so the equilibrium of the aggregate insurance is given in Proposition 1. We assume $\gamma_i = 1$ for each $i = 1, \cdots, N$. There are $N = 10$ banks.

Bank	α	σ	Risk-Adjusted Variance	Sharpe Ratio
1	0.1	0.40	0.170	0.243
2	0.1	0.35	0.133	0.275
3	0.1	0.30	0.100	0.316
4	0.1	0.26	0.078	0.359
5	0.1	0.23	0.063	0.399
6	0.1	0.20	0.050	0.447
7	0.1	0.18	0.042	0.486
8	0.1	0.15	0.033	0.555
9	0.1	0.12	0.024	0.640
10	0.1	0.10	0.020	0.707

Table 2. Example 2 of a disordering loss market. This table displays a disordering loss market when the percentage of specific risk in individual risk increases with respect to individual risk. Therefore, aggregate insurance is a better insurance program than the classical insurance program by Proposition 6. It can be checked that the condition in Proposition 1 is satisfied, so the equilibrium of the aggregate insurance is given in Proposition 1. We assume $\gamma_i = 1$ for each $i = 1, \cdots, N$. There are $N = 10$ banks.

Bank	α	σ	Risk-Adjusted Variance	Sharpe Ratio
1	0.10	0.200	0.050	0.447
2	0.15	0.315	0.122	0.430
3	0.20	0.440	0.234	0.414
4	0.25	0.575	0.393	0.399
5	0.30	0.720	0.608	0.385
6	0.35	0.875	0.888	0.371
7	0.40	1.040	1.242	0.359
8	0.45	1.215	1.679	0.347
9	0.50	1.400	2.210	0.336
10	0.55	1.595	2.847	0.326

On the other hand, when the individual risk, $Var(X_i)$, is opposite of the percentage of the specific risk, $\frac{\sigma_i^2}{Var(X_i)}$, classical insurance is better. In general, when a higher systemic risk corresponds to a smaller specific risk, classical insurance is better than aggregate insurance. Table 3 displays an example of the ordering loss market in which the classical insurance program should be preferred to aggregate insurance.

Table 3. An Example of an ordering loss market. This table displays an ordering loss market when the percentage of specific risk in individual risk decreases with respect to individual risk. Therefore, classical insurance is a better insurance program than the aggregate insurance program by Proposition 6. We assume $\gamma_i = 1$ for each $i = 1, \cdots, N$. There are $N = 10$ banks.

Bank	α	σ	Risk-adjusted Variance	Sharpe ratio
1	0.10	0.400	0.170	0.243
2	0.15	0.350	0.145	0.394
3	0.20	0.300	0.130	0.555
4	0.25	0.260	0.130	0.693
5	0.30	0.230	0.143	0.794
6	0.35	0.200	0.163	0.868
7	0.40	0.180	0.192	0.912
8	0.45	0.150	0.225	0.949
9	0.50	0.120	0.264	0.972
10	0.55	0.100	0.313	0.984

Through these examples, we have shown that specific risk is critical in comparing those capital insurance programs. If the specific risks can be ignored, these three insurance contracts offer similar welfare. Equivalently, when the systematic risk is *extremely large*, it does not matter which capital insurance program should be issued, as is demonstrated by Proposition 5.

4.2. Low Correlation Market and High Correlation Market

The correlation structure affects the capital insurance program. On the one hand, we have seen by Proposition 4 that aggregate-cross insurance is not a good choice in a low-correlated market. A low correlation parameter comes from large specific risks. In other words, if specific risks are sufficiently large enough compared with the systemic risk component, aggregate-cross insurance does not add welfare. On the other hand, when the specific risks are very small, Proposition 5 ensures that aggregate-cross insurance does not add welfare over aggregate insurance either. Low specific risks correspond to a high (or even perfectly correlated) correlation coefficient among the loss portfolios. Therefore, aggregate-cross insurance does not work better in either a low or a high correlation environment under Assumption I and Assumption II.

Actually, in the absence of asymmetric information, we argue that aggregate-cross insurance does not work better than aggregate insurance in general. To see this, we assume that α_i is the same for all i and σ_i is the same for all i. Then, each pair of banks has the same correlation coefficient written as τ. By straightforward calculation, we have:

$$\mathbb{E}(W^{*,ac}) = \tau^2 \mathbb{E}(W^{*,a}) = \tau^2 \mathbb{E}(W^{*,c}). \tag{25}$$

Therefore, the lower the correlation coefficient τ, the smaller expected welfare of the aggregate-cross insurance. Overall, $\mathbb{E}(W^{*,ac}) < \mathbb{E}(W^{*,a}) = \mathbb{E}(W^{*,c})$. When all banks contribute to systematic risk equally, then specific risks are also similar; the aggregate-cross insurance is not as good as the two other insurance programs.

4.3. Systemic Risk

There are many different interpretations about systemic risk. Some authors suggest using the default probability of the whole financial system (see, for instance, [10]). Other authors suggest using Shapley values to estimate systemic risk (see [3]).[12] It is beyond the scope of this paper to develop a

---

[12] See [5,7,8].

systemic risk theory, as we focus on the effect of capital insurance. Rather, we indicate that aggregate insurance is a useful tool to deal with systemic risk by using two interpretations of systemic risk.

First, we view systemic risk as the likelihood of aggregate loss meeting a threshold. Precisely, the higher probability $P(X \geq L)$, the higher the systemic risk. In aggregate insurance, post-aggregate insurance becomes (by using Equation (??)):

$$\sum X_i - \sum \beta_i X = \frac{1}{2} X. \tag{26}$$

Clearly, the *ex post* aggregate loss is smaller than the *ex ante* aggregate loss, X. Therefore, aggregate insurance, indeed, reduces systemic risk.

Second, we consider the systemic risk for each individual bank in a one-factor model. Before purchasing aggregate insurance, the systematic risk contribution of the bank, i, is α_i. We assume that γ_i is the same across the banks. Then, the coinsurance percentage for the bank, i, is:

$$\beta_i \geq \frac{\alpha_i \alpha Var(Y)}{\alpha^2 Var(Y) + \sigma^2} - \frac{1}{2N}. \tag{27}$$

Hence, the contribution to the systematic risk of the bank, i, after purchasing aggregate insurance, is:

$$\alpha_i - \beta_i \alpha \leq \frac{\alpha_i \sigma^2}{\alpha^2 Var(Y) + \sigma^2} + \frac{1}{2} \frac{\alpha}{N}. \tag{28}$$

When the number of banks, N, is large enough or when the variability of the systemic risk, $Var(Y)$, is sufficiently large, we see that $\alpha_i - \beta_i \alpha < \alpha_i$. Therefore, the systemic risk of each bank, i, is reduced after purchasing aggregate insurance.

4.4. Identification and Implementation of "Too Big to Fail"

Suppose the disordering loss market occurs; according to our theory, the aggregate insurance program is a desired regulatory tool to solve the "too big to fail" issue. Nevertheless, there are two fundamental questions to be solved as follows.

1. How to implement the aggregate insurance program, i.e., how to characterize the equilibrium in a general situation.
2. How to distinguish the "too big to fail" banks that are forced to purchase aggregate insurance from the other banks. Alternatively, how to identify those "too big to fail" banks.

We illustrate our solutions to these questions by an example, while a general solution is given in Appendix B.

To explain the answers to the questions above, we consider 15 banks, and the loss portfolio of each bank follows a one-factor model. The systematic risk factor is represented by Y with $\mathbb{E}[Y] = Var(Y) = 1$. Each bank has the same expected loss, $0.05\mathbb{E}[Y]$, but the specific risk varies differently. In fact, σ_i moves from 40% to 12%. Proposition 6 implies that aggregate insurance is more desirable than classical insurance. It is also easy to see that $\frac{Cov(X_i,X)}{\gamma_i}$ is decreasing from $i = 1$ to $i = 15$. However, as shown in Table 4, condition (??) in Proposition 1 is not always satisfied. To be precise, for the last five banks, $\frac{Cov(X_i,X)}{Var(X)} < \frac{1}{2N}, i = 11, 12, 13, 14, 15$.

Table 4. Example 3 of a disordering loss market. This table displays a disordering loss market when each bank has the same expected loss in a one-factor model. Therefore, aggregate insurance is a better program by Proposition 6. However, the condition in Proposition 1 is not satisfied, as shown for $i = 11, 12, \cdots, 15$. There are $N = 15$ banks, and each $\gamma_i = 1$.

Bank	α	σ	Risk-Adjusted Variance	Sharpe Ratio	$\frac{Cov(X_i,X)}{Var(X)}$
1	0.05	0.40	0.1625	0.124	0.1170
2	0.05	0.38	0.1469	0.130	0.1070
3	0.05	0.36	0.1321	0.138	0.0990
4	0.05	0.34	0.1181	0.145	0.0907
5	0.05	0.32	0.1049	0.154	0.0829
6	0.05	0.30	0.0925	0.164	0.0755
7	0.05	0.28	0.0809	0.176	0.0686
8	0.05	0.26	0.0701	0.189	0.0622
9	0.05	0.24	0.0601	0.204	0.0563
10	0.05	0.22	0.0509	0.222	0.0509
11	0.05	0.20	0.0425	0.243	0.0459
12	0.05	0.18	0.0349	0.268	0.0414
13	0.05	0.16	0.0281	0.298	0.0374
14	0.05	0.14	0.0221	0.336	0.0338
15	0.05	0.12	0.0169	0.385	0.0307

Appendix B presents a general solution of the equilibrium without Condition (??). The equilibrium problem and how to identify the "too big to fail" problem are solved simultaneously. As the risk-adjusted covariance sequence, $\frac{Cov(X_i,X)}{\gamma_i}$, is decreasing for $i = 1, \cdots, N$, we know that the sequence, $\frac{\sum_{j=1}^{i} Cov(X_j,X)}{2\sum_{j=1}^{i} \gamma_j}$, is decreasing for $i = 1, \cdots, N$, as well. The first step is to find a unique number, n, such that:

$$\frac{Cov(X_i, X)}{\sum_{k=1}^{n} Cov(X_k, X)} \geq \frac{\gamma_i}{2\sum_{k=1}^{n} \gamma_k}, i = 1, \cdots, n \quad (29)$$

and

$$\frac{Cov(X_i, X)}{\sum_{k=1}^{n} Cov(X_k, X)} < \frac{\gamma_i}{2\sum_{k=1}^{n} \gamma_k}, i = n+1, \cdots, N. \quad (30)$$

In this example, we find out that $n = 13$ (see Table 5). Therefore, the first 13 banks, but not the first 10 banks, are "too big to fail" banks that should be required to purchase the aggregate insurance. The last two banks can be ignored in this aggregate insurance program. The second step is to determine the optimal load factor, ρ^*, in the aggregate insurance program, which is:

$$\rho^* = \frac{1}{\mathbb{E}[X]} \frac{\sum_{i=1}^{n} Cov(X_i, X)}{2\sum_{i=1}^{n} \gamma_i} = 0.081. \quad (31)$$

At last, the optimal co-insurance parameters for the first 13 banks are:

$$\beta^{i,a}(\rho^*) = \frac{Cov(X_i, X) - \rho^* \gamma_i \mathbb{E}[X]}{Var(X)}, i = 1, \cdots, 13. \quad (32)$$

The last two banks do not buy the aggregate insurance as $\beta^{i,a}(\rho^*) = 0, i = 14, 15$. The equilibrium and relevant computation are displayed by Table 5. We observe that the optimal co-insurance parameter decreases with respect to $\frac{Cov(X_i,X)}{\gamma_i}$, a measure of the systemic risk of these "too big to fail".

Table 5. Implementation of Example 3. This table displays the equilibrium of Example 3. We note that when i starts from 14, $\frac{Cov(X_i,X)}{\gamma_i}$ is strictly greater than $\frac{\sum_{j=1}^{i} Cov(X_j,X)}{2\sum_{j=1}^{i} \gamma_j}$. Then, the last two banks are not "too big to fail". The optimal load factor is $\rho^* = 8.1\%$.

Bank	$\frac{Cov(X_i,X)}{\gamma_i}$	$\frac{Cov(X_i,X)}{Var(X)}$	$\frac{\sum_{j=1}^{i} Cov(X_j,X)}{2\sum_{j=1}^{i} \gamma_j}$	$\beta^{i,a}$
1	0.1975	0.1170	0.09875	8.10 %
2	0.1819	0.1070	0.09485	7.18 %
3	0.1671	0.0990	0.09108	6.30 %
4	0.1531	0.0907	0.08745	5.47 %
5	0.1399	0.0829	0.08395	4.69 %
6	0.1275	0.0755	0.08058	3.95 %
7	0.1159	0.0686	0.07735	3.27 %
8	0.1051	0.0622	0.07425	2.63 %
9	0.0951	0.0563	0.07128	2.03 %
10	0.0859	0.0509	0.06845	1.49 %
11	0.0775	0.0459	0.06575	0.99 %
12	0.0699	0.0414	0.06318	0.54 %
13	0.0631	0.0374	0.06075	0.14 %
14	0.0571	0.0338	0.05845	0
15	0.0519	0.0307	0.05628	0

5. Conclusion

In this paper, we present a welfare analysis of several capital insurance programs in equilibrium. We show that aggregate insurance ensures a higher welfare if each big bank has similar systematic risk. The classical insurance program, however, has a higher welfare when the individual bank's risk is positively related to the expected loss per each volatility unit. In general, aggregate-cross insurance does not add more welfare if there exists no asymmetric information concern. Overall, we demonstrate that the capital insurance program is a useful regulatory tool to address the "too big to fail" issue.

Acknowledgments: We are grateful to two anonymous referees for comments which greatly improved the exposition.

Conflicts of Interest: The authors declare no conflict of interest.

Appendix Proofs

The proofs rely on the following simple lemma.

Lemma 1 *Given positive numbers b_i, c_i, κ_i for each $i = 1, \cdots, n$,*

1. *If the vector $\kappa = (\kappa_i)$ is co-monotonic to the vector $\frac{b}{c} = (\frac{b_i}{c_i})$, then:*

$$\frac{\sum_{i=1}^{n} b_i \kappa_i}{\sum_{i=1}^{n} b_i} > \frac{\sum_{i=1}^{n} c_i \kappa_i}{\sum_{i=1}^{n} c_i}.$$

2. *If the vector $\kappa = (\kappa_i)$ is counter-monotonic to the vector $\frac{b}{c} = (\frac{b_i}{c_i})$, then:*

$$\frac{\sum_{i=1}^{n} b_i \kappa_i}{\sum_{i=1}^{n} b_i} < \frac{\sum_{i=1}^{n} c_i \kappa_i}{\sum_{i=1}^{n} c_i}.$$

Proof: $\sum b_i \kappa_i \sum c_i - \sum b_i \sum c_i \kappa_i = \sum_{i,j} b_i \kappa_i c_j - \sum_{i,j} b_j c_i \kappa_i = \sum_{i,j} (b_i c_j - b_j c_i) \kappa_i = \sum_{i,j,i<j} (b_i c_j - b_j c_i)(\kappa_i - \kappa_j) = \sum_{i,j,i<j} c_i c_j \left(\frac{b_i}{c_i} - \frac{b_j}{c_j} \right) (\kappa_i - \kappa_j)$. □

Given a vector $a = (a_1, \cdots, a_n)$, we use $VAR(a) = \sum a_i^2 - (\sum a_i)^2$ to represent the variability of the vector, a. A small $VAR(a)$ means that those components in a are close to each other. Similarly, we write $\mathbb{E}[a] = \sum a_i$. It is easy to see that $VAR(a) = \frac{1}{2} \sum (a_i - a_j)^2$.

Lemma 2 *Given two sequences of positive numbers, $a_i, b_i, i = 1, 2, \cdots, n$,*

- *If those numbers, $a_1, \cdots, a_n$, are close enough in the sense that $VAR(a) \leq \mathbb{E}[a]^2 VAR(b)/\mathbb{E}[b]^2$, then $\frac{\sum a_i^2}{\sum b_i^2} \leq \frac{(\sum a_i)^2}{(\sum b_i)^2}.$*
- *If those numbers, $b_1, \cdots, b_n$, are close enough in the sense that $VAR(b) \leq \mathbb{E}[b]^2 VAR(a)/\mathbb{E}[a]^2$, then $\frac{\sum a_i^2}{\sum b_i^2} \geq \frac{(\sum a_i)^2}{(\sum b_i)^2}.$*

Proof: By straightforward calculation, we obtain:

$$\begin{aligned}\sum a_i^2 (\sum b_i)^2 - (\sum a_i)^2 \sum b_i^2 &= \frac{1}{2}\left\{\sum_{i,j,k}(a_i - a_j)^2 b_k^2 - \sum_{i,j,k} a_i^2 (b_j - b_k)^2\right\} \\ &= \sum b_i^2 VAR(a) - \sum a_i^2 VAR(b).\end{aligned} \quad (A-1)$$

When the numbers, a_i, are close enough, the first term in (A-1) is dominated by the second term. This is the first case. It is the classical Cauchy-Schwartz inequality when $a_1 = \cdots = a_n$. In the second case, the second term is close to zero. □

Proof of Proposition 4. Under the uncorrelated assumption, $\mathbb{E}[W^{*,a}] = \frac{\sum Var(X_i)}{4 \sum \gamma_i}$. As $\mathbb{E}[X_i] \geq 0$ for each i, we have $\mathbb{E}[W^{*,c}] \geq \frac{\sum \mathbb{E}[X_i]^2}{4 \sum_i \gamma_i \mathbb{E}[X_i]^2 / Var(X_i)}$. For each $i \neq j$, if $\frac{Var(X_i)}{\gamma_i} < \frac{Var(X_j)}{\gamma_j}$, then by the co-monotonic assumption, $\frac{\mathbb{E}[X_i]}{\sqrt{Var(X_i)}} \leq \frac{\mathbb{E}[X_j]}{\sqrt{Var(X_j)}}$. So, $\frac{\mathbb{E}[X_i]^2}{Var(X_i)} \leq \frac{\mathbb{E}[X_j]^2}{Var(X_j)}$. Therefore:

$$\frac{Var(X_i)}{\mathbb{E}[X_i]^2} \geq \frac{Var(X_j)}{\mathbb{E}[X_j]^2}. \quad (A-2)$$

This means that vectors $\left(\frac{Var(X_i)}{\gamma_i}\right)$ and $\left(\frac{Var(X_i)}{\mathbb{E}[X_i]^2}\right)$ are counter-monotonic. Then, by Lemma 1, we obtain (using $b_i = \gamma_i, c_i = \gamma_i \mathbb{E}[X_i]^2 / Var(X_i)$ and $\kappa_i = Var(X_i)/\gamma_i$):

$$\frac{\sum \mathbb{E}[X_i]^2}{\sum_i \gamma_i \mathbb{E}[X_i]^2 / Var(X_i)} > \frac{\sum Var(X_i)}{\sum \gamma_i}. \quad (A-3)$$

We have proven the first part. As for the second part, assume that the risk-adjusted variance is counter-monotonic to the Sharpe ratio vector. Then, by the same idea, we have that:

$$\frac{\sum \mathbb{E}[X_i]^2}{\sum_i \gamma_i \mathbb{E}[X_i]^2 / Var(X_i)} < \frac{\sum Var(X_i)}{\sum \gamma_i} = \mathbb{E}[W^{*,a}]. \quad (A-4)$$

Therefore, when $\mathbb{E}[X]^2$ is close to $\sum \mathbb{E}[X_i]^2$, we obtain that $\mathbb{E}[W^{*,c}] \leq \mathbb{E}[W^{*,a}]$. The proof is complete. □

Proof of Proposition 5. The welfare of each insurance contract in the one-factor model is computed as follows.

$$\mathbb{E}(W^{*,a}) = \frac{1}{4} \frac{\alpha^2 Var(Y) + \sigma^2}{\sum_i \gamma_i} \quad (A-5)$$

$$\mathbb{E}(W^{*,c}) = \frac{1}{4} \frac{\alpha^2}{\sum_i \gamma_i \frac{\alpha_i^2}{\alpha_i^2 Var(Y) + \sigma_i^2}} \qquad (A\text{-}6)$$

and:

$$\mathbb{E}(W^{*,ac}) = \frac{1}{4} \frac{\left(\sum_i \hat{\alpha}_i E(Y) \frac{\alpha_i \hat{\alpha}_i Var(Y)}{\hat{\alpha}_i^2 Var(Y) + \hat{\sigma}_i^2} \right)^2}{\sum_i \gamma_i \frac{\hat{\alpha}_i^2 E(Y)^2}{\hat{\alpha}_i^2 Var(Y) + \hat{\sigma}_i^2}} = \frac{1}{4} \frac{\left(\sum_i \frac{\alpha_i \hat{\alpha}_i^2 Var(Y)}{\hat{\alpha}_i^2 Var(Y) + \hat{\sigma}_i^2} \right)^2}{\sum_i \gamma_i \frac{\hat{\alpha}_i^2}{\hat{\alpha}_i^2 Var(Y) + \hat{\sigma}_i^2}}. \qquad (A\text{-}7)$$

Clearly, when the total $\sigma^2 = 0$, the welfare is identical for all three types of contracts. The second part follows from the same idea. □

Proof of Proposition 6.

First, note that $\alpha^2 \geq \sum \alpha_i^2$, and the function $f(x) \equiv \frac{x^2 Var(Y) + \sigma^2}{x^2}$ is decreasing with respect to x. Then:

$$\frac{\alpha^2 Var(Y) + \sigma^2}{\alpha^2} \leq \frac{\sum (\alpha_i^2 Var(Y) + \sigma_i^2)}{\sum \alpha_i^2}. \qquad (A\text{-}8)$$

To prove $\mathbb{E}[W^{*,a}] < \mathbb{E}[W^{*,c}]$ under the co-monotonic condition, it suffices to show that:

$$\frac{\sum (\alpha_i^2 Var(Y) + \sigma_i^2)}{\sum \gamma_i} < \frac{\sum \alpha_i^2}{\sum_i \gamma_i \frac{\alpha_i^2}{\alpha_i^2 Var(Y) + \sigma_i^2}}. \qquad (A\text{-}9)$$

In fact, by using the co-monotonic relationship between the risk-adjusted variance and the Sharpe ratio, the risk-adjusted variance is counter-monotonic to the vector, $\left(\frac{Var(X_i)}{\mathbb{E}[X_i]} \mathbb{E}[Y]^2 \right)$. Note that $\mathbb{E}[X_i] = \alpha_i \mathbb{E}[Y]$ and $Var(X_i) = \alpha_i^2 Var(Y) + \sigma_i^2$. Then, the last inequality (??) follows from Lemma 1 for $b_i = \gamma_i$, $c_i = \gamma_i \frac{\alpha_i^2}{\alpha_i^2 Var(Y) + \sigma_i^2}$, and $\kappa_i = Var(X_i) / \gamma_i$.

If the risk-adjusted variance is counter-monotonic to the Sharpe ratio across the banks, then by the same proof, we obtain:

$$\frac{\sum (\alpha_i^2 Var(Y) + \sigma_i^2)}{\sum \gamma_i} > \frac{\sum \alpha_i^2}{\sum_i \gamma_i \frac{\alpha_i^2}{\alpha_i^2 Var(Y) + \sigma_i^2}}. \qquad (A\text{-}10)$$

For a large positive number, x, $f'(x) = -\frac{2\sigma^2}{x^3}$ is close to zero; so, the curve $y = f(x)$ is almost flat. Then, for a large $\mathbb{E}[X]$, the numbers, $\frac{\alpha^2 Var(Y) + \sigma^2}{\alpha^2}$ and $\frac{\sum (\alpha_i^2 Var(Y) + \sigma_i^2)}{\sum \alpha_i^2}$, are close enough that:

$$\frac{\alpha^2 Var(Y) + \sigma^2}{\alpha^2} \sim \frac{\sum (\alpha_i^2 Var(Y) + \sigma_i^2)}{\sum \alpha_i^2} > \frac{\sum \gamma_i}{\sum_i \gamma_i \frac{\alpha_i^2}{\alpha_i^2 Var(Y) + \sigma_i^2}}.$$

Equivalently, $\mathbb{E}[W^{*,a}] > \mathbb{E}[W^{*,c}]$. □

Proof of Proposition 7. As the risk-adjusted variance is co-monotonic to the Sharpe ratio across each bank, Lemma 1 yields that:

$$\frac{1}{4} \frac{\sum \mathbb{E}[X_i]^2}{\sum \gamma_i \mathbb{E}[X_i]^2 / Var(X_i)} > \frac{1}{4} \frac{\sum Var(X_i)}{\sum_i \gamma_i}. \qquad (A\text{-}11)$$

By using the Cauchy-Schwartz inequality, $Var(X_i) Var(\hat{X}_i) \geq Cov(X_i, \hat{X}_i)^2$ for each i. We obtain:

$$\frac{1}{4} \frac{\sum \mathbb{E}[X_i]^2}{\sum \gamma_i \mathbb{E}[X_i]^2 / Var(X_i)} > \frac{1}{4} \frac{\sum Cov(X_i, \hat{X}_i)^2 / Var(\hat{X}_i)}{\sum_i \gamma_i}. \qquad (A\text{-}12)$$

Note that $\frac{Cov(X_i,\hat{X}_i)^2}{Var(\hat{X}_i)\gamma_i} = \rho_i^2 \frac{Var(X_i)}{\gamma}$, where ρ_i is the correlation coefficient between X_i and $\hat{X}_i$. If the Sharpe ratio of the "dual" risk $\frac{\mathbb{E}[\hat{X}_i]}{\sqrt{Var(\hat{X}_i)}}$ is counter-monotonic to the risk-adjusted correlated variance, $\rho_i^2 \frac{Var(X_i)}{\gamma}$, then $\rho_i^2 \frac{Var(X_i)}{\gamma}$ is co-monotonic to $\frac{Var(\hat{X}_i)}{\mathbb{E}[\hat{X}_i]^2}$. Again by Lemma 1 (for $b_i = \gamma_i, c_i = \gamma_i \frac{\mathbb{E}[\hat{X}_i]^2}{Var(\hat{X}_i)}$ and $\kappa_i = \rho_i^2 \frac{Var(X_i)}{\gamma}$), we have:

$$\frac{\sum Cov(X_i,\hat{X}_i)^2/Var(\hat{X}_i)}{\sum_i \gamma_i} > \frac{\sum \mathbb{E}[\hat{X}_i]^2 \frac{Cov(X_i,\hat{X}_i)^2}{Var(\hat{X}_i)^2}}{\sum \gamma_i \frac{\mathbb{E}[\hat{X}_i]^2}{Var(\hat{X}_i)}} \tag{A-13}$$

By combining (A-12) with (A-13) together, we obtain:

$$\frac{\sum \mathbb{E}[X_i]^2}{\sum \gamma_i \frac{\mathbb{E}[X_i]^2}{Var(X_i)}} > \frac{\sum \mathbb{E}[\hat{X}_i]^2 \frac{Cov(X_i,\hat{X}_i)^2}{Var(\hat{X}_i)^2}}{\sum \gamma_i \frac{\mathbb{E}[\hat{X}_i]^2}{Var(\hat{X}_i)}}. \tag{A-14}$$

Equivalently:

$$\frac{\sum \mathbb{E}[X_i]^2}{\sum \mathbb{E}[\hat{X}_i]^2 \frac{Cov(X_i,\hat{X}_i)^2}{Var(\hat{X}_i)^2}} > \frac{\sum \gamma_i \frac{\mathbb{E}[X_i]^2}{Var(X_i)}}{\sum \gamma_i \frac{\mathbb{E}[\hat{X}_i]^2}{Var(\hat{X}_i)}}. \tag{A-15}$$

When $\mathbb{E}[X_i]$ is distributed equally, or the expected losses are fairly close enough, Lemma 2 ensures that:

$$\frac{(\sum \mathbb{E}[X_i])^2}{\left(\sum \mathbb{E}[\hat{X}_i]^2 \frac{Cov(X_i,\hat{X}_i)}{Var(\hat{X}_i)}\right)^2} > \frac{\sum \mathbb{E}[X_i]^2}{\sum \mathbb{E}[\hat{X}_i]^2 \frac{Cov(X_i,\hat{X}_i)^2}{Var(\hat{X}_i)^2}}. \tag{A-16}$$

Finally, by using (A-15) and (A-16), we obtain:

$$\frac{(\sum \mathbb{E}[X_i])^2}{\left(\sum \mathbb{E}[\hat{X}_i]^2 \frac{Cov(X_i,\hat{X}_i)}{Var(\hat{X}_i)}\right)^2} > \frac{\sum \gamma_i \frac{\mathbb{E}[X_i]^2}{Var(X_i)}}{\sum \gamma_i \frac{\mathbb{E}[\hat{X}_i]^2}{Var(\hat{X}_i)}}. \tag{A-17}$$

By using Proposition 2 and Proposition 3, we obtain that $\mathbb{E}[W^{*,c}] > \mathbb{E}[W^{*,ac}]$. □

Appendix A General Solution of the Equilibrium of Aggregate Insurance

The regulator's problem is to solve the optimal load factor, such as:

$$\rho^* = argmax_{\{\rho \geq 0\}} \rho \sum_{i=1}^{N} \max\left(\frac{Cov(X_i,X) - \rho\gamma_i \mathbb{E}[X]}{Var(X)}, 0\right) \tag{B-1}$$

and the optimal coinsurance percentage for each bank $i = 1, \cdots, N$ is:

$$\beta^{i,a}(\rho^*) = \max\left(\frac{Cov(X_i,X) - \rho^*\gamma_i \mathbb{E}[X]}{Var(X)}, 0\right). \tag{B-2}$$

For this purpose, we reorder the bank index and still use $i = 1, \cdots, N$, such that:

$$\frac{Cov(X_1,X)}{\gamma_1} \geq \frac{Cov(X_2,X)}{\gamma_2} \geq \cdots \geq \frac{Cov(X_N,X)}{\gamma_N}. \tag{B-3}$$

In other words, we examine the risk-adjusted covariance of the loss portfolio with the aggregate loss for each bank and reorder these banks from the largest risk-adjusted covariance one to the lowest risk-adjusted covariance one. Intuitively, a large risk-adjusted covariance of the loss portfolio with the aggregate loss ensures a large systemic risk. Therefore, the regulator pays more attention to these banks and makes sure those banks purchase the aggregate insurance to resolve the issue of "too big to fail". The risk-adjusted covariance $\frac{Cov(X_i, X)}{\gamma_i}$ and the beta $\frac{Cov(X_i, X)}{Var(X)}$ can be viewed as two measures of the systemic risk.

The next lemma is trivial.

Lemma 3 *Given a decreasing sequence, $\frac{a_i}{b_i}$, for $i = 1, \cdots, N$ and $a_i, b_i > 0$, the sequence, $\frac{c_i}{d_i}$, is also decreasing, where $c_i = \sum_{j=1}^{i} a_j, d_i = \sum_{j=1}^{i} b_j$.*

By using Lemma 3 and (B-3), we have:

$$\frac{Cov(X_1, X)}{2\gamma_1} \geq \frac{\sum_{j=1}^{2} Cov(X_j, X)}{2\sum_{j=1}^{2} \gamma_j} \geq \cdots \geq \frac{\sum_{j=1}^{N} Cov(X_j, X)}{2\sum_{j=1}^{N} \gamma_j}. \tag{B-4}$$

By comparing these two decreasing sequences, $\left\{\frac{Cov(X_i, X)}{\gamma_i}; i = 1, \cdots, N\right\}$ and $\left\{\frac{\sum_{j=1}^{i} Cov(X_j, X)}{2\sum_{j=1}^{i} \gamma_j}; i = 1, \cdots, N\right\}$, we can easily find a unique number, n, such that:

$$\frac{Cov(X_i, X)}{\gamma_i} \geq \frac{\sum_{k=1}^{n} Cov(X_k, X)}{2\sum_{k=1}^{n} \gamma_k}, i = 1, \cdots, n \tag{B-5}$$

and:

$$\frac{Cov(X_i, X)}{\gamma_i} < \frac{\sum_{k=1}^{n} Cov(X_k, X)}{2\sum_{k=1}^{n} \gamma_k}, i = n+1, \cdots, N. \tag{B-6}$$

Equivalently:

$$\frac{Cov(X_i, X)}{\sum_{k=1}^{n} Cov(X_k, X)} \geq \frac{\gamma_i}{2\sum_{k=1}^{n} \gamma_k}, i = 1, \cdots, n \tag{B-7}$$

and:

$$\frac{Cov(X_i, X)}{\sum_{k=1}^{n} Cov(X_k, X)} < \frac{\gamma_i}{2\sum_{k=1}^{n} \gamma_k}, i = n+1, \cdots, N. \tag{B-8}$$

Define:

$$\rho^* = \frac{1}{\mathbb{E}[X]} \frac{\sum_{i=1}^{n} Cov(X_i, X)}{2\sum_{i=1}^{n} \gamma_i}. \tag{B-9}$$

It is easy to see that:

$$\beta^{i,a}(\rho^*) = \frac{Cov(X_i, X) - \rho^* \gamma_i \mathbb{E}[X]}{Var(X)}, i = 1, \cdots, n \tag{B-10}$$

and $\beta^{i,a}(\rho^*) = 0, i = n+1, \cdots, N$. Moreover, ρ^* is the optimal solution of the following problem:

$$\max_{\rho} \rho \sum_{i=1}^{n} \left(\frac{Cov(X_i, X) - \rho \gamma_i \mathbb{E}[X]}{Var(X)}\right).$$

Finally, it is straightforward to check that $\{\rho^*, \beta^{i,a}(\rho^*), i = 1, \cdots, N\}$ is the optimal solution in equilibrium. The bank, i, is considered to be "too big to fail" for $i = 1, \cdots, n$. $\beta^{i,a}(\rho^*) > 0$ for these "too big to fail" banks. The other bank, i, such that $i = n+1, \cdots, N$, does not buy the aggregate insurance.

References

1. V.V. Acharya, L.H. Pedersen, Th. Philippon, and M. Richardson. "A Tax on Systemic Risk." In Proceedings of the 2010 KDI International Conference: Post-Crisis Regulatory Reforms to Secure Financial Stability, Seoul, Korea, 27–28 May 2010; pp. 3–39.
2. K.J. Arrow. *Essays in the Theory of Risk Bearing*. Chicago, IL, USA: Markham Publishing Co., 1971.
3. M. Bluhm, E. Faia, and J.P. Krahnen. "Endogenous Bank's Networks, Cascades and Systemic Risk, SAFE Working Paper 12." New York, NY, USA: SSRN. [CrossRef]
4. K. Borch. "Equilibrium in a reinsurance market." *Econometrica* 30 (1962): 424–444. [CrossRef]
5. M. Billio, S. Getmansky, A. Lo, and L. Pelizzon. "Measuring Systemic Risk in the Finance and Insurance Sectors, Working Paper." Cambridge, MA, USA: Massachusetts Institute of Technology, 2009.
6. P.A. Chiappori, and B. Salanié. "Testing for asymmetric information in insurance market." *J. Polit. Econ.* 108 (2000): 56–78. [CrossRef]
7. Y. Choi, and R. Douady. "Financial crisis dynamics: Attempt to define a market instability indicator." *Quant. Financ.* 12 (2012): 1351–1365. [CrossRef]
8. L. Eisenberg, and T. Noe. "Systemic risk in financial systems." *Manag. Sci.* 47 (2001): 236–249. [CrossRef]
9. C. Gollier. *The Economics of Risk and Time*. Cambridge, MA, USA: MIT Press, 2011.
10. M. Pritsker. "Enhanced Stress Testing and Financial Stability." New York, NY, USA: SSRN. [CrossRef]
11. A. Kashyap, R. Rajan, and J.C. Stein. "Rethinking Capital Regulation." In Proceedings of the Economic Policy Symposium: Maintaining Stability in a Changing Financial System, Jackson Hole, WY, USA, 21–23 August 2008; pp. 431–471.
12. R. Mace. "Full insurance in the presence of aggregate uncertainty." *J. Polit. Econ.* 99 (1999): 928–956. [CrossRef]
13. A. Raviv. "The design of an optimal insurance policy." *Am. Econ. Rev.* 69 (1979): 84–96.
14. W. Wagner. "Diversification at financial institutions and systemic crises." *J. Financ. Intermedian* 19 (2010): 373–386. [CrossRef]

© 2013 by the authors. Licensee MDPI, Basel, Switzerland. This article is an open access article distributed under the terms and conditions of the Creative Commons Attribution (CC BY) license (http://creativecommons.org/licenses/by/4.0/).

Article

Optimal Reinsurance: A Risk Sharing Approach

Alejandro Balbás [1,*], Beatriz Balbás [2] and Raquel Balbás [3]

1. University Carlos III of Madrid. CL. Madrid 126. 28903 Getafe, Madrid, Spain
2. University of Castilla la Mancha Avda. Real Fábrica de Seda, s/n. 45600 Talavera, Toledo, Spain; beatriz.balbas@uclm.es
3. University Complutense of Madrid. Department of Actuarial and Financial Economics. Somosaguas-Campus. 28223 Pozuelo de Alarcón, Madrid, Spain; raquel.balbas@ccee.ucm.es
* Author to whom correspondence should be addressed; alejandro.balbas@uc3m.es.

Received: 11 June 2013; in revised form: 21 July 2013; Accepted: 24 July 2013; Published: 5 August 2013

Abstract: This paper proposes risk sharing strategies, which allow insurers to cooperate and diversify non-systemic risk. We deal with both deviation measures and coherent risk measures and provide general mathematical methods applying to optimize them all. Numerical examples are given in order to illustrate how efficiently the non-systemic risk can be diversified and how effective the presented mathematical tools may be. It is also illustrated how the existence of huge disasters may lead to wrong solutions of our optimal risk sharing problem, in the sense that the involved risk measure could ignore the existence of a non-null probability of "global ruin" after the design of the optimal risk sharing strategy. To overcome this caveat, one can use more conservative risk measures. The stability in the large of the optimal sharing plan guarantees that "the global ruin caveat" may be also addressed and solved with the presented methods.

Keywords: optimal reinsurance; general risk measure; risk sharing; systemic risk

1. Introduction

The optimal reinsurance problem is a classic topic in Actuarial Mathematics. A common approach is to minimize some measure of the first insurer risk after reinsurance. Seminal papers by Borch [1] and Arrow [2] used the variance as the risk measure and proved that the stop-loss reinsurance minimizes the retained risk if premiums are calculated with the Expected Value Premium Principle ($EVPP$). The subsequent research followed similar ideas and tried to take into account more general risk measures and premium principles, which may give optimal contracts other than stop-loss. Recently, Gajec and Zagrodny [3] considered more general symmetric and even asymmetric risk functions, such as the absolute deviation and the truncated variance of the retained loss, under the standard deviation premium principle. Kaluszka [4] studied reinsurance contracts with many convex premium principles (exponential, semi-deviation and semi-variance, Dutch, distortion, *etc.*). Other well known financial risk measures, such as the Value at Risk (VaR) or the Conditional Value at Risk ($CVaR$, also called $AVaR$, $TVaR$, CTE,Expected Shortfall, *etc.*), are also being considered. For example, Kaluszka [4] uses the $CVaR$ as a premium principle, and Cai and Tan [5] calculate the optimal retention for a stop-loss reinsurance by considering the VaR and the $CVaR$, under the $EVPP$. Important extensions are also presented in Cai *et al.* [6] and Bernard and Tian [7]. Balbás *et al.* [8] seem to be the first authors proving that the stop-loss reinsurance is still optimal for the $EVPP$ and the $CVaR$, though the reinsurance budget does not have to be always saturated. An interesting summary of all of these findings may be found in Centeno and Simoes [9], though there are still many open problems, and more recent papers may be found (Seng *et al.* [10], Cui *et al.* [11], Chi and Tanb [12], *etc.*).

It is not so usual in the literature to include the reinsurer point of view. The main reason is that the final decision is made by the ceding company. However, the reinsurer must also accept the selected strategy. A third approach considers the objectives of both companies and proposes a "reciprocal reinsurance". A very recent study may be found in Cai et al. [13], though there are more analyses involving both optimization methods and the theory of cooperative games.

This paper deals with "reciprocal reinsurance contracts" involving a general number of companies. In other words, we propose a risk sharing approach in order to diversify the risk as much as possible, so as to make the "global market risk" (or systemic risk, in this paper) as close as possible to the total sum of partial risks. Risks are measured in a very general setting, since Coherent Risk Measures (Artzner et al. [14]), Deviation Measures (Rockafellar et al. [15] and Expectation Bounded Risk Measures (Rockafellar et al. [15]) may be used.

The paper outline is as follows. Section 2 will be devoted to introducing the main notations and the framework. In Section 3, we will present an "Optimal Risk Sharing Problem" ($ORSP$) in such a way that every insurer attempts to conserve the size of his portfolio (market share) and simultaneously reduce his risk. As said above, it may be done by means of Game Theory or Vector Optimization, and we have selected the second approach, due to the mathematical problems that the use of risk measures may cause. Thus, we propose a two stage $ORSP$, such that, first of all (stage 1), every insurer computes his ideal value (minimum risk with a non-lower market share). As usual, in Vector Optimization, the ideal values compose the Ideal Point (Nakayama et al. [16]), and a vector optimization problem (second stage) enables the insurers to look for a risk sharing plan respecting the ideal point and every market share, as well as approaching the systemic risk as much as possible.

The proposed problems are not easy to solve in practice, since it requires the minimization of general risk functions, which are barely differentiable. Standard mathematical methods do not apply, and Section 4 is devoted to extending a methodology of Balbás et al. [8,17]. We will see that Linear Programming linked methods will be sufficient to overcome the mathematical difficulties, despite the fact that we may deal with both discrete and continuous random variables and the risk measure is quite general.

Sections 5 and 6 present illustrative numerical examples. We only try to clarify how the developed mathematical methods allow us to solve, in practice, the proposed optimization problems in a simple manner. Simultaneously, the examples will illustrate the practical properties of the optimal risk sharing strategy and a caveat that might arise from time to time. The existence of huge disasters might lead to wrong solutions of our $ORSP$, in the sense that the involved risk measure could ignore the existence of a non-null probability of "global ruin" (*i.e.*, the ruin of every involved company) after the design of the optimal risk sharing strategy. To overcome this caveat, one can use more conservative risk measures. The stability in the large of the optimal sharing plan guarantees that "this global ruin caveat" may be also addressed with the presented methods.

The last section of the paper summarizes the most important conclusions.

2. Preliminaries and Notations

Consider the probability space, $(\Omega, \mathcal{F}, \mathbb{P})$, composed of the set of "states of the world" Ω, the σ-algebra $\mathcal{F}$ and the probability measure, $\mathbb{P}$. Denote by $\mathbb{E}(y)$ the mathematical expectation of every $\mathbb{R}$-valued random variable y, defined on Ω. Let $p \in (1, \infty)$ and denote by L^p the Banach space of random variables, y, on Ω, such that $\mathbb{E}(|y|^p) < \infty$, endowed with the norm:

$$E(|y|^p))^{1/p} \qquad \| y \|_p = (I$$

for every $y \in L^p$. According to the Riesz Representation Theorem, L^q is the dual space of L^p, where $q \in (1, \infty)$ is characterized by $1/p + 1/q = 1$.

Let $[0, T]$ be a time interval. From an intuitive point of view, one can interpret that $y \in L^p$ may represent claims at T for some arbitrary insurer.

Consider n insurance companies, whose final (within $[0, T]$) claims will be represented by the non-negative random variables, $y_1, y_2, \ldots y_n \in L^p$, respectively. In order to simplify notations, let us assume that all of them deal with the Expected Value Premium Principle with the same loading rate, γ. Thus, the random final (at T) of the wealth of the jth—company will be $(1+\gamma)\mathrm{IE}(y_j) - y_j$, $j = 1, 2, ..., n$.

In order to simplify the framework, assume that all of the insurers deal with the same risk measure:

$$\rho : L^p \longrightarrow \mathrm{IR}$$

Consider the sub-gradient of ρ:

$$\Delta_\rho = \{z \in L^q; -\mathrm{IE}(yz) \leq \rho(y), \forall y \in L^p\} \subset L^q. \tag{1}$$

We will assume that Δ_ρ is convex and $\sigma(L^q, L^p)$—compact, and:

$$\mathrm{E}(yz) : z \in \Delta_\rho\} \quad \rho(y) = Max\{-\mathrm{I} \tag{2}$$

holds for every $y \in L^p$. Furthermore, we will also assume the existence of $\widetilde{E}_\rho \geq 0$, such that the constant random variable, $z = \widetilde{E}_\rho$, is in Δ_ρ and:

$$\Delta_\rho \subset \left\{z \in L^q; \mathrm{IE}(z) = \widetilde{E}_\rho\right\}. \tag{3}$$

Summarizing, we have:

Assumption 1. The set, Δ_ρ, given by (1) is convex and $\sigma(L^q, L^p)$—compact, (2) holds for every $y \in L^p$, $z = \widetilde{E}_\rho$ is in Δ_ρ and (3) holds. □

Assumption 1 is not at all restrictive, since it is satisfied by every expectation bounded risk measure (Rockafellar et al. [15]) with $\widetilde{E}_\rho = 1$ and by every deviation measure (Rockafellar et al. [15]) with $\widetilde{E}_\rho = 0$. Examples of expectation bounded risk measures are the Conditional Value at Risk (*CVaR*) and the Weighted Conditional Value at Risk (*WCVaR*), amongst many others. Examples of deviation measures are, amongst others, the classical p—deviation:

$$\sigma_p(y) = \left[\mathrm{IE}(|\mathrm{IE}(y) - y|^p)\right]^{1/p},$$

or the upside and downside p—semi-deviation:

$$\sigma_p^+(y) = \left[\mathrm{IE}(|Max\{y - \mathrm{IE}(y), 0\}|^p)\right]^{1/p}$$

and:

$$\sigma_p^-(y) = \left[\mathrm{IE}(|Max\{\mathrm{IE}(y) - y, 0\}|^p)\right]^{1/p}.$$

If $\widetilde{E}_\rho = 1$, then it is easy to see that ρ is also coherent in the sense of Artzner et al. [14], if and only if:

$$\Delta_\rho \subset L_+^q = \{z \in L^q; \mathrm{IP}(z \geq 0) = 1\}.$$

Further details may be also found in Balbás et al. [8,17].

Under the framework above, we can consider the risk of the jth—company, given by:

$$\rho((1+\gamma)\mathrm{IE}(y_j) - y_j) \tag{4}$$

$j = 1, 2, ..., n$, and the systemic risk, given by:

$$\rho((1+\gamma)\mathrm{IE}(y) - y) \tag{5}$$

where:
$$y = \sum_{j=1}^{n} y_j \in L^p$$

denotes "global claims". Since Assumption 1 implies that ρ is sub-additive, we have that:

$$\rho((1+\gamma)\mathrm{IE}(y) - y) = \rho\left((1+\gamma)\sum_{j=1}^{n}\mathrm{IE}(y_j) - \sum_{j=1}^{n} y_i\right)$$
$$\leq \sum_{j=1}^{n} \rho((1+\gamma)\mathrm{IE}(y_j) - y_j). \tag{6}$$

3. The Risk Sharing Problem

Expression (6) may suggest that every company can reduce risk and simultaneously improve expected profits. Actually, companies might attempt to modify their portfolios in such a manner that (6) almost becomes an equality. This purpose may be addressed with two stages.

In the first stage, every insurer can compute his ideal risk level, *i.e.*, the minimum risk associated with the expected wealth of his portfolio. The optimization problem for the jth-company becomes:

$$\begin{cases} \mathrm{Min}\,\rho((1+\gamma)\mathrm{IE}(x_j) - x_j) \\ \mathrm{IE}(x_j) \geq \mathrm{IE}(y_j) \\ 0 \leq x_j \leq y \end{cases} \tag{7}$$

$x_j \in L^p$ being the decision variable.

Fix an ideal point,
$$I = (I_1, I_2, ..., I_n)$$

i.e., I_j is not higher than the optimal value attained by (7), $j = 1, 2, ..., n$. In the second stage, all the companies, such that:

$$I_j < \rho_j = \rho((1+\gamma)\mathrm{IE}(y_j) - y_j) \tag{8}$$

could collaborate, so as to improve their particular risk. Without loss of generality, we can assume that (8) holds for $j = 1, 2, ..., n$, so the insurers could look for a risk sharing plan solving the optimization problem:

$$\begin{cases} \mathrm{Min}\,\sum_{j=1}^{n} w_j \rho((1+\gamma)\mathrm{IE}(x_j) - x_j) \\ \mathrm{IE}(x_j) \geq \mathrm{IE}(y_j), & j = 1, 2, ..., n \\ \sum_{j=1}^{n} x_j \leq y \\ 0 \leq x_j, & j = 1, 2, ..., n \end{cases} \tag{9}$$

$x = (x_1, x_2, ..., x_n) \in (L^p)^n$ being the decision variable and $w_j > 0$ being a weight associated with the jth-insurer, $j = 1, 2, ..., n$. Every company is guaranteeing that his portfolio size (or market share) will not decrease, and the weights $w = (w_j)_{j=1}^{n}$ must be chosen in such a manner that:

$$I_j < \rho((1+\gamma)\mathrm{IE}(x_j) - x_j) \leq \rho_j, \tag{10}$$

$j = 1, 2, ..., n$ must hold. Thus, every company will be approaching its ideal risk level, and the solution:

$$x^* = (x_1^*, x_2^*, ..., x_n^*) \in (L^p)^n$$

of (9) will be a Pareto optimum, in the sense that there is not any (9)−feasible allocation,

$$x = (x_1, x_2, ..., x_n) \in (L^p)^n$$

,such that:
$$\rho((1+\gamma)\mathrm{IE}(x_j) - x_j) \leq \rho\left((1+\gamma)\mathrm{IE}\left(x_j^*\right) - x_j^*\right),$$

$j = 1, 2, ..., n$, with one strict inequality at least (Nakayama *et al.* [16]).

Notice that the constraints of (9) lead to:

$$\mathrm{IE}(x_j) = \mathrm{IE}(y_j) \tag{11}$$

and:

$$\sum_{j=1}^{n} x_j = y \tag{12}$$

$j = 1, 2, ..., n$, so, if necessary, we can slightly modify the restrictions of (9).

4. Mathematical Tools

Both optimization problems, (7) and (9), involve the risk function, ρ, which is non-differentiable in general, and therefore, the standard mathematical methods do not apply any more. In order to overcome this caveat, several authors have proposed equivalent linear problems that apply for discrete random variables and particular interesting examples, such as the *CVaR* or the absolute deviation (Konno *et al.* [18], Mansini *et al.* [19], *etc.*). Balbás *et al.* [8] dealt with a particular optimal reinsurance problem and gave a new linear dual problem characterizing the primal solutions and applied in a much more general setting, since the probability space, $(\Omega, \mathcal{F}, \mathrm{IP})$, does not have to be discrete, and the fulfillment of Assumption 1 is the unique hypothesis about the risk measure, ρ. This section is devoted to pointing out how the approach of Balbás *et al.* [8] may be significantly extended, and both (7) and (9) have a linear dual problem characterizing their solutions. This is important from a computational point of view, since it will allow us to find, in practice, the optimal allocation, $x = (x_1, x_2, ..., x_n) \in (L^p)^n$.

With regard to Problem (7), following Balbás *et al.* [8], and bearing in mind (2) and (3), there is an equivalent linear problem with infinitely many constraints, namely:

$$\begin{cases} Min\theta \\ \mathrm{IE}(x_j z_j) - (1+\gamma)\tilde{E}_\rho \mathrm{IE}(x_j) \leq \theta, \quad \forall z_j \in \Delta_\rho \\ \mathrm{IE}(x_j) \geq \mathrm{IE}(y_j), \\ 0 \leq x_j \leq y \end{cases} \tag{13}$$

$(\theta, x_j) \in \mathrm{IR} \times L^p$ being the decision variable. Indeed, bearing in mind Expression (2), one can easily prove the equivalence between (7) and (13) with quite parallel arguments to those in Balbás *et al.* [8]. Problem (13) shows an advantage with respect to Problem (7), because it is linear, but the drawback is provoked by the existence of infinitely many constrains (there is one constraint per every element, $z_j \in \Delta_\rho$). Nevertheless, the dual problem of (13) overcomes this caveat, since it remains linear and may be given as follows:

$$\begin{cases} Max\mathrm{IE}(y_j)\lambda_j - \mathrm{IE}(yv_j) \\ z_j + v_j \geq (1+\gamma)\tilde{E}_\rho + \lambda_j \\ \lambda_j \geq 0, z_j \in \Delta_\rho, v_j \in L^q, v_j \geq 0 \end{cases} \tag{14}$$

$(\lambda_j, z_j, v_j) \in \mathrm{IR} \times L^q \times L^q$ being the decision variable. We can take I_j as the optimal value of the linear dual problem above, so as to define the ideal point, I.

With respect to Problem (9), the equivalent linear problem with infinitely many constraints becomes:

$$\begin{cases} \operatorname{Min} \sum_{j=1}^{n} \theta_j \\ w_j \operatorname{IE}(x_j z_j) - w_j(1+\gamma)\tilde{E}_\rho \operatorname{IE}(x_j) - \theta_j \leq 0, & \forall z_j \in \Delta_\rho, j = 1, 2, ..., n \\ \operatorname{IE}(x_j) \geq \operatorname{IE}(y_j), & j = 1, 2, ..., n \\ \sum_{j=1}^{n} x_j \leq y \\ 0 \leq x_j, & j = 1, 2, ..., n \end{cases}$$

$\left((\theta_j)_{j=1}^n, (x_j)_{j=1}^n \right) \in \mathrm{IR}^n \times (L^p)^n$ being the decision variable, while the linear dual problem is:

$$\begin{cases} \operatorname{Max} \sum_{j=1}^{n} \operatorname{IE}(y_j)\lambda_j - \operatorname{IE}(y\nu) \\ -(1+\gamma)w_j \tilde{E}_\rho + w_j z_j - \lambda_j + \nu \geq 0, & j = 1, 2, ..., n \\ \lambda_j \in \mathrm{IR}, \lambda_j \geq 0, \nu \in L^q, \nu \geq 0, z_j \in \Delta_\rho & j = 1, 2, ..., n \end{cases} \quad (15)$$

$$\left((\lambda_j)_{j=1}^n, (z_j)_{j=1}^n, \nu \right) \in \mathrm{IR}^n \times L^q \times L^q$$

being the decision variable.

We are dealing with infinite-dimensional Banach spaces, so the existence of a duality gap between (9) and (15) might hold, *i.e.*, both problems might attain different optimal values (Luenberger, [20]). However, similar methods to those in Balbás *et al.* [8] enable us to prove the duality gap absence, and (15) totally characterizes the optimal allocation, $\left(x_j^* \right)_{j=1}^n$, solving (9). Thus, in practice, one can solve the dual problem, which is linear and, therefore, easy to solve, even if the probability space, $(\Omega, \mathcal{F}, \mathrm{IP})$, is complex and (15) is an infinite-dimensional problem (Anderson and Nash, [21]), and then, one can find the optimal allocation, $\left(x_j^* \right)_{j=1}^n$, by applying the Karush-Kuhn-Tucker conditions below.

Suppose that $\left(x_j^* \right)_{j=1}^n$ is (9)-feasible and:

$$\left((\lambda_j^*)_{j=1}^n, (z_j^*)_{j=1}^n, \nu^* \right) \quad (16)$$

is (15)-feasible. Then, they solve (9) and (15), if and only if the following Karush-Kuhn-Tucker-like conditions:

$$\begin{cases} \operatorname{IE}\left(x_j^* z_j \right) \leq \operatorname{IE}\left(x_j^* z_j^* \right), & \forall z_j \in \Delta_\rho, j = 1, 2, ..., n \\ \operatorname{IE}\left(x_j^* \left(-(1+\gamma)w_j \tilde{E}_\rho + w_j z_j^* - \lambda_j^* + \nu^* \right) \right) = 0, & j = 1, 2, ..., n \\ \operatorname{IE}\left(x_j^* - y_j \right) = 0, & j = 1, 2, ..., n \\ \sum_{j=1}^{n} x_j^* = y \end{cases} \quad (17)$$

hold. □

In practice, we can consider that (16) is known, since it may be computed by solving the dual problem (15). Thus, (17) becomes a linear system of equations, leading to the optimal allocation, $\left(x_j^* \right)_{j=1}^n$.

5. Numerical Experiment

Let us deal with a simple numerical example in order to illustrate how the theorem above allows us to solve Problems (7) and (9) and obtain the optimal allocation, $\left(x_j^* \right)_{j=1}^n$. This numerical experiment will be used in Section 6 to point out how the optimal allocation may increase the "probability global of ruin".

Consider three companies and a set of states composed of five scenarios, $\Omega = \{\omega_1, \omega_2, \omega_3, \omega_4, \omega_5\}$. Suppose that the probability of all of them equals 0.2. Matrix:

$$C_y = \begin{pmatrix} 2, & 4, & 6, & 8, & 10 \\ 10, & 8, & 6, & 4, & 2 \\ 1, & 1, & 1, & 1, & 1000 \end{pmatrix} \quad (18)$$

gives the random cost for annual claims, the jth−row being associated with the jth−company, $j = 1, 2, 3$. Suppose, finally, that $\gamma = 0.05$ and that ρ is the CVaR with the confidence level, 60% (so $\tilde{E}_\rho = 1$). Though higher levels of confidence are usually recommended, the selected one, 60%, will enable us to illustrate many effects we are interested in. Furthermore, the CVaR is consistent with the second order stochastic dominance (and the standard utility functions) for every level of confidence (Ogryczak and Ruszczynski, [22]).

It is easy to verify that:

$$\begin{pmatrix} \text{IE}(y_1) = 6, & \text{IE}(y_2) = 6, & \text{IE}(y_3) = 200.8, & \text{IE}(y_1 + y_2 + y_3) = 212.8 \\ \rho_1 = 2.7, & \rho_2 = 2.7, & \rho_3 = 289.66, & \rho(1.05\text{IE}(y) - y) = 289.06 \\ & & & \rho_1 + \rho_2 + \rho_3 = 295.06 \end{pmatrix} \quad (19)$$

and the systemic risk, $\rho(y) = 289.06$, is strictly lower than the sum of the partial risks, $\rho_1 + \rho_2 + \rho_3 = 295.06$. The three companies may attempt to remove the difference (six monetary units) by means of a risk sharing plan.

Bearing in mind that (Rockafellar et al., [15])

$$\Delta_\rho = \left\{ z = (z_1, ..., z_5); 0 \leq z_i \leq 2.5 \text{ and } \sum_{i=1}^5 z_i = 5 \right\},$$

Problem (14) becomes:

$$\begin{cases} \text{Max} \text{IE}(y_j)\lambda - 0.2 \sum_{i=1}^5 y_i v_i \\ -\lambda + z_i + v_i \geq 1.05, & i = 1, 2, ..., 5 \\ \sum_{i=1}^5 z_i = 5 \\ 0 \leq z_i \leq 2.5, & i = 1, 2, ..., 5 \\ 0 \leq \lambda, 0 \leq v_i, & i = 1, 2, ..., 5 \end{cases}$$

$\left(\lambda, (v_i)_{i=1}^5, (z_i)_{i=1}^5 \right) \in \mathbb{R}^{11}$ being the decision variable and $\text{IE}(y_j)$ equaling six for $j = 1, 2$ or 200.8 for $j = 3$. By solving these simple linear problems, we can obtain the optimal value of (7) for the three involved insurers, and the ideal point becomes

$$I = (-0.65, -0.65, 271.66).$$

As can be seen, the ideal point would significantly improve the risk level of the three companies, while their expected profit would remain the same. The first and second company could reach a negative CVaR, and the risk reduction could equal $\frac{2.7+0.65}{2.7} = 124.07\%$, whereas this percentage would become $\frac{289.66-271.66}{289.66} \simeq 6.21\%$ for the third insurer. In this situation, a risk sharing plan could be interesting for them all, but recall that the ideal point above is not reachable (actually, the systemic risk, $\rho(1.05\text{IE}(y) - y) = 289.06$, can never be lower than the sum of partial risks; see (6)). Besides, a significant fall of the third risk could provoke a positive increment of the rest of the ones, so the weights, $(w_j)_{j=1}^3$, should be selected, so as to prevent this situation. Suppose that the three companies choose $(w_j)_{j=1}^3 = (10, 10, 1)$. Then, Problem (9) will lead to a Pareto optimum, and Problem (15) will become:

$$\begin{cases} Max 6(\lambda_1 + \lambda_2) + 200.8\lambda_3 - 0.2 \sum_{i=1}^{5} y_i v_i & \\ -\lambda_j + w_j z_{j,i} + v_i \geq 1.05 w_j, & j = 1, 2, 3 \\ & i = 1, ..., 5 \\ \sum_{i=1}^{5} z_{j,i} = 5, & j = 1, 2, 3 \\ \lambda_j \geq 0, 0 \leq z_{j,i} \leq 2.5, 0 \leq v_i, & j = 1, 2, 3 \\ & i = 1, ..., 5 \end{cases}$$

with

$$\left((\lambda_j)_{j=1}^3, \left((z_{j,i})_{j=1}^3 \right)_{i=1}^5, (v_i)_{i=1}^5 \right)$$

being the decision variable and

$$(y_i)_{i=1}^5 = (13, 13, 13, 13, 1012).$$

Solving this problem with standard linear optimization methods and using Conditions (17), we get the optimal allocation:

$$C_x = \begin{pmatrix} 6, & 6, & 6, & 6, & 6 \\ 6, & 6, & 6, & 6, & 6 \\ 1, & 1, & 1, & 1, & 1000 \end{pmatrix} \quad (20)$$

and the summary (19) becomes:

$$\begin{pmatrix} IE(x_1) = 6, & IE(x_2) = 6, & IE(x_3) = 200.8, & IE(x_1 + x_2 + x_3) = 212.8 \\ \rho_1 = -0.3, & \rho_2 = -0.3, & \rho_3 = 289.66, & \rho(1.05 IE(y) - y) = 289.06 \\ & & & \rho_1 + \rho_2 + \rho_3 = 289.06 \end{pmatrix}. \quad (21)$$

Thus, the equality:
$$E(y) - y) = \rho_1 + \rho_2 + \rho_3 \quad \rho(1.05I \quad (22)$$

shows that the three companies can totally diversify the non-systemic risk in this case. Notice that the ideal risk level is not reached by any company.

6. Systemic Risk Reduction and Global Bankruptcy

Consider the numerical example above, but suppose that the second stage is addressed with the alternative weights, $(\tilde{w}_j)_{j=1}^3 = (1, 1, 1)$. Then, it is easy to repeat the process and get the new allocation:

$$C_{\tilde{x}} = \begin{pmatrix} 0, & 0, & 0, & 0, & 30 \\ 0, & 0, & 0, & 0, & 30 \\ 13, & 13, & 13, & 13, & 952 \end{pmatrix}.$$

Thus, (19) and (21) become:

$$\begin{pmatrix} IE(\tilde{x}_1) = 6, & IE(\tilde{x}_2) = 6, & IE(\tilde{x}_3) = 200.8, & IE(\tilde{x}_1 + \tilde{x}_2 + \tilde{x}_3) = 212.8 \\ \rho_1 = 8.7, & \rho_2 = 8.7, & \rho_3 = 271.66, & \rho(1.05 IE(y) - y) = 289.06 \\ & & & \rho_1 + \rho_2 + \rho_3 = 289.06 \end{pmatrix}. \quad (23)$$

Obviously, this new solution would not be accepted by the first and second insurers, since their particular risk increases from 2.7 to 8.7. As indicated in Section 4, the weights in (9) must be selected in such a manner that (10) holds. However, we could also provide other numerical examples, such that (10) would hold, and the caveat below would also apply.

Indeed, the risk sharing strategy, $C_{\tilde{x}}$, shows the existence of serious caveats that cannot be ignored when designing optimal reinsurance problems. Expression (21) implies that $C_{\tilde{x}}$ also satisfies (22), and therefore, both C_x and $C_{\tilde{x}}$ diversify the non-systemic risk. There is only systemic risk after both reinsurance strategies. However, the major difference is caused by the state of nature, $\omega_5 \in \Omega$. If ω_5 comes out, then the three companies will be facing significant capital losses. In other words, if one compares Strategies C_y and $C_{\tilde{x}}$, the probability of ruin for the three insurers is clearly higher for $C_{\tilde{x}}$, despite the fact that this risk sharing plan eliminates the non-systemic risk, while the initial one, C_y, does not.

In general, the existence of very negative catastrophes implying high capital losses generates loss-distributions very asymmetric and with very heavy tails, as well as very closely correlated risks in the insurance industry. In a risk sharing plan, it is very important to diversify the risk provoked by very severe disasters, which can only be done by dealing with very conservative risk measures, related to very risk averse decision makers. Otherwise, more aggressive risk measures will not detect this contagion effect and might indicate a global diversification of the non-systemic risk and, simultaneously, lead to risk sharing strategies, making it grow the ruin probability of the whole system.

The analysis of Balbás *et al.* [17] may be easily adapted to the setting of this paper. The implication is that, under weak conditions, the optimal risk sharing strategy remains stable as the risk measure becomes more and more conservative. In fact, there is a limit in the large of this strategy. Thus, the method proposed in Section 3 must be complemented with a new analysis verifying the ruin probability of the involved companies. If the result is not adequate, then the optimal strategy must be reached with a more risk averse risk measure. The stability of the optimal strategy in the large will guarantee that "the probability of global ruin" may be controlled, even when facing heavy tails and high correlations. The example in Section 5 shows that the methodology of Section 3 usually leads to successful solutions (C_x in (20) totally diversifies the non-systemic risk and does not make it grow any probability of ruin), but strategies, such as $C_{\tilde{x}}$, should be discarded if they were obtained.

7. Conclusions

The optimal reinsurance problem is a classical topic in Actuarial Mathematics. The usual viewpoint only considers the ceding company objective, though there are other approaches, taking into account the reinsurer opinion, too. This paper proposes a "reciprocal reinsurance" involving a general number of companies. The main purpose is the diversification of the non-systemic risk conserving every market share.

We have addressed the objective above by means of two stage Vector Optimization Problems. In the first step, every insurer computes his ideal risk level, and the second step provides an optimal risk sharing plan that integrates the objectives of all of the involved insurers and respects ideal points and market shares.

The usual mathematical methods do not apply to solve the proposed optimization problems, due to the lack of differentiability, so we have provided specific mathematical tools permitting us to give explicit solutions of the presented problems. These tools apply in a very general framework, since we can deal with both discrete and continuous probability spaces, and the risk measure assumptions are quite weak.

Numerical examples have shown how the proposed tools apply in practice, as well as the properties of the reached optimal risk sharing strategy. Furthermore, the examples have shown that under some particular conditions, the selected risk sharing plan might provoke the existence of scenarios that are very negative for all of the involved companies, making it grow the "probability of global bankruptcy", with respect to this probability value, before the reinsurance contract. If so, the risk sharing plan should be modified, and a good way to do that is to choose a more conservative risk measure. The stability in the large of the optimal sharing plan guarantees that this "global ruin caveat" may be always solved. □

Acknowledgments: Research partially supported by "*Comunidad Autónoma de Madrid*" (Spain, Grant *S2009/ESP*–1594) and "*MEyC*" (Spain, Grants *ECO2009*–14457–*C04* and *ECO2012*–39031–*C02*–01). The usual caveat applies.

References

1. K. Borch. "An attempt to determine the optimum amount of stop loss reinsurance." *Transactions of the 16th International Congress of Actuaries I* 1 (1960): 597–610.
2. K.J. Arrow. "Uncertainty and the welfare of medical care." *Am. Econ. Rev.* 53 (1963): 941–973.
3. L. Gajec, and D. Zagrodny. "Optimal reinsurance under general risk measures." *Insur. Math. Econ.* 34 (2004): 227–240. [CrossRef]
4. M. Kaluszka. "Optimal reinsurance under convex principles of premium calculation." *Insur. Math. Econ.* 36 (2005): 375–398. [CrossRef]
5. J. Cai, and K.S. Tan. "Optimal retention for a stop loss reinsurance under the *VaR* and *CTE* risk measures." *ASTIN Bull.* 37 (2007): 93–112.
6. J. Cai, K.S. Tan, C. Weng, and Y. Zhang. "Optimal reinsurance under *VaR* and *CTE* risk measures." *Insur. Math. Econ.* 43 (2008): 185–196. [CrossRef]
7. C. Bernard, and W. Tian. "Optimal reinsurance arrangements under tail risk measures." *J. Risk Insur.* 76 (2009): 709–725. [CrossRef]
8. A. Balbás, B. Balbás, and A. Heras. "Optimal reinsurance with general risk measures." *Insur. Math. Econ.* 44 (2009): 374–384. [CrossRef]
9. M.L. Centeno, and O. Simoes. "Optimal reinsurance." *RACSAM* 103 (2009): 387–405. [CrossRef]
10. K.T. Seng, C. Wenga, and Y. Zhang. "Optimality of general reinsurance contracts under *CTE* risk measure." *Insur. Math. Econ.* 49 (2011): 175–187.
11. W. Cui, J. Yang, and L. Wu. "Optimal reinsurance minimizing the distortion risk measure under general reinsurance premium principles." *Insur. Math. Econ.* 53 (2013): 74–85. [CrossRef]
12. Y. Chi, and K.S. Tanb. "Optimal reinsurance with general premium principles." *Insur. Math. Econ.* 52 (2013): 180–189. [CrossRef]
13. J. Cai, Y. Fang, Z. Li, and G.E. Willmot. "Optimal reciprocal reinsurance treaties under the joint survival probability and the joint profitable probability." *J. Risk Insur.* 80 (2012): 145–168. [CrossRef]
14. P. Artzner, F. Delbaen, J.M. Eber, and D. Heath. "Coherent measures of risk." *Math. Finance* 9 (1999): 203–228. [CrossRef]
15. R.T. Rockafellar, S. Uryasev, and M. Zabarankin. "Generalized deviations in risk analysis." *Financ. Stoch.* 10 (2006): 51–74. [CrossRef]
16. H. Nakayama, Y. Sawaragi, and T. Tanino. *Theory of Multiobjective Optimization*. Waltham, MA, USA: Academic Press, 1985.
17. A. Balbás, B. Balbás, and A. Heras. "Stable solutions for optimal reinsurance problems involving risk measures." *Eur. J. Oper. Res.* 214 (2011): 796–804. [CrossRef]
18. H. Konno, K. Akishino, and R. Yamamoto. "Optimization of a long-short portfolio under non-convex transaction costs." *Comput. Optim. Appl.* 32 (2005): 115–132. [CrossRef]
19. R. Mansini, W. Ogryczak, and M.G. Speranza. "Conditional value at risk and related linear programming models for portfolio optimization." *Ann. Oper. Res.* 152 (2007): 227–256. [CrossRef]
20. D.G. Luenberger. *Optimization by Vector Spaces Methods*. Hoboken, NJ, USA: John Wiley & Sons, 1969.
21. E.J. Anderson, and P. Nash. *Linear Programming in Infinite-Dimensional Spaces*. Hoboken, NJ, USA: John Wiley & Sons, 1987.
22. W. Ogryczak, and A. Ruszczynski. "Dual stochastic dominance and related mean risk models." *SIAM J. Optimiz.* 13 (2002): 60–78. [CrossRef]

© 2013 by the authors. Licensee MDPI, Basel, Switzerland. This article is an open access article distributed under the terms and conditions of the Creative Commons Attribution (CC BY) license (http://creativecommons.org/licenses/by/4.0/).

MDPI
St. Alban-Anlage 66
4052 Basel
Switzerland
Tel. +41 61 683 77 34
Fax +41 61 302 89 18
www.mdpi.com

Risks Editorial Office
E-mail: risks@mdpi.com
www.mdpi.com/journal/risks

www.ingramcontent.com/pod-product-compliance
Lightning Source LLC
LaVergne TN
LVHW070607100526
838202LV00012B/591